TAKE YOUR
SOUL
TO WORK

TAKE YOUR
SOUL

TO WORK

Transform Your Life and Work

TANIS
HELLIWELL

RANDOM HOUSE OF CANADA

Canadian Cataloguing in Publication Data

Helliwell, Tanis

   Take your soul to work

ISBN 0-679-30958-6

1. Work – Religious aspects.   2. Self-actualization (Psychology) – Religious aspects.   3. Spiritual life.   I. Title.

BL65.W67H44 1999   248.8   C98-931197-X

Cover and interior design: Sharon Foster Design
Cover image: © Dorling Kindersley Ltd.

Excerpt from "East Coker" in the "Four Quartets," from *Collected Poems 1909–1962* by T. S. Eliot, © 1974. Reprinted by permission of Faber and Faber, London, England.

Excerpt from *The Collected Works of St. John of the Cross*, translated by Kieran Kavanaugh and Otilio Rodriguez © 1979, 1991 by Washington Province of Discalced Carmelites, ICS Publications, Washington, DC.

Printed and bound in Canada

10 9 8 7 6 5 4 3 2 1

This book is dedicated to
all people who are committed
to creating a healthy world.

Table of Contents

Acknowledgments

I wish to thank Samaya Ryane of *Shared Vision* magazine, who, in 1996, invited me to write a monthly column called "Take Your Soul to Work." Those installments led to this book and gave me the needed impetus. Also, my gratitude to Lionel Wilson for providing current data compiled from many different sources.

I also want to thank Jill McBeath, Barbara Siskind and Julia Cipriani for their insightful comments, and my deep appreciation goes to Ann Mortifee, who helped me find the thread on which to string the pearls. I'm grateful to Tonya Rehder, Joanne Broatch and Bert Simpson for suggestions for improvement on the final draft. Thanks also to Debbie Albrecht and Dave Clarke for their computer assistance, to Lynn Young for her speedy re-typing and to Dan Martin for his e-mails.

Special thanks to Barbara and Barry Siskind, Ann and Harper Graham and Margaret Hope for inviting me to their peaceful cottages to write. My gratitude also goes to Sandy Penrose, the Banff Centre for Management and many others for giving me a chance to teach what I teach best. Lastly, I thank Sarah Davies and others at Random House of Canada, including David Kent and Jennifer Shepherd, who all believed in this book from the first and helped birth it.

Introduction

Our souls are starving. Everywhere I go, I sense a chronic low-grade depression in people, a soul sickness. Psychotherapist Thomas Moore writes of this spiritual illness in *Care of the Soul.* The most common complaints his clients have are feelings of "emptiness, meaninglessness, vague depression, disillusionment about marriage, family, relationships, loss of values, yearning for personal fulfillment, and hunger for spirituality." These are all symptoms of the unhappiness that people feel when their lives and work are not in keeping with their soul's purpose.

Happiness results from satisfying both our personality and soul needs. Ideally, the two work together in partnership because the soul knows the purpose for our life, and the personality is the vessel we have been given to fulfill that purpose. The soul cannot accomplish its goals without the cooperation of the personality, and the personality—operating without the direction of the soul—tends to seek momentary pleasures that can lead to long-term disillusionment. Psychological pain stems, in part, from overfeeding our personality needs at the expense of the soul. However, negating our personality needs often leads to pain as well. If we satisfy our personality needs by obtaining financial and occupational security, for example, or by being liked and respected by others, then we might be better able to satisfy the needs of our soul.

The soul and personality working together create a soul-infused personality. This interdependent partnership is necessary if we are to fully develop our potential. Having a soul-infused personality means being self-actualized, joyful, creative, truthful and self-directed. It also means being committed to working with others to create healthy workplaces and to become a creator of good in the world. As we become more soul-infused, we actively seek to take our soul to work and experience increasing discontent if we are not able to do so.

We humans have come to a juncture in our evolutionary path with two choices facing us. One path is regressive. A disconnection to our soul leads to isolation—not only with our essential selves, but with others and our world. Along this path we find pollution of our physical bodies and the planet, emotional suffering caused by our lack of concern for others, mental suffering due to working in jobs that use only a small part of our potential and spiritual suffering because we are leading lives not in keeping with our soul's calling.

The second choice facing us is the progressive path—the path of transformation. Individually and collectively this is evidenced in our world by an increased interest in spirituality. Consider the number of spiritual books and workshops that have become available over the last few decades and the more recent entrance of spirituality into the business world. Discussing spirituality in the workplace would have been unthinkable even five years ago! Now, throughout North America, conferences devoted to this topic are springing up. Participants include union members, government and health organizations, multi-national corporations, as well as self-employed consultants and people of all ages, religions and genders. And these conferences are not one-time occurrences. Participants often form ongoing discussion and support groups to catalyze change in society, donate money to worthy causes and plan new conferences for succeeding years.

Spirituality in the workplace is not only a topic for discussion at conferences; it must be applied to our everyday work. It involves true partnership between the souls and personalities of both ourselves and others. Fortunately, organizations, large and small, are taking positive steps towards providing better places to work. The dress code has changed from the prescribed blue suit of the '80s to casual clothes that reflect our individuality. A different way of thinking is emerging as organizational structures move from autocratic to democratic, seeking to utilize and promote the best ideas and talents of each individual. Granted, sometimes there are gaps between the theory of "empowerment" and the actual practice of this concept in the workplace, but these are closing as more individuals and organizations push their boundaries to try new behaviors that satisfy both their soul and personality needs.

As individuals and organizations walk the progressive path of transformation, they move away from attitudes of dependence on others or independence from others to a new attitude of interdependence. But this process is not without pain. The journey of transformation is accompanied by confusion, frustration and setbacks, but also excitement, optimism and the joy of discovering a better way of living and being in the world. We start to ask ourselves the hard questions: "Who am I?" "What do I want to do with my life?" "How can I make my work meaningful?" Indeed, the question of work becomes essential. Work might be paid or unpaid and is not just *what* we do but also *how* we do it. Our attitude towards coworkers, clients and the service we are providing is of great importance. Do we have the right motivation for our actions? Do we seek to help, not harm? These are crucial questions.

Western society has fostered beliefs—about what kind of work we should do, how we should do it and for how long we should do it—which may not be in accord with our individual soul's calling. Meaningful work is essential to human evolution, and it could be anything so long as it improves us and adds value to the world. Two decades ago, philosopher and economist E.F. Schumacher wrote in *Good Work* that individuals should "*reject* meaningless, boring, stultifying, or nerve-racking work in which a man [or woman] is made the servant of a machine or a system.... Work is the joy of life and is *needed* for our development, but meaningless work is an abomination."

I'd like to clarify "meaningless." This refers to work that the individual finds meaningless. It has nothing to do with any particular job or occupation. We are all unique and what suits one of us will not necessarily be right for another. The rejection of meaningless work of which Schumacher speaks is happening right now. The large organizations where people are just "cogs in the wheel" are falling apart, and small organizations that develop people's potential are increasing in number. This doesn't mean that all large organizations are limiting employees or that all small organizations are encouraging them. What is necessary is an environment of high trust, respect and the appropriate amount of work to interest the individual, regardless of the size of the organization.

Ultimately, however, change begins with the individual. *Take Your Soul to Work* was written with the individual in mind. Its purpose is to assist you in balancing your life by discovering and acting upon your soul's needs and finding more meaning in your work. It is a "how to" book that gives you the tools and techniques I've found work best to develop your potential in your life and work. But it's more than that. This book also grapples with the issues arising globally concerning the deep need to heal ourselves, our relationships with others and our world. In that sense, *Take Your Soul to Work* is also a "why to" book.

Individuals searching for ways to transform themselves and their organizations will not find their answers in technology, in statistics or in logic alone. The tools of which I speak depend less on doing and more on being, less on quantity and more on quality. Their basis, to some extent, is a combination of the world's myths, psychology and the spiritual laws on which our world was formed and continues to function. For two decades I have studied Native American, Christian, Buddhist, Western Metaphysical and other traditions to learn more about these spiritual laws. It is not always easy to interpret these spiritual teachings and apply them in a concrete and practical way in our everyday life and work so I have tried in this book to incorporate these essential spiritual truths in a way easily understood by all readers.

Take Your Soul to Work is divided into three sections. The first, *Defining Personality, Soul and Work*, examines the different needs of the personality and soul and illustrates what "taking your soul to work" means. The second section, *Inner Transformation: The Soul-Infused Personality*, assists readers—through self-assessment exercises—in determining their soul's purpose, examining their talents and gifts and overcoming fears. The third section, *Outer Transformation: Taking Your Soul to Work*, offers readers concrete, practical ways to bring soul into their present work.

Take Your Soul to Work mirrors my own soul journey—both past and present—and the journey of so many others whom I have known and worked with over the years. It is my hope that this book will assist you in bringing together your spiritual and material, individual and collective, personal and work worlds, while at the same time convince you that you are here for a purpose and that your life makes a difference.

Defining Personality, Soul and Work

In any way that men love me in that same way they find my love: for many are the paths of men, but they all in the end come to me.

SONG OF GOD, BHAGAVAD GITA

The Evolution of Work

*The work ethic is alive and well; the fact is,
it's under-employed.*

DANIEL YANKOLOVICH

What Is Meaningful Work?

There is a difference between a "job" and "work." A job is what
we do to satisfy our financial and physical needs; work satisfies
our emotional, mental and spiritual needs and gives us meaning
in life. Our personalities think more in terms of doing a job and
our souls long for meaningful work. In an ideal world our job
and our work would be the same, but, unfortunately, in today's
world more people have a job than have their true work. The
desire for meaningful work which supports both personality and
soul needs is increasing in our society, throwing our entire concept of the nature of work into question. Matthew Fox discusses
this in *The Reinvention of Work*:

> We should not allow ourselves to be deceived that today's cri-
> sis in jobs is just about more jobs; it is not. The job crisis is
> something deeper: a crisis in our relationship to work and the

challenge put to our species to reinvent it.... Work comes from inside out; work is the expression of our soul, our inner being. It is unique to the individual; it is creative. Work is an expression of the Spirit at work in the world through us.

Essentially, Fox is saying that only by listening to the soul will we be able to hear what it is that we are meant to do in life. Avoiding the soul's cries results in us seeking meaning and happiness in the wrong places.

Of course, not everyone will be able to do the work they prefer. Perhaps you want to be a full-time artist but still need to find a way to support your family. Life has dealt you a challenging set of circumstances for a purpose. Healing and self-knowledge lie in discovering that purpose. Perhaps you are confusing soul work from personality desires, or maybe the choice of work is correct but your timing is off. You might even understand a part of your soul's work, but not all of it. The soul does not move from Point A to Point B. It takes a circuitous route and as it does so you learn a little bit here and a little bit there about your life's purpose.

James, now in his late forties, spent the last twelve years balancing the needs of the personality with those of the soul. His journey began when he decided to write a book on a large topic, not easily defined, and unique in its subject area. He felt "called" to write the book and yet could not support himself financially by doing so full time. Over the years he found several ways of making ends meet, from crafting jewelry to minimizing expenses by living a frugal country life. Throughout this journey he learned patience, humility, persistence and many other wonderful qualities. But still the book was not finished.

A few years ago, James became romantically involved with a powerful, successful woman whose work directly affected thousands of people. Initially, James thought that his soul was rewarding him for his long-term commitment and that, with his money worries ended, he would now be able to finish the book. This has not happened. This new relationship has called on still deeper aspects of himself. It has become obvious to James, through ongoing struggles with his ego, that in supporting his new partner emotionally so that she can better offer her work in the world, James is doing more good than he could do by writing his book. That's not to say that James has let go of the book. He's still writing but now sees it as only one piece of his soul's work and maybe not the central piece at that.

This journey to balance soul and personality concerns has not been easy for James, because of our society's tendency to judge people's worth by their occupation or by how much money they make. More money equals more worth. This idea may seem unpleasant, because most of us prefer to declare that money and success doesn't matter. However, if we are honest with ourselves, most of us tend to look down on those who are unemployed and view them as lazy and a drain on those who are working. And, if we become unemployed, are laid off or forced into early retirement, we often think these same things about ourselves.

Our self-esteem and self-image are so strongly connected with our work that many of us, even if we do not like our jobs, are afraid to leave. The thought of being unemployed incites incredible anxiety and even fear because so much of our self-concept is identified with the job we perform. If people are asked, "What do you do?" how often do they mention that they are hikers, environmentalists or fathers? So strong is the feeling of identifying our Self with our work and how much we earn that people who are not working in paid jobs, perhaps raising their children or working as volunteers, often feel apologetic and non-valued when they are asked this question. Similarly, individuals who are working in "alternative" professions such as massage therapy, astrology, or the arts, or who are self-employed may feel that their work doesn't count as much as traditional occupations. That their work is even considered "alternative" is a good indicator of this underlying suspicion and lack of acceptance.

We must change this view of work and see that all work that helps the common good has value. As long as our work is in keeping with our soul's purpose, we are doing what we came to do.

The idea that we *have to* work in order to make enough money to survive—whether surviving means having enough food, owning a home, supporting our children or looking after ourselves in our old age—is a commonly held notion of why we work. As soon as we believe that we *must* work, feelings of victimization and resentment creep in. This is common in those of us who don't enjoy our work, but it can even occur in those of us who like it.

We have to consider our personality and the set of circumstances we have been given in this life and find our work within these boundaries. Bewailing that it isn't fair, that it's easier for others, that it's not what we want, none of this will do any good. We must search through the rubble of our genetic, historical and cultural circumstances to find the pearl of countless value that lies buried. Some lives call for excellence in the outer world and others for excellence in the inner. The soul and personality need to learn to work together to determine their joint purpose and then embrace it with joy.

We have a choice. We can look at work as labor and exertion that we are obligated to do, or we can see work as something we *choose* to do because it gives us joy and a sense of purpose. It involves sharing our unique gifts in the ways that seem most meaningful to us at any given time. Defining work this way allows for continual growth and redefinition. The work we may want at twenty may not be what we feel called to do at fifty. Rather than attempt to make ourselves fit into someone else's idea of a job, we need to focus on the combination of talents and skills and temperament we each have and then find or create the work in which we can excel.

Taking our soul to work means doing the work that we have an inner calling for. We want to do this work regardless of how much it pays, how much status is involved, or what our friends and family may think. In doing this work we feel good about ourselves, others and our world. Our life has meaning and we are on track with our purpose. Psychologist Abraham Maslow said that a person is both "actuality and potentiality," and that developing our potential leads to self-actualization. By taking our soul to work we bring the totality of who we are to our job. When we do what we love, we draw energy to ourselves, resulting in the manifestation of our dreams in the material world. This leads both to inner and outer fulfillment.

In Sanskrit the word "karma" means work and creation. We work and create every minute and, examined in this light, anything can be our work. These thoughts are reflected in the *Bhagavad Gita*:

> When work is done as sacred work, unselfishly, with a peaceful mind, without lust or hate, with no desire for reward, then the work is pure. But when work is done with selfish desire, or feeling it is an effort, or thinking it is a sacrifice, then the work is impure.

I can hear some of you saying, "That's all well and good, but I work for a large company that tells me what to do."

And who chose that company and work? We all make choices about where we'll work and should consider both the benefits and the restraints these choices entail.

Some of you might reply, "But I *have* no choice. I have too many responsibilities. I have young kids, no education, no support…"

While hearing the commitment and heartfelt concern for others in these words, I also sense desperation, despair and feelings of victimization. We must remember that life continually offers us choices. Granted, we cannot choose the talents we are born with, but we can choose whether to develop them. Also, we do not always choose—at least on a personality level—the painful situations we encounter, but we *can* choose how we respond to them.

I once heard a motivational speaker comment on the power of choice. This man, a physically active ex-marine, had been in a fire that left him severely burned, his face was disfigured and most of his fingers were missing. After recovering from the deep depression that resulted from that tragedy, this man re-entered the world by running for mayor. He won. Then he decided to take up flying. One day, he was forced to make an emergency landing, and the crash left him paralyzed from the waist down. When I heard this man tell his story from his wheelchair, what captured my attention was his attitude to the restrictions that had been placed on his life. He said, "Before my accidents there were 10,000 things I could do. Now there are 9,000."

This man's life has been a challenge to say the least but we've all had our share of difficulties—what I like to call "opportunities for growth." I have a deep belief that we are never given any challenges in life that we cannot rise above. Joseph Campbell wrote something similar in *Reflections on the Art of Living*: "Every failure to cope with a life situation must be laid, in the end, to a restriction of consciousness."

All of us need to examine the restrictions we place on ourselves that keep us from doing our soul's work. This does not mean that we won't flounder, sometimes with a lack of grace, in difficult situations. But we can learn to "fearlessly flounder" and look for the opportunities our soul is affording us.

Many of the responsibilities we have are the result of choices we have made in life. Some of these choices have been soul choices and some have been personality choices. When we make soul choices, we feel fulfilled, and there's a certain rightness about our decisions. Personality choices are more variable, and what satisfies our personality at one time may not do so forever. Because our personality and soul inhabit us simultaneously, it is not always easy to decide which one is speaking to us. A rule of thumb I use to differentiate personality from soul concerns is to ask myself, do I act out of guilt, fear or how others will perceive me? or do I feel a sense of calm or exhilaration about my choice? Soul choices have an inner sense of rightness, even though the path may be difficult for myself and others and I may not know the final outcome.

Marjorie is representative of many people I have encountered in my seminars. She is forty years old and works as the manager of a large company. She is divorced and has two children, eleven and fourteen, who visit their father on weekends. Over time, Marjorie felt an increasing pull towards social work, in particular the planning of healthy communities. This would entail returning to university for further studies. No matter how many times she told herself that it was not practical financially, Marjorie found herself facing a soul call that would eventually deeply affect her own life as well as the lives of her children.

Marjorie realized she had two choices. She could try to ignore the call, but knew that to do so would likely make her miserable. Or, she could attempt to get her personality and soul working together to find a solution. Time and effort and many sacrifices and compromises from both Marjorie, her children and even her ex-husband would be required, but all of it was possible. For instance, her children could get paper routes to pay for extras and their father could have the children over one night during the week so that Marjorie could take the necessary courses. And this would not be a short-term plan; it could take years for Marjorie to achieve the goal.

One of the first questions Marjorie asked herself was, "What if my ex-husband and children don't want to assist me in meeting my soul's choice of work?" Obviously, this can and does happen. The first thing Marjorie needed to consider was whether she had been assisting her children and ex-husband in meeting their needs in the past. If she had, there was a greater possibility that they would be interested in supporting her. Up until that time, Marjorie might have been putting her life on hold to serve her children's needs, but relationships can change. Interdependence is the balance between meeting our needs and the needs of others. Perhaps the children could help with the dishes, fold some laundry, look after their own rooms and feed the dog—all work that Marjorie presently does. But what if her ex-husband will not look after the kids an additional night during the week? Is it possible that they could fend for themselves for a few hours if Marjorie prepared their meal the night before? Eventually, with the support of her children and ex-husband, Marjorie decided to stay in her present job while pursuing her educational plans one night a week. Marjorie realized that at this point in her life she needed to move persistantly but slowly because her soul work was to provide her children with security. In taking care of her children her soul was meeting a higher need by serving others.

Our relationships with others are integral to our lives and we need to search for creative ways to meet their needs while also meeting those of our own soul. I'm not saying that we should do what we want regardless of the impact on others, but we should never ignore a soul call. We have a choice. Finding a solution that *best* suits the needs of both others and our soul is imperative if we are to achieve balance.

Our souls, like our personalities, are unique, and we must find a combination of life work that suits both. Personality choices alone can never lead to happiness; only by following the soul's choices in relationship with the personality will we be happy in our life's work.

Personality and Soul Roles

Every transformation of man...has rested on a new metaphysical and ideological base; or rather, upon deeper stirrings and intuitions whose rationalized expression takes the form of a new picture of the cosmos and the nature of man.

LEWIS MUMFORD

Transformation of Ourselves and Our World

We are witnessing a time of transformation for both individuals and humanity. By understanding our place in human history, we can find a context for discussing our individual lives and work. There have been three major stages in recorded time through which humanity has risen, from Neolithic hunter-gatherer societies to agrarian communities to large industrialized nations, and we are now participating in the flowering of the fourth cycle in our mainstream culture.

In the first stage, people lived in tribal societies dependent both on others and the physical environment for survival. Their lives were dictated by the changing seasons and the migration of animals. There was little time for art or culture as people scrambled daily to ensure they didn't starve or die of exposure. Gradually, as these basic needs were met and certain inventions made life easier, humans moved to the second stage of their development. Riane Eisler, in *The Chalice & the Blade*, has argued that this was a time of living in harmony with nature and honoring the feminine principle which creates life. This second stage was birthed in the Middle East; clay and stone earth goddess figures as old as twelve thousand years have been found from the beginnings of that era. These agricultural, peaceful societies in the Middle East and in Europe peaked between 6000 and 4000 B.C. and were replaced by more aggressive ones. Warlords flourished throughout Europe from 4000 to 2000 B.C., bringing with them the third stage in humanity's evolution. Independence, from others, from nature and from the spirit, and the masculine principle of "might is right," where the strongest took what they wanted, were characteristic of this third stage and this mind-set contrived to dominate until recently in human history.

The fourth stage—where humans learn to be interdependent and treat others as themselves—builds on what was *best* in the three preceding stages. From stage one we learned connectiveness to the land and the physical environment and the ability to survive harsh conditions. In stage two we learned to live in harmony with others and nature, and in stage three we learned independence and the use of free will to create the reality we wanted. The fourth stage of human evolution—that of interdependence—is based on the fundamental principles that all life is sacred; that life exists in all forms seen and unseen; that humans must work with spiritual laws to create in the physical world; and that their creations serve not only themselves but all living beings.

These four stages, which have taken humanity thousands of years to undergo, are the same stages each of us goes through in our lives. As babies and young children we are completely dependent on our mothers to satisfy our basic physical needs. In later childhood and teenage years we desire to fit in and be accepted—first by family, and then by friends and teachers. In this second stage of development we are concerned not that we will survive, but that we will be liked by others. In our twenties and even thirties, after we have learned to conform to societal laws, we seek to follow our own path in life towards financial, physical, mental and even religious independence. The fourth stage—that of interdependence—is where we as individuals choose to love and care for other races, countries, species and the planet itself. The natural order of individual and human evolution follows this pattern, but it is possible to get stuck and not be able to develop past the earlier stages because of woundings or lack of support.

For example, some people in the workforce have remained dependent on their employers. These individuals believe that, if they work hard and are loyal employees, they will be looked after by their companies. This dependent parent and child relationship carries over into their entire lives. They trust their government to ensure their safety and feel comfortable with the rules. The gift these individuals bring to the fourth stage of human evolution is a belief in the importance of relationship and of giving to others. What they lack, however, is a sense of independence. Fortunately, this is changing. Most people are now taking responsibility for their lives, through self-employment, managing their own finances, ongoing education and questioning their previous views of themselves and others.

Other individuals get stuck in the independent stage of development and use their work as a way to get as much as they can for themselves. The gifts that these people bring to the fourth stage are independence and the ability to stretch one's boundaries. These are important qualities to learn if we are to become conscious creators in our world. Independence, however, when not in balance with a healthy recognition of our dependence on other humans and nature, often leads to greed and violence. Independent thinking, without concern for others, is no longer working in the world of work. Previously successful local and national companies have been forced to realize that they are part of a global economy. The rise and fall of the Japanese yen affects the New York Stock Exchange, and companies with head offices in the United States manufacture their products in Taiwan and sell them in Europe.

In fact, neither dependent nor independent thinking is working. Interdependence is needed and is created by bringing together the best of the dependent mind-set, relationship with others, and the best of the independent mind-set, relationship with oneself. Interdependent people are committed to creating a better world for others and are already working in mutually beneficial business partnerships and personal relationships, and are involved in community building and healing the environment.

These men and women are attempting to live consciously in a time when our old world view is collapsing and the new one has not yet come completely into form. They may not be sure what the entire new paradigm will be, but they see glimpses of it and are confident enough to experiment with different forms and beliefs until they find ones that work. Progressive individuals from a wide range of backgrounds and talents are taking responsibility for creating a new world. Some are doing it for egocentric reasons, others for altruistic ones. Nonetheless, they have chosen the path of growth which will lead them—however painfully—into the new stage of interdependence.

This emerging world view is affecting not only individuals but the collective soul of humanity. Psychiatrist Carl Jung said that the stories of each person's life are linked to the universal truths found in humanity's soul, which he termed the *collective unconscious*. Hindus refer to these truths as "the Akashic records," and biologist Rupert Sheldrake calls them "morphogenetic fields." Sheldrake discovered that the repetition of individual behaviors has an evolutionary effect upon a species over time, and that these morphogenetic fields are inherited and include the collective ability and knowledge of our race.

For example, humans once believed that the Earth was flat and now—even though only astronauts have actually seen it—

everyone believes it is round. This change of belief did not occur overnight. It took a few individuals such as Copernicus and Galileo to "discover" the truth that had always existed and then others—some reluctantly—followed suit. Science is not always about inventing something. Often it's about rediscovering a deeper truth, the spiritual laws on which all life is based.

The growing number of people who have been searching for spiritual meaning both in their lives and their work over the last few decades is causing a change in the morphogenetic field of humanity. Spirituality, which used to be the passion of just a few people, is now becoming the interest of the many. In the last ten years, spiritual books have created lots of book sales and news-oriented magazines like *Time* and *Maclean's* have featured articles on angels and life after death. And the quest for spirituality, once considered a personal search, has now entered the world of work. Companies are donating billions of dollars annually towards humanitarian causes at home and abroad, and environmental and ethical funds are a growing area for investment. The collective soul of humanity affects our individual lives as much as we affect it. What happens in the microcosm of the individual is reflected in the macrocosm of the human species, and vice versa. This is the underlying spiritual principle on which our material world is grounded.

> *Like millions of trees which are all rooted in one and the same earth, so millions of human minds are rooted in one and the same universal being.*
>
> PAUL BRUNTON

Through all four stages of evolutionary development—both as individuals and as a species—we become increasingly conscious of the relationships between the spiritual and material realms. In the first stage, we live in harmony with both the spiritual and physical laws but in the innocent, unconscious way of a child with its mother. In the second and third stage, we consciously start our climb towards control of our physical world by first gaining support from others and then by asserting our independence from them. Only in the fourth stage of human evolution do the spiritual and physical worlds start reuniting and this time not in childhood innocence but in mature adult consciousness. We begin to realize that the world literally does not work for us unless it also works for others. The disconnection between the world of form and the world of spirit ends when these two are reunited. In this fourth stage of individual and human transformation we must be able to bring both the personality and soul together if we want to create good for both ourselves and the world.

This process of transformation is not always easy. Recently, I received an e-mail from a man who had taken a course with me some months earlier. He described his physical and psychological anguish in turning away from a career path for which he had worked for many years, in order to follow his heart and soul down an unknown road. Like Dan, all of us will encounter difficulties as we start moving from being personality-focused to becoming soul-focused.

Dan's Story

Dear Tanis,

I have been working as an engineer for twenty months— four months short of becoming accredited as a professional engineer. For the last year I have been debating a career change. My intent was to give my notice early this month, travel for one to two years, then return to Canada and pursue a new career path—either a Ph.D. in psychology or an M.B.A. specializing in tourism.

I was feeling wonderful on Monday, having just returned from holidays. My brother—a forty-five-year-old risk-taking entrepreneur—and I started talking on the telephone that night. He spent almost three hours trying to convince me of the benefits of staying at work the extra four months to become a professionally accredited engineer. He explained how professional accreditation would serve me well in many areas of life, far beyond whether or not I worked as an engineer.

As our conversation continued I began to get very cold and started shaking uncontrollably. I continued talking with my brother, during which time I put on a jacket, wrapped myself in blankets and turned the heat up. Only when I was overcome by complete body pains, especially in the back and neck, did I halt our talk. After our conversation, as I was continuing to shake and shiver uncontrollably, I turned the heat up even more and drank several large mugs of hot chocolate. My legs felt weak and I barely had enough energy to make it up the stairs. I got into bed fully clothed, using a winter sleeping bag and two heavy comforters. My shaking continued for several hours until I finally fell asleep.

During this period of trying to get to sleep, I began to feel noticeably better after the thought of asking for your advice came into my head. Tuesday I felt physically drained and got dizzy if I moved too quickly. Today I feel almost 100 percent, with no residual signs of the "illness" which felt like a horrible flu less than two days ago.

This could be a coincidence, but I firmly believe that my body was reacting to an extreme difference of opinion between my logical and emotional sides. Every logical thought tells me to stay four months more in my job and finish my professional engineering accreditation. My emotional side has very little support, except for an incredibly strong feeling, like nothing I have ever felt before, that I should listen to my gut and quit. If this feeling was not so overwhelming, the decision would be easy and logic would win out.

I realize that this answer is one I must come to on my own, by looking deep inside of myself. I have never had such strong emotions pulling me in a direction, and I am unsure which side of myself to listen to as the future is so unknown. Do you have any advice on how I can find my answers?

Best regards, Dan

Dan and others like him are searching for the work that their soul calls them to do. This is a difficult process and often we must make sacrifices without knowing what the resulting gains will be. Friends and family, like Dan's brother, although well intentioned, might urge us to stay on the safe, known path of financial and job security. This opinion is often in accord with one's own personality, listing many of the same arguments. However, our soul may not agree and has other plans, which we, as Dan did, start to grasp intuitively. This inner turmoil and seeming conflict between the soul and personality impels us in the search for meaningful work and life purpose. The process of transformation in which Dan finds himself is the same one calling thousands of individuals in our world and that number is increasing exponentially.

When we are engaged in the struggle between conflicting needs of the soul and personality, we might think that we can only satisfy one to the loss of the other. This is not always the case. I suggested to Dan that he reassure his soul that he was going to act on its wishes, but also ask it to support him in staying at his present job for four months, so he could get his accreditation. This compromise served the needs of both his personality and his soul over the long run by demonstrating to both of them that their needs would be met. Dan did decide to stay in his present job, while simultaneously finding ways to satisfy his soul. He started by taking up yoga and firming up his travel plans.

The Marriage between the Personality and the Soul

The soul knows your life's purpose and the personality has the gifts to fulfill it. The union of the two creates a third entity, the soul-infused personality. We are neither a soul being nor a physical being; we are both. And only by recognizing their interdependence can we become true creators.

When personality is cut off from soul—as happens far too often in our world—it wanders aimlessly and in despair. The body vessel can become physically, emotionally, mentally and spiritually ill. We can see aspects of this "dis-ease" everywhere—illness caused by a toxic environment, destruction of our habitat, war, violence and hopelessness.

When soul is cut off from personality, it cannot fulfill its destiny because it has no vessel in the physical world through which it can grow and learn and express its innate creativity. The soul's essence is *being* and the personality's is *doing*, and we need to bring both into balance in order to create a life worth living, not only for ourselves, but for all other creatures and for the planet as well. This is our ultimate task and work on the Earth. We have no other.

Another way of considering the marriage of personality and soul is through the ancient Chinese yin/yang symbol. The yin is the female, receptive, nurturing force connected to the earth and the world of form; the yang is the male, active, creative force of the spiritual world. When these two forces of energy are balanced in the vessel of our body, a dynamic fusion is created. Our work is not separate from who we are as a spiritual and physical being. It is an extension of who we are. Personality and soul are equal partners, both separate and interconnected. In any marriage, there are two individuals with their individual needs, but also a third—the marriage itself—with its needs. The soul must learn to work within the confines of the personality and the personality must surrender to the divine will of the soul. Catholic priest and mystic Teilhard de Chardin, in *The Phenomenon of Man*, wrote of the personality/soul relationship:

> Without the slightest doubt *there is something* through which material and spiritual energy hold together and are complementary.... Yet, seductive though it be, the idea of the direct transformation of one of these two energies into the other is no sooner glimpsed than it has to be abandoned. As soon as

we try to couple them together, their mutual independence becomes as clear as their interrelation.

Locked in physical reality, the personality does not always accept this interdependent role gracefully. It forgets that it has no life apart from the universal life force that created it. Confined to physical time and space, the personality fears that merging with the soul might cause its destruction and death. It resists surrender. But the soul courts the personality, offering it moments of insight, love, ecstasy, purpose and, ultimately, union with the divine. The soul is patient, knowing that over time the personality will become frustrated and exhausted after it has suffered and failed to find meaning in life and will return to the soul. And, like the prodigal son, the personality will be greeted by the soul with joy and thanksgiving. There is no blame or guilt, only love and acceptance. As the divine marriage of personality and soul takes place, the two partners become ready to fulfill their joint destiny—their conscious work in the world.

Personality and Soul Roles

The word "personality" is derived from the Greek word *persona*, meaning mask. Our personality is a construct we use to experience the world, but it is not the essential part of us. Whereas the soul is eternal, the personality is transitory. It's the clothing that our soul wears in this life. Carl Jung, in describing the different strengths of the *persona* and soul, said that persona facilitates relationship with the outer world as the soul does with the inner world.

Unlike the personality, our soul has no fear, pride or attachment to the things of this world, no concern with time and no judgment of right and wrong. Its perspective is eternity. The soul knows the divine laws of creation and sends down a part of itself into our personality, so we can learn to manifest these laws in the world of time and space. Whether we believe that the soul does this in one life, or in a succession of lives, is ultimately not important. Whether our lives are easy or difficult, whether we are a Caucasian man or an Asian woman, a carpenter, a homemaker or a mathematical genius, what is ultimately important is that we learn to manifest our gifts and encourage others to manifest theirs.

Not limited by space or time, the soul is infinite. It has many viewing points on how our individual life fits into the overall divine plan for humans. Our personality, on the other hand, has one point of view because it is finite and anchored in the physical world. Fortunately, the infinite is attracted to the finite and the finite to the infinite and, as we become a soul-infused personality, we merge these two principles in our life and work.

> *The personality's wish is to have power over experience, to control all events and consequences, and the soul's wish is to have power through experience, no matter what that may be.*
>
> DAVID WHYTE

The personality can use its free will to dominate the soul, but this is not the path to happiness. Some people's souls come knocking in their twenties and are told to go away. For others, the knock at the door happens in their thirties or forties. Even then the soul may be rejected. The personality believes that the soul leaves and returns occasionally to see if we've changed our mind. Our personality may fight what it sees as its opponent; and if the personality is too strong, the soul may never gain "legitimate" entrance. What the personality fails to realize is that the soul is already inside. Although we are free to ignore our soul's call, we cannot evolve as conscious creators until we act on our soul's desires.

Poets, mystics and teachers in all spiritual traditions have spoken of the soul for hundreds, even thousands, of years. Some, like the sixteenth-century mystic St. John of the Cross, see the soul as a lover:

> One dark night
> Fired with love's urgent longings
> —Ah the sheer grace!—

I went out unseen
My house now all stilled;

. . .

On that glad night,
In secret, for no one saw me,
Nor did I look at anything,
With no other light or guide
Than the one that burned in my heart;

. . .

O guiding night!

O night more lovely than the dawn!
O night that has united
The lover with his beloved,
Transforming the beloved in her Lover.

These words are uplifting and inspiring, yet we must not sentimentalize the soul. It is not a soft romantic lover. It has, as Carl Jung observed, an objective, distant quality, and merging the soul with the personality is not an easy task. When our personality falls in love with the soul, it initially sees only the positive aspects and has many illusions as to the relationship. One by one, as we painfully confront our projections and shadows, our soul destroys these illusions. The soul is unmoved by our psychic pain and accepts no bribes offered by our personality. However, as with any good marriage, through commitment, hard work and love, our personality and soul can eventually find a healthy and loving relationship through which both are able to accomplish their task better than either by itself.

This relationship is not always equal. Some people are dominated by the soul and have not mastered the reality of their everyday world. They find it impossible to have relationships, cook meals, pay bills and are incompetent in "real" life. However, it is much more common for people to be personality-dominated and to live too much in the everyday world while shutting out the soul's call. We see this in ego-driven individuals who strive for the outward trappings of success at the expense of their family, their own soul and their relationship with the world that supports them.

How the Soul and the Personality Work Together

It is important to understand that the personality has its own consciousness quite apart from that of the soul. This consciousness is anchored in the earth element of the body, just as the soul's realm is that of spirit. If there were no separate consciousness there would be no struggle in the personality for its independence. It would do as the soul wished and that would be that. However, we know from our own personal experience that this is not the case. We see this, for example, when our soul wants us to leave our present job but our personality fears a loss of income, respect from others and fear of the unknown. This resistance comes from fears held and programmed into our body by a bodily consciousness, which is much different than soul consciousness.

Some people have difficulty believing that we have even one soul, but many aboriginal cultures think we have two—a spiritual soul and a body soul. The North American Fox tribe believe—as do the Plains Cree, the West Coast Tlingit and the Shawnee—that the body soul enters the body at conception whereas the spiritual soul enters at birth. The body soul carries our memories from life to life and builds the body, utilizing the information it has gained. In order to better understand the connection between our spiritual and physical natures, it is helpful to understand the different functions of these two "souls."

But why is it important to know how many souls we have? And what has this got to do with taking our soul to work? In order to take our soul to work we need two things. The first is the ability to listen to our soul to discover our life purpose. The second is being able to manifest that purpose by eliminating disharmonious behaviors or habits found in the cellular memory of the body. If these negative programs are not eliminated, they sabotage our efforts to fully manifest our potential. I was a transformational therapist for sixteen years and found that the consciousness of the soul and of the body greatly affect each other. One of the exercises I did with my clients was to take them, by guided visualization, to a time before birth in order to determine their purpose for this life. Almost all of those participating in the visualizations had foreknowledge of their life purpose, why they had chosen their parents and the difficulties they would face. They even knew the causes of certain diseases and weaknesses in their bodies. Also, they were able to remember that they had specifically chosen their particular physical vessel and personality to accomplish the task that their soul had set for them.

Don't forget that the soul and body need to work together as equal partners. If the soul consciousness does not work in harmony with the body consciousness, we become ill, but it is equally unhealthy to exaggerate the importance of the soul. If we see our soul as being better than the body, then we lose touch with the sacredness of the body and of all matter. If we do this, we may find peace in meditation and seclusion, but will be unable to live and work amongst our fellow human beings.

You may have forgotten your spiritual purpose at this moment, but it is encoded in your blood and cells. The soul continually helps the personality recall its purpose by whispering. If whispers don't work, the soul increases the volume until the shouting gets so loud—as it did in Dan's situation—that it becomes difficult for the personality to ignore. In heeding the soul, the personality will often need to re-define its relationship with life and work, as Dan did. We may need to *learn* to listen and to practice listening to our soul just as we practice anything at which we wish to excel. Fortunately, many of humankind's most popular stories and myths can teach us how to do this.

Predictable Steps to Consciousness

*Into deep darkness fall those who follow
the immanent. Into deeper darkness fall
those who follow the transcendent.*

ISA UPANISHAD

Quest for the Holy Grail

Humanity's great myths provide clues and signposts in the quest
to lead a soul-infused life. As Joseph Campbell, internationally
recognized expert on myth, wrote in *Reflections on the Art of
Living*, "Myth makes a connection between our waking consciousness and the mystery of the universe." The myth of the
quest for the Holy Grail, as told over eight centuries, transcends
time and has re-emerged in the present as a potent guide to understanding the steps we must take to reunite with our soul. The
Grail can be seen to represent both the body soul and the spiritual soul described earlier. The personality is the vessel that
houses the soul and the soul continually refills the personality,
another example of the marriage and interdependence between
the world of form and spirit.

For our purposes, I will restrict the discussion of the myth of the Holy Grail to one of its heroes, Perceval. His struggles, I believe, most nearly reflect our own.

Perceval was born to a noble woman and a knight, who had fought and died in the Crusades. His mother, afraid to lose her son to the same fate as her husband, tried to protect Perceval by moving to a forest near Mount Snowdon in Wales, where she kept his origins a secret from him. One day, the story goes, Perceval saw knights so glorious he thought they must be angels. When he learns the truth, Perceval immediately decides to become a knight and leaves home to follow that path.

On his own and without the guidance of his mother, Perceval —not knowing the rules of knightly conduct—makes a big mistake. He kills a knight and is banished from court to temper his warrior talent and learn the laws of his world. During his banishment, Perceval is mentored by an elderly knight, who teaches him the rules of knightly conduct. It is only after Perceval masters these that he remembers his mother and decides to seek her. On his way home, Perceval encounters the Grail Castle and sees the Grail.

We, like Perceval, are cut off—either at birth or in our early years—from our soul and the knowledge of who we really are. Perceval's mother—in one sense—represents our own parents, who with good intentions have imposed society's value systems on us just as they were imposed on them by their own parents. When they do this, they separate us from our souls. But there is a purpose to all of this; the separation strengthens our personality and we need a strong vessel to house our soul. And, as with Perceval, our soul will tell us our life's work when we are ready, regardless of where we live or who our parents are. For each of us this is the stage where, innocent of the ways of the world, we start our journey towards becoming a conscious creator in the world.

But the journey is not easy and we will undoubtedly make mistakes along the way. Perceval had raw, uncensored talent but lacked experience and we, like him, must learn the laws of our society before we are able to do our soul's work. It is only after we have learned these laws that our search for the Grail—our soul—begins. We might see the Grail early on and get a glimpse of our soul's purpose, but won't be able, at that time, to receive the entire revelation.

As the story continues we learn that the lord of the Grail Castle—the Fisher King—is wounded in the groin, his creative center. Perceval, we are told, could have helped the king, but, adhering to the correct laws of knightly conduct, neglects to ask the question that would have healed him. The next morning, Perceval awakes to discover that the Grail and the castle have disappeared. He is cast into the Wasteland because he was more concerned about being a polite guest than in showing compassion for the king and in seeking to heal him.

Perceval spends the next five years wandering in the Wasteland, seeking the Grail and overcoming many trials. He feels abandoned by God and continues to make his way alone, homeless and lawless. Although he doesn't know it at this time, he is remolding and ensouling himself. Finally, on Good Friday, feeling tired and empty, Perceval meets a hermit, a spiritual guide. Perceval begs God for forgiveness for his sins of omission. He has learned his lesson; his personality and soul unite and, transformed, he is now able to transform others. Perceval returns to the Fisher King; he asks him the correct question and, through compassion and humility, heals both him and the Wasteland.

We are both Perceval and the Fisher King—hero *and* victim. In our modern world, the Fisher Kings are the psychically and spiritually wounded individuals who run many corporations and governments, and who are creating a Wasteland of the Earth. None of us is innocent. If we are sacrificing both our body and soul to the desires of our personality, we wound ourselves. When what we do is not in accordance with the greatest good, we create a physical and spiritual Wasteland.

To heal ourselves and our world we must ask difficult questions. However, like Perceval, we might neglect to do this. In learning to fit into the laws of society, we sometimes lose the power to see or speak the unadulterated truth. Only by speaking the truth can we restore ourselves and our world to health. "Whom does the Grail serve?" (Does the personality serve itself and the material world or the soul and the higher good of all?) This is the question we must seek to ask *and* answer.

On the surface it may seem unfair that Perceval, a good and noble person who did nothing more than keep his mouth shut, should suffer such a painful penance. But all of us need to learn to speak our soul's, and not our culture's, truth. During this difficult time we must confront whatever we are attached to. If we regard ourselves as being kind, powerful, or competent, we will be forced to see and incorporate our shadow side—often the complete opposite. This is the road to true humility, compassion and wisdom.

When Perceval learns this lesson, he enters into a new relationship with his soul. His soul does not abandon him but gives him solutions to solve his difficulties. When we confront our shadow side, the personality becomes a partner with the soul.

Our paths might not be identical to Perceval's, but many steps that we take to find the Grail are common to us all. We wander in the Wasteland in order to find our purpose in life and to learn compassion for all beings. Only when we have achieved this do we then become a soul-infused personality.

Four Stages in Creating a Soul-Infused Personality

In the ancient world people studied what were called the "inner mysteries," spiritual truths that governed humanity. The marriage between the personality and soul was one of these mysteries. Students of these mysteries were given many tests or "initiations," similar to the ones Perceval faced in his quest for the Holy Grail. Individuals who passed these tests were referred to as "the twice-born" and became the spiritual leaders of their people.

Some religious traditions and indigenous cultures still teach these mysteries—in various stages of purity—and have made them available to spiritual seekers regardless of race, religion or gender. And psychologists and therapists—to a limited extent—have replaced the spiritual counselors and teachers of the ancient world. In this day and age, very few individuals in the Western world feel compelled to journey into monastic caves in the Himalayas to achieve spiritual revelation.

Instead, most of us work and live in the world and undergo these initiations while doing so. We might require a temporary retreat in our thirties, forties or fifties, when the tests are most severe, and some of us may take a few years off work to rethink our lives and change our lifestyles. This is a healthy soul choice. However, after re-focusing our life priorities, most of us re-enter the world of work in order to be of service to others and to the world. We may even return to the same kind of work we had done prior to our spiritual crisis but, although what we do is the same, how we do it is now different. We make different choices when we begin to work from the soul rather than from the personality. There are four major stages that the personality undergoes in its journey to fuse with the soul. These stages deeply affect our attitude towards work and life in general.

Stage One: Creating the Vessel

In the first part of our life—usually until sometime in our twenties—we learn society's rules so that we can fit in and not be a danger either to it or to ourselves. Stage one builds our foundation, our roots in the material world. It is during this first stage that people learn from society whether they are considered winners or losers, the haves or the have nots. Will they become doctors, lawyers, gas jockeys or unemployed? It is during stage one that more than half the people in North America are shunted into back streams, never to become successful within our culture's standards. But don't forget that each individual has the potential to fulfill their soul's purpose, even if they are not considered successful by society.

Almost all of us receive wounds in our early life, from losing a parent to death, divorce or alcoholism, to psychological, emotional or physical abuse, to being physically, socially or academically inept and therefore rejected by either our peers or authority figures. I don't believe for a moment that life is supposed to be easy. These wounds are the grit in the oyster that transforms us into a beautiful pearl. Our transformation is born out of difficulties, pain and the challenges we face in life. That is, of course, if we rise to face these challenges. I'm not attempting to make this sound easy as many people have very difficult challenges to face. However, we still have many choices in life.

For example, it is true—in fact, nothing is more true—that what we think of is what we become. So do we think positive or negative thoughts about ourselves and do we speak positively or negatively to others? What we think and say to ourselves and others greatly impacts our reality, as does how we see.

When we watch violence, verbal abuse or gratuitous sex on television or films, or watch the news and read newspapers, which concentrate on violence and tragedies, we might create negative thoughtforms that preoccupy our minds. By exposing themselves to this kind of pollution on a daily basis, many people become depressed. This exposure is fouling our spiritual, emotional and mental environment. What is worse, it affects not just the television watcher, but even the atmosphere of the innocent, just as cigarette smoke damages not just the smoker, but all those who breathe the smoke.

To keep our soul's vessel healthy and strong, we must refrain from exposing ourselves to negative news, people and situations and, to some extent, we can all do this. Our soul is mirrored by nature—we pollute ourselves when we pollute nature. We can also create an atmosphere more conducive to soul health by lobbying to clean up our psychic space just as we would lobby to clean up our environment. Finally, we can substitute positive thoughts for negative ones, such as love for fear, forgiveness for betrayal. Just as recovering alcoholics band together to support each other, we can associate with others who will encourage us, love us and have our best interests at heart. Such people are healers of others and of the world.

We must first set our own house in order before we can move to the next stage. If our personality has been badly wounded in stage one, we need first to repair our damaged vessel before moving on to stage two. Some of us might spend our entire life healing our vessel. As Jack Kornfield, psychologist and spiritual teacher, said in *A Path with Heart*, "When we have not completed the basic developmental tasks of our emotional lives or are still quite unconscious in relation to our parents and families, we will find that we are unable to deepen our spiritual practice." The goal, after all, is not to be a soul without a body, but to become a soul-infused personality so that we can become a conscious creator in the world. And before we can master the public world, we must first master the private world of our own childhood and upbringing and become a healthy, productive member of our community.

Stage Two: Strengthening the Vessel

When we have successfully completed stage one, we can begin stage two by asking the question, "What do I want to do with my life?" In our twenties and thirties the personality, not the soul, usually answers this question because we have only the information that our culture has provided with which to answer. We examine society's existing options and see which option suits us best. The world of work has many standard jobs available to us and these are like boxes of various sizes, shapes and colours. We find the box that looks most like us and then, having found it, we try to fit ourselves into that box.

This is a difficult time for individuals who cannot find a box that suits them. It often does not occur to people at this stage that there are other options, many of which are less obvious, or that there is nothing "wrong" with them because they can't find a good match between themselves and standard options. People who have the easiest time with stage two are those who are most highly socialized to the traditional values and expectations of society. For example, successful men and women might want to be teachers, doctors or lawyers and their academic records suit these professions. In other words, the boxes fit. We see this stage exemplified in Perceval's life when he practices the qualities of knighthood until he becomes the best knight in the world. He makes himself fit into the existing box and learns how to succeed using the knightly rules of his world.

What determines the initial success of our personality is how well we fit in the boxes. Yes, there are the Bill Gateses of this world who drop out of university to follow their passion, but these are rare individuals, and those who succeed by going against society's values need great self-esteem, willpower and a talent in something that society believes it needs. Without these three qualities it can be difficult for the person to succeed. And succeeding in the material world is an important criteria for forming a strong enough vessel to contain the soul.

The goals of the personality and the soul are not necessarily at cross purposes in this stage because the qualities that our personality is developing may also meet the soul's need. A talented, young musician, for instance, might earn a good livelihood and respect from society while meeting the needs of their soul. This person is fortunate, but it is not the path that most of us walk. It is more common to discover our soul's purpose later on.

To strengthen the personality vessel we might work in several successive jobs, trying to find a better fit between our qualities and the box available to us in the workplace. We might not be aware of it, but subconsciously the search for the soul's work has begun. Mostly, however, we are interested in satisfying the needs of the personality, acquiring the material attributes of success such as a car and a house. We also follow the dictates of society in our personal life by getting married and having children. In stage two, our focus is "out there" in the material world of doing, not "in here" in the spiritual world of being. The personality is fed but the soul is starved.

So far, we have been discussing the predictable steps to consciousness that "successful" people—those that fit reasonably well into existing boxes—take. What happens to the other half of the population, those who have "learned" by age twenty that they are not going to be successful in the world, because they don't have what society deems valuable? These individuals are probably not happy with their jobs. Our culture sees people as less successful when they have jobs in physical labor or in repetitive office tasks such as word processing. I am not saying that people cannot find their souls in repetitive, more mundane tasks. Soul can be found in *any* work, paid or unpaid, but it must be a matter of choice, or we feel victimized and have great difficulty working with our soul. And, if we have not succeeded according to the rules of our society, we often feel inadequate.

> *Material progress is a preliminary step to spiritual awakening.*
>
> GOPI KRISHNA

Less-valued members of society may feel condemned to a meaningless life and seek to fill the emptiness by acquiring the trappings of success—cars, homes, clothes—that they cannot afford. This only serves to reinforce their negative thoughts about themselves. For low achievers not working in interesting physical, emotional or intellectual environments, the personality *as well as* the soul is starving.

In stage two, our major motivation is to satisfy our personality—not our soul—so we seek extrinsic rewards such as money, status and material goods. If we have not achieved this external success in society, it is hard for us to move fully into stage three. We need to complete one phase before moving to the next, and it is possible to get stuck in stage two by trying to find a job that is emotionally and mentally satisfying but which may not be spiritually satisfying. This happens when we like the people with whom we work and find our job intellectually challenging but that it doesn't create meaning in our lives. Our "real" life still happens outside our work.

Stage Three: Emptying the Vessel

> *We spend the first half of our lives becoming some-*
> *body. Now we can work on becoming nobody,*
> *which is really somebody.*

RAM DASS

Sometime in our thirties, forties or, occasionally, fifties, we realize that living according to society's rules and values is not enough. At this time we usually go through a soul crisis no matter what we have achieved in the outer world. Often labeled a "mid-life crisis," this period can be characterized by depression and a feeling of emptiness and meaninglessness in life. In stage three, no outside accomplishments will suffice to fill the growing void within. At this time people often feel that they are nobodies, going nowhere, doing nothing. We have proven in stage two that we can hold down a job, raise children and keep friends. We are safe by our world's standards to move from being other-directed to being self-directed. Therefore, stage three is a time when we can ruthlessly assess what we are doing, both personally and professionally. Our central question may be, "What have I been doing with my life?"

Stage three is a time of no compromise. Like Perceval in his quest for the Holy Grail, most of us will undergo trials in the Wasteland where we must be *willing* to give up all we have achieved in our life. We may not have to literally surrender our jobs, marriages or financial security, but we need to reexamine them to see if they serve our soul, and if they do not, then we must let them go. T.S. Eliot, in his poem *Four Quartets*, which to my mind is one of the world's best descriptions of the journey of the soul to consciousness, writes:

I said to my soul, be still, and wait without hope
For hope would be hope for the wrong thing; wait
without love

For love would be love of the wrong thing; there is yet faith
But the faith and the love and the hope are all in the waiting.
Wait without thought, for you are not ready for thought;

What the soul asks of us is no less than everything. Eliot continues:

To arrive where you are, to get from where you are not,
You must go by the way wherein there is no ecstasy.
In order to arrive at what you do not know
You must go by a way which is the way of ignorance.
In order to possess what you do not possess
You must go by the way of dispossession.

This journey can take years, as it did for Perceval. Our health may be compromised, we might be fired or downsized, or suffer through a divorce. We might even endure a combination of many hardships; perhaps we have an especially strong personality and need more than one thing to break it down. However much happens to us is the right amount for the soul to work its magic; and however long it lasts is the right length of time for the soul to subdue the personality. For, make no mistake, there is a battle taking place. The personality will strive to keep the power it has gained and will not relinquish control willingly. Buddhist teacher Chogyam Trungpa Rinpoche says that from the ego's point of view, this step in spiritual progress is "one insult after another."

For some people, the personality never relinquishes control; these people often repeat the same mistakes, refusing to learn their lessons. Life for them is an endless cycle of frustration as they hold willfully to the goals of the personality and refuse to move towards the goals of the soul. What these individuals want most eludes them. They don't find the career or partner of their dreams. What is called for in stage three is complete surrender and it is only when these individuals comply, expecting nothing but the death of all they hold dear, that life will be rekindled in them. Only then, as for Perceval, does the soul's task present itself, enabling them to see what they need to do to take their soul to work.

It is often the men and women who have achieved the greatest success who have the most difficult time. Individuals who never fit in the traditional boxes are often more willing to surrender what they have achieved because they feel they have less to lose.

Poet and writer David Whyte captures the importance of stage three in his words, "Some things cannot be spoken of or discovered until we have been stuck, incapacitated, or blown off course for a while. Plain sailing is pleasant, but you are not going to explore many unknown realms that way." The gift for us in this third stage, in totally relinquishing control and emptying our vessel of all to which we were attached, is the opportunity to explore the unknown realms of the psyche, the unconscious and the power that lies hidden there. This power is needed to fuel soul growth and integration in the final stage.

Stage Four: Re-Filling the Vessel

The last stage in becoming a soul-infused personality is to take responsibility for creating a better world. Perceval, united in soul and body, rediscovers the Grail and asks the Fisher King the difficult question. In order to help heal the king, Perceval, for the first time, consciously links himself to a higher power. The king is healed, the Wasteland is restored to fertility and Perceval becomes the next guardian of the Grail Castle. He comes into his power in the world by uniting his soul and personality. Perceval embodies the principle of taking his soul to work because his work is not separate from his soul, but an extension of it. As such, he points the way for each of us. Only by undergoing these four stages can we fully know our purpose in both life and work. Trying to skip steps, refusing to take steps, or denying we are in a certain stage will not serve us. We cannot cheat or trick the soul.

It is important to remember that moving through these steps is definitely linked to age. Whereas it is possible to find many people in their sixties and seventies who have not gone through these four stages in their development, it is rare to find someone in their teens or twenties who has. Abraham Maslow summarizes the reasons for this:

> Self-actualization does not occur in young people. In our culture at least, youngsters have not yet achieved identity, or autonomy, nor have they had time enough to experience an enduring, loyal, post-romantic love relationship, nor have they generally found their calling, the altar upon which to offer themselves. Nor have they worked out their *own* systems of values; nor have they had experiences enough (responsibility for others, tragedy, failure, achievement, success) to shed perfectionistic illusions and become realistic; nor have they generally made their peace with death; nor have they learned how to be patient; nor have they learned enough about evil in themselves and others to be compassionate; nor have they had time to become post-ambivalent about parents and elders, power and authority; nor have they generally become knowledgeable and educated enough to open the possibility of becoming wise; nor have they generally acquired enough courage to be unpopular, to be unashamed about being openly virtuous, etc.

The qualities of self-actualization of which Maslow speaks are the same ones that both we and Perceval attain on our journey to becoming a soul-infused personality. Perceval was highly successful at each step along the way. He was a dutiful son before his journey began and then learned the rules of knightly conduct so well that he missed the opportunity to heal the Fisher King on their first meeting. Next, Perceval became skilled in his profession, and was soon regarded as "the best knight in the world." But only by letting go of each of the roles and rules of the preceding stages of development was he able, and this applies to us as well, to master the new ones. By the final stage, Perceval was able to rededicate his talents and gifts to the law of love and compassion, and hence could heal the king and the Wasteland. Perceval's journey mirrors the stages of humanity, as we walk from dependence to independence to interdependence. First, we need to master the laws of our material world—the low road— and then we are called to the high road.

The High Road of Work

When work is done for a reward, the work brings pleasure or pain, or both, in its time; but when man does work in Eternity, then Eternity is his reward.

BHAGAVAD GITA

Taking the High Road

I've briefly touched upon the concept of the high and low roads of work. When taking the high road, we are concerned both with *what* we do and *how* we do it. The high road is connected to the soul. It means using our jobs as vehicles to create something for the betterment of ourselves, others and the world. High road work alleviates physical, emotional, mental or spiritual suffering in the long term. High road work is based on the principles of interdependence—that what hurts one of us hurts all and what helps one of us helps all. Sometimes in high road work we help others directly, for example, a social worker who helps the homeless or a scientist who finds cures for diseases. Other times we help indirectly by supporting individuals and organizations who are doing high road work. This is true of office managers, administrative assistants and accountants.

Low road work, on the other hand, more often serves the short-term personality needs of individuals and organizations and does not, in and of itself, feed the soul. Some low road work might alleviate short-term suffering but it creates more long-term suffering. This is true of the pornography industry, weapons manufacturing and the drug trade. But it's important to emphasize that not all low road work has a negative impact on ourselves or others. Some low road work, in fact, might be important and necessary.

You might work as a waitress, a plumber or a lawyer for one reason only: money. You know that this is not what your soul calls you to do but you are doing it in order to support your family. Low road work meets your financial and security needs—which satisfy your personality—and without it you might not be able to afford to do any high road work. This high road work could be raising your family, coaching a soccer team or becoming involved in community projects and volunteer activities.

Most of our jobs, in fact, contain aspects of both high and low road work—aspects that satisfy the soul and others that satisfy the personality. The waitress might be doing that job for financial reasons but her way of doing it could be high road. By treating her customers with kindness and interest she can make their experience a pleasant one and ensure that they feel good about themselves and others.

It might be helpful to view work on a continuum, with some work being 100 percent high road and some 100 percent low road, but the great majority somewhere in the middle.

Some low roads may be desirable for society at this time. Law enforcement and the military, for example, have two roads. The lower road caters to people's need to be protected from crime in our country and from encroachment by others. These needs will be with us for some time and there will continue to be jobs in these areas. But high road jobs within these professions are growing. In the last ten years, for example, the military has taken a more active role in peacekeeping and disaster relief. Also, in the

United States, the army recently created a corps of environmental engineers who assist with ecological restoration.

There are two main ways we can do high road work. We might be "called" by our soul to the high road of a certain occupation. The word "vocation" means a calling to a specific kind of work and these jobs create good in our world. Or, we might transform our workplace with high road conduct by being compassionate, joyful, wise, ethical and courageous in speaking the truth. If we bring these qualities to our workplace, we can create good for our colleagues, clients and organization, regardless of the work we do. Both paths are equally important, but it may be difficult to discern the high road in some occupations.

Brenda is a housecleaner—often considered a low road job. She would prefer to be a healer—typically a high road job—and has taken many courses towards her goal. But Brenda has not yet been able to support herself in this vocation so in the meantime she is bringing the spirit of healing to her present work. She uses organic products and takes pride in her ability to create a pleasant atmosphere for those whose homes she cleans. Brenda goes out of her way to make herself useful, including hanging pictures, moving furniture and ironing clothes. She even bakes cookies and babysits her clients' pets when they are away. Because of how she does her work, Brenda is a "home healer," the high road of soul in her profession.

All of us can examine our work in this light to discover whether the way in which we work is creating a better environment for those with whom we come in contact. How we do our work is as important as what we do, just as long as what we're doing is not harming others. We take the high road by celebrating people, building their self-confidence, encouraging them and keeping our promises. We can do this even if the work itself isn't interesting or challenging.

It is possible that you'll never be able to do your *ideal* high road job, but you can be the bridge to high road work so that others following you will benefit. Perhaps you've always wanted to work with the poor in Third World countries. But you're married and are raising three young children. It would hardly be considered the high road if you abandoned your children to pursue this ideal job. Instead, you could support foster children and send money, letters and clothes to help, while at the same time continuing to take good care of your own children.

The amount of risk we are willing to take in order to do high road work may change. If we have enough money and have done low road work for some time, no longer finding it challenging or soul satisfying, we may take greater risks to work on the high road in our occupation. But some individuals will not be satisfied by practicing high road behavior in an otherwise low road job. Their soul will call them to high road occupations as well. Let's examine several areas—finance, law, medicine, politics, education and forestry—that collectively employ great numbers of people. Presently, I see in all of these occupations many hopeful signs that deserve recognition.

Accounting, Economics and Finance

Environmental audits and resource-based accounting are the high roads in accounting. The low road is traditional cost-based accounting, where a company is seen to be doing well if its sales outweigh its costs. I understand that we need to make a profit or we won't stay in business, but taking the high road in business means ensuring that profits are not our *only* motive for working and not our only criteria for success. Cost-based accounting is not concerned with how many non-renewable resources the company uses up in order to make its profits. To measure success using the high road of accounting, we need to calculate how much pollution is produced and energy consumed in order to make our products and how much energy will be needed to recycle our used computers, cars, televisions and paper when their useful life is past.

Our GNP is based on the low road of economics. Hazel Henderson, a well-recognized high road economist, says, "GNP values very highly bullets, tanks and cars; and it values at zero the environment, clean air, clean water, etc. It also values at zero our children, managing household activities, serving on our school board.... In so many countries of the world, the contribution of unpaid workers is far larger than the GNP." Ted Halstead has developed a GPI (Genuine Progress Indicator) and this, and other tools like it, helps redefine progress for our nations and organizations. The higher our GPI, the higher our household and volunteer work, and the greater our leisure time, life span of consumer durables, public infrastructure and income distribution to raise the quality of life for the poor. The lower our GPI, the greater our resource depletion, pollution, long-term environmental damage, defense expenditures and dependence on foreign assets.

High road economist Schumacher sums up the problem with the GNP in *Good Work*:

> The quality of life—not the quantity—yes, that's what matters. GNP, being a purely quantitative concept, bypasses the real question: how to enhance the quality of life.

Schumacher tells a story to illustrate his point. As a young man during the war he worked as a farm laborer and his job was to count the number of cattle in the fields. There were always thirty-two. One morning an old farmer saw him doing this and remarked, "If you count them every day they won't flourish." Schumacher wrote the old fellow off as a country yokel and proceeded with his count. One day, to his surprise, there were only thirty-one. He found the missing cow dead under a bush. He realized that he'd been so busy counting *quantity* that he'd missed the *quality* of each cow, which would have helped him prevent this one's death.

Within the last decade, many financial institutions and mutual funds specializing in the high road have sprung up in answer to people's concern about how they invest their money. The financial institution VanCity is a pioneer in ethical investing in Canada. The Ethical Growth Fund, which it founded, currently invests roughly $5 billion in socially and environmentally responsible organizations. In the United States, Shore Trust Bank, partner with Eco-Trust, goes one step further. Opened in July of 1997, it is North America's first fully fledged environmental bank. It lends money to businesses and community groups that embrace sound environmental principles.

Law

Many years ago, I knew a criminal lawyer who explained to me that his job was to defend his clients and to prevent them from being convicted of crimes even if he knew they were guilty. His work was not to seek justice but to win his case. The soul road of law is justice based on truth, not on deceit or falsehood. Eventually, this lawyer began using drugs to numb himself against the pain of his soulless work and ended up with an addiction.

His plight is not uncommon. When we do something that is not serving the highest good, our soul rebels and we become very unhappy. People might not be able to consciously attribute their unhappiness to the fact that their work is not in accord with their soul. They may have numbed themselves through drugs, sex, food, shopping or television—to name just a few addictions—but satisfying personality cravings fails to satisfy soul needs. To do this, we must seek high road work.

I appreciate that this lawyer was doing his job and working within the parameters of the law, but I believe that our laws need to be revised so that lawyers are better able to follow the high road. In fact, law is founded on the high road principle that all people are entitled to a fair trial. In practice, there are many difficulties in ensuring this happens. Money too often determines the outcome, as we have seen when the poor are unable to afford to take rich companies or individuals to trial for injustices and crimes.

Meanwhile, many high road areas within law are growing, such as environmental law, consumer advocacy and mediation.

In mediation, for example, a couple who are divorcing can work out a fair settlement that is acceptable to both of them. Under the traditional adversarial system and low road of law, both parties try to get as much as they can for themselves, and fairness is not necessarily part of the process.

In law, as with these other occupations, the high road is concerned with the greatest good for all parties involved long term. I understand that this is not always easy to determine, but if that remains our underlying motivation in our work, we can be sure we are moving towards the high road.

Medicine

There are also high and low roads in medicine. In some places in China, people pay their doctors to keep them well and if they get sick, their doctor looks after them for free. That system's emphasis is on health, not illness. It is certainly easier for physicians to follow the high road when the system they are working in reinforces it.

Currently, North American medical plans do not do this. Physicians are paid for the number of people they see. Therefore, they are not financially supported if they take the time to thoroughly discuss possible underlying emotional, mental or spiritual causes of their patients' illnesses. This leads to their dealing only with the bodily symptoms, often frustrating for both the physician and patient. Surgery fee structures also create difficult ethical decisions. For example, doctors might receive four times as much money for doing a Cesarean section than for a vaginal delivery. Rather than being called in the middle of the night and spending twelve hours delivering a baby, it must be tempting to book an appointment for a half hour during daylight hours. And yet, despite considerably less remuneration for more time invested, overworked physicians follow the high road year after year. But this does not mean that the system does not frustrate and depress them.

A physician once said to me that there are two kinds of doctors—gardeners and plumbers. Our present medical system in North America often emphasizes illness over health, plumbing over gardening. Billions of dollars are spent each year to treat heart disease and cancer, dealing only with the symptoms, not the causes. Yet, we continue to sell cigarettes, pollute our air and lead high-stress lives—the causes of these diseases. In fairness to physicians, many do an excellent job of informing the public about the hazards of smoking and the importance of proper nutrition and exercise in ensuring good health. In advocating these things, they are following the high road of their profession, and it is not their responsibility if people refuse to follow their advice.

The low road of healing focuses only on the body, while the high road or holistic healing is concerned with treating the body, mind and soul of the patient. The high road emphasizes prevention and non-invasive healing processes. In British Columbia, the Vancouver General Hospital has opened a clinic for alternative healing methods, including Chinese medicine, acupuncture and colour and touch therapy. This is a good example of how both roads of medicine can peacefully co-exist and support each other. One physician I know works four days a week in his traditional practice and a fifth day at a holistic clinic. He is so busy at the clinic that it takes three months to get an appointment. Unfortunately, only higher wage earners can afford continual holistic treatment, so this system of medicine is inaccessible for a great number of low-income patients.

Something that costs nothing and that has been shown to have an affect on healing is prayer. This is because our physical and emotional well-being is intricately connected to our spiritual well-being. Dr. Larry Dossey, author of *Prayer Is Good Medicine* and a pioneer in the area of high road healing, believes that prayer heals people in less time, saves more lives and reduces pain. Medical schools are starting to investigate and teach the benefits of spirituality to their students and in doing so are moving towards the high road of healing. Johns Hopkins University School of

Medicine in Baltimore has been so impressed by the research on prayer that it has started offering courses on faith and healing to doctors in training. Teaching physicians to balance their personal and work lives helps them to live the high road of a healthy life and in turn be better doctors for their patients.

Politics

The low road in politics is desiring power and control over people's lives and destinies. The high road is creating a government which anticipates the needs of the masses and which establishes policies and structures that allow people to flourish physically through health care, emotionally through a world at peace, mentally through interesting work and spiritually by helping them to develop their potential.

One example of a high road politician is Al Gore, the Vice-President of the United States. In addition to being a successful politician, he is also an active environmentalist and author of *Earth in Balance: Ecology and the Human Spirit*. Other examples of high road politics are exemplified by Corinne McLaughlin, who has taught transformational politics at American University in Washington, D.C., and Gordon Davidson, former executive director of the Social Investment Forum who has worked with President Clinton's Council on Sustainable Development. In their courageous ground-breaking book *Spiritual Politics*, they talk about working with higher spiritual principles. McLaughlin and Davidson advocate that all politicians resolve conflict for the good of all, further cooperation for mutual benefit, create sustainability for future generations, co-create with the natural world, uphold human rights, support sharing and personal initiative, act honestly and be an example for others of serving the whole and not one's self.

Svend Robinson, a Canadian member of Parliament, is just such a politician. Svend was first elected in 1979 and has put his values on the line on several occasions. As a result of participating in a blockade to a logging road in Clayoquot Sound in 1993, He was found guilty of criminal contempt and sentenced to fourteen days in jail. Despite cries from those who felt he should lose his parliamentary seat for breaking the law, Svend stated that it was his right to take a stand despite the consequences and that he might do so again. On August 4, 1994, he was quoted in *The Vancouver Sun* as saying, "I intend to continue working as a member of Parliament, to speak out against destruction of the environment, to speak out for aboriginal rights and I will do that in every possible way."

Another outspoken Canadian, Maurice Strong, millionaire businessman, veteran diplomat and active environmentalist, has also taken the high road in business and statesmanship. He once cut his own salary as chair of Ontario Hydro to $1 to demonstrate his belief in public service. In 1996, as undersecretary-general of the United Nations, he was awarded the U Thant peace award for his commitment to the UN and his environmental protections efforts. Government has a great responsibility in establishing laws that make it easier for individuals in all areas of work and life to follow the high road.

Education

The low road in education reveals itself in cramming our children's heads full of "readin', writin' and 'rithmitic'" at the expense of developing their talents and fostering in them a love of learning. In education, as with many professions, there is a need to incorporate both low and high roads to fully educate the whole person. If children can't read or write they will not find employment, so teaching these basic skills is important. However, if we kill our children's sense of joy and hope by not encouraging more soulful ways of learning, how can there be a possibility of hope for them and our world? Matthew Fox, in *The Reinvention of Work*, gives us a vision to aspire towards:

> Our era is in need of *wisdom schools*, as opposed to *knowledge factories* that have characterized education during the industrial era.... A wisdom school would...honor the heart and body, the right brain of awe and wonder, as much as it would the analytic or left brain.

My first career was as a high school teacher in what was then called an "open concept" school. Although all traditional subjects were taught, there were few physical walls, which was intended to promote team teaching and open thinking. However, I found that although the school "looked" open physically, the teaching was still quite traditional. From this I learned that the *spirit* of the high road must accompany the physical form if we are to make long-lasting changes in educational institutions.

There are several systems, such as Montessori and Waldorf, that attempt to offer the high road in education, but these are private schools and do not suit all students, nor can all parents afford the tuition fees. We need a flexible education system where students can find teachers and schools that will help them learn in the best way for them. This does not apply to just elementary and secondary schools. More and more we are seeing graduate schools that are offering alternative educational systems. Jean Houston has a Mystery School devoted to studying the philosophical and spiritual truths behind human existence, and Matthew Fox recently founded The University of Creation Spirituality. Also, there is a multitude of other educational institutions where students can study on weekends, in summers or by correspondence.

Waste Disposal and Forestry

Even getting rid of garbage can be high road work. Most organizations, and not just the more obvious not-for-profit ones such as Greenpeace or Earth Save, can follow the high road. Dynamotive, a company in British Columbia, has developed the technology to transform common garbage into a clean fuel. Winner of several awards, Dynamotive works to develop better industrial technologies that solve major environmental problems. It has created two products: Bio-Oil, which can be used as fuel on its own, and Bio-Lime, which can remove hazardous sulfur dioxide emissions from coal-burning plants that cause acid rain and contribute to the greenhouse effect.

Forest companies are also starting to walk the high road. In working with MacMillan Bloedel, Canada's largest forest products company, I have noticed a progressive move towards high road thinking. In the past ten years there has been more tree replanting and fewer toxic chemicals being dumped from pulp mills into streams. Recently, MacMillan Bloedel made a leap to the high road by announcing that they will eliminate clearcutting of old growth forests in British Columbia within five years. In the *MB Journal Bulletin* they offered their reasons: "This is about changing public values. Generally speaking, the public values on issues like clearcutting and old growth are increasingly clear.... We hope our program can be a big step forward in reconciling the differences between environmental and economic interests." MacMillan Bloedel is also trying to devise new ways of doing business by asking the question, Are there other ways of making paper without harvesting old-growth forests? One alternative they have come up with is growing poplar trees that can be harvested for pulp in twelve years instead of sixty.

Another high road option in the pulp and paper industry is to create "agripulp" mills. Arboken Incorporated, another Canadian company, puts out ten thousand tons of office grade paper annually made from farm products such as corn, wheat and oat straw. There is also increasing interest worldwide in growing some crops, such as flax, hemp and kenaf, as alternatives to tree farming. Hemp, for instance, grows so fast—6–16 feet in 70–110 days—that herbicides are not needed, and its natural resistance means that pesticides are not necessary either. Washington State University's Wood Composite Laboratory has tested hemp for use in medium-density fiberboard and results show that hemp is up to twice as strong as wood. The French have been building hemp houses for years and hemp products, such as Canobite, Mehabit, Canosmose and medium-density fiberboard are now available in North America. Hemp as a crop is at least 400 percent more efficient than tree farming.

Other companies specialize in harvesting the urban forest. Big City Forest in New York City turns industrial pallets (most of which are made of oak and other hardwoods) into flooring and industrial mill work. CanFibre Group of Canada is building two new plants in Riverside, California, and Lackawanna, New York. Each facility will be able to process 150,000 tons annually of wood residuals from construction, demolition and manufacturing into seventy-five million square feet of pressure-treated medium-density fiberboard.

Walking the high road in the forestry industry is not a new thing, and some people have done so for most of their lives. Harper Graham, a sixty-seven-year-old logger, is a two-time winner of British Columbia's Forests Excellence Award for his self-managed woodlot. As a third generation logger, logging is in Harper's blood. Working his way across Canada, his grandfather hewed ties for the CPR railway and was present in Craigellachie, B.C., in 1885 when the last spike of the first trans-Canadian railway was driven. His father also spent most of his days logging either for himself or others. Harper first joined the family tradition in 1949 by driving a logging truck around Campbell River and later moved into contract hauling. By 1962, Harper had saved enough money to buy his own woodlot. "To my knowledge," he says, "we were the first ones to plant trees on Read Island. This was done by my daughter, who was studying forestry at the time. These trees are now over thirty feet tall and doing very well. We're still working this woodlot today."

Activities on Harper's lands include logging, custom log sorting, a portable sawmill and free ranging of livestock. Considerable economic benefits have been generated—all enjoyed by the personality—and yet the land has retained its esthetic appeal and wildlife habitat—qualities important to the soul. Harper has increased the possible inventory fourfold while maintaining the integrity of the land in a sustainable manner. "If I were younger, I would take up the challenge again," says he. "What is better than having your lunch on the butt of a fresh cut log and your feet planted firmly in the sawdust wondering how many trees you can grow here the second time around?"

It is possible, as Harper Graham found, to walk the high road in industries that have previously appeared to be traveling in low road ways. As illustrated by the previous examples, there are momentous changes occurring in most occupations that allow for high road thinking. Although we do not have the space to examine the high and low roads of all occupations, I encourage you to apply this way of thinking to your own work.

Are You Doing High Road Work?

Here are a few questions to help you identify whether your work is on the high road.

1. Does your work diminish or increase you?
2. Does your work give you joy, creativity, meaningful learning, love?
3. Do others experience joy, creativity, meaningful learning or love because of you or your work?
4. Does your work benefit the world in both the short and long term?
5. Which parts of your work are low road?
6. Which parts of your work are high road?
7. Are you satisfied with the combination of low and high road aspects of your work?
8. If not, what would you like to do differently?

You may find that you are working mostly on the high road of your occupation and yet it is still not your soul's work. For example, you might have been in politics for many years attempting to make changes to governmental policies in areas of benefit to the community, environment and health care. Now you feel burnt out and are no longer putting your whole heart into your work and your soul is urging you to retire to the country to write a book that will summarize your previous learnings. Your soul work can change. As you continue to work on what you consider to be the high road in your job, you move away from being personality-dominated to being soul-infused. Organizations, like people, also can take either the high or low roads and can be either personality- or soul-infused.

Soul-Infused Organizations: An Organic Model

Soul-infused organizations recognize work in accordance with natural and spiritual laws, thereby helping their employees to develop their potential and creating goods and services that better the world.

Personality-dominated organizations, on the other hand, have a tendency to treat their employees as "objects" which serve the organization and, if they break down through overwork, they are replaced. These types of organization are interested in making the most money with the least regard for others inside or outside the organization. They demonstrate little concern about whether their products or services are helping or damaging the world, or if their workplace is helping or harming their employees.

Because the systems and policies of so many personality-dominated companies treat people as inanimate, it is useful to examine the impact of this thinking on the companies' efficiency and health. To do this, let's examine the difference between open and closed systems. Machines and technology, at present, are examples of closed systems and, based on the second law of thermodynamics, the products of closed systems move from usable to unusable. Under these laws, the more energy a system gives off, the more entropy there is and the less the system is capable of changing. This means that computers, television sets, airplanes and most of the products that we manufacture take a lot of energy to produce, have a limited span of useful time and end up as junk littering our environment.

Many organizations are run on this closed system principle, based on a mechanical model, and this model is not healthy for human beings. Organizations stressing technology at the expense of humanity and placing profit over long-term sustainability may have thrived in the previous stage of independence, but now many individuals are finding their jobs incompatible with the needs of their soul and are leaving in droves. Personality-dominated organizations are losing their best people and are crumbling with decay from within. Fortunately, some are considering changing to open, living systems.

Nobel Prize-winning chemist Ilya Prigogine proved that open systems are able to extract energy from entropy in their environment and recycle waste into order. For example, plants utilize the sun's energy in a way humans cannot, to make vegetables, grass and trees, to sustain every living organism on Earth. Margaret Wheatley, writing of Prigogine's work in *Leadership and the New Science*, said, "Equilibrium is neither the goal nor the fate of living systems, because open systems are partners with their environment." Wheatley goes on to say that open, living systems work best when they have a clear sense of their own identity so that they are not threatened by change, but welcome new information from their environment.

There are many formerly personality-dominated organizations, such as IBM and General Motors, which used to operate as closed systems and which are now moving towards open system organic practices. Like a person having a mid-life crisis who finds that their old way of living isn't working, traditional organizations are losing ground and downsizing. With the former organizational structure dissolving, employees have the opportunity to re-examine their way of working and are moving towards strategies that better suit the soul—forming teams, empowering themselves and helping to create partnerships with other companies. This can be a jerky process as the personality of the organization fights for control. The process of becoming a soul-infused organization is no different from the process for an individual whose personality resists encroachment by the soul.

Some organizations are evolving into soul-infused ones; others are starting up that way. These types of businesses are usually the progeny of soul-infused owners who want to create goods and services that will serve the world long term. They often attract like-minded individuals as both staff and clientele.

Soul-infused organizations see themselves as living entities. In fact, the word "organization" is derived from the word "organism," which means an animal or plant considered as a totality of *interdependent* parts functioning to maintain vital activities. As with living organisms, employees and their organization have a symbiotic relationship—the health of one affects the other. Organizations that are physically, emotionally, mentally and spiritually healthy are ones that obey the natural laws.

The metaphor of a garden works well in helping us understand the relationship between employees and their organizations. Plants in a garden need to be given good soil with proper nutrients in which to grow. Appropriate training and enough time to do their work are soil and nutrients to employees. It is also important that there is no competition among the plants for these nutrients or some plants, like people, will wither and fail to flourish. Young seedlings must be carefully nurtured and not be expected to bear as much fruit at first, just as new employees need time to learn the ropes before being expected to produce in the same way as an experienced employee. There must be enough sun—in the form of praise—to encourage the people to blossom. If employees are deprived of praise or are kept in the dark—by being given negative feedback or not enough information to do their job—they suffer. And, like plants who need water to grow, people must receive appropriate opportunities to develop their potential. If people are given too much water, because of others' unrealistic expectations of them, or too little, through non-creative, repetitive work, they will not develop into healthy organisms.

Strong plants create strong seeds that will thrive anywhere there is good soil. Good leaders—like good gardeners—need to thin out the less sturdy plants to give the healthy ones room to grow. This means letting go of employees who—given training and time—have proven unable to do the job. And don't forget that a pear tree cannot bear oranges. Individuals will never be happy in their work or develop their potential if they are expected to be something they are not.

Does your workplace meet these organic criteria for good health? When there is a good fit between you and your organization, you both thrive and help to create a healthy environment for staff, customers and suppliers. If you are dissatisfied with your organization, you might pressure it to change or crowd the other plants; or you might withdraw your roots and become passive, a dwarfed plant that doesn't get enough nourishment. If the organization is not meeting your needs, you may need to seek out more fertile soil or find a more nourishing environment.

Healthy organizations, like gardens, are able to resist encroachment from others and create room for plants that are beneficial to them. Joel Solomon, an entrepreneur, has a great saying about competition: "You don't have to protect every piece of corn from the raccoons." Joel is the president of Hollyhock, a personal growth center in Canada. He is also the managing partner of Renewal Partners, a company that gives seed capital to small community-based businesses where multiple partners own shares of each other's businesses. His principles are founded on a gardening model. "Build healthy soil, find healthy seed stock, focus on perennials, work hard and carefully nourish young plants, create diversity, try to align with cosmic and natural laws and the garden will gradually take care of itself and be abundant with less and less effort. Share cuttings and seeds with neighbors and feed the soil, feed the soil, feed the soil."

For Joel, the soil represents relationships with others, reputation, clarity of values, personal growth, self-mastery, knowledge, skill-building and a clean system, meaning a healthy physical body. Joel and his partners own a part of approximately fifty businesses in both Canada and the United States, all run by values-driven individuals who are attempting to have a positive social impact on the world. Joel was born into a well-to-do family in Tennessee that owned numerous shopping malls. He showed leadership qualities early, and by age nineteen was the national youth coordinator for the Jimmy Carter presidential campaign. But what Joel saw in politics distressed him, as did working in the family business. As he says, "Working with shopping mall real estate literally hurt my soul." He withdrew to the land and began working as an organic gardener. He commenced a life-long quest for consciousness and sought to align himself and his work with higher spiritual laws. After many years, Joel realized that he had a responsibility to others to use his inheritance wisely. He took the tools and talents he had been given—money, business acumen and leadership skills—and applied them towards generating community and small start-up businesses.

Joel's business rules include only doing business with friends or people who could be; becoming a minority partner in support of other people's dreams and life work; developing community by having many cross-ownerships where multiple partners own shares of others' businesses; allowing employees to own a part of the business or organization to build loyalty and commitment; fostering gender partnerships that have a balance of men and women to create a more holistic organization and heal the wounds of men and women in business; and investing for long-term gradual growth. Joel's business principles are based on interdependence.

Soul at Work: A Corporate Story

Xantrex, one of the winners of Canada's fifty best-managed private companies award which is given annually by Arthur Andersen & Co., is another example of a company committed to soulful business practices. Nazir Mulji, the thirty-seven-year-old president, started with this high-tech manufacturing company many years ago as a student doing work placement for the summer. Upon graduation, he was hired as an engineer and soon told his fellow employees that one day he was going to be president. One of the ways he achieved his goal was to make himself useful by serving others' needs. As one co-worker said of him, "Because Nazir said that he wanted to be president and demonstrated his talent for leadership, it was easy to hand him the responsibility."

Nazir conveys his vision and empowers his staff to do their tasks by having monthly meetings with employees where they can see the financial picture, their key customers and areas that need improvement. Individuals at Xantrex work in three large teams—called focused factories—that plan and carry out their work according to this updated information. The staff in each of these factories have the responsibility and power to make things happen. If individuals have complaints or suggestions, they are aired publicly and even Nazir and senior management are expected to act on them. These "requests" are posted in the lunchroom and are handled within a month of their submission. In this way, employees see immediately that their suggestions are being taken seriously and become committed to offering more.

Xantrex has a yearly gathering of all staff, which they call an "advance." Nazir says, "It's not a retreat; we're not moving back, we're moving forward, so we call it an advance." Last year I was invited to conduct their advance on Taking Your Soul to Work. On day one, employees sought solutions to problems that were affecting the progress of the company. On the second day, employees determined their career, personal and soul goals— whether inside or outside Xantrex—and the company committed itself to supporting their employees in achieving them. By helping their employees to develop their potentials, Xantrex is creating a soul-infused organization.

Xantrex has created a family feeling within the company; they care about the whole person, not just the person who has come to work. Employees hail from approximately thirty different countries. To celebrate employee diversity, Xantrex hung up a map of the world where employees could stick pins indicating their country of origin. Xantrex has also conducted ESL training and celebrates the cultural and religious traditions—such as Chinese New Year—of its employees. Xantrex makes a point of hiring for attitude and not for race or gender. As Nazir says, "We are origin blind."

Nazir, himself an Ismali Moslem, stresses that his training as a leader began with his volunteering for his spiritual community. Starting as an event planner in his local place of prayer, Nazir learned the skills of organizing people and resources. Recently, the Aga Khan appointed him head of twelve thousand Ismali Moslems in British Columbia, where—in addition to being president of Xantrex—he coordinates eight hundred volunteers in a dozen different centers. Nazir is a good example of how soul-infused personalities create or encourage soul-infused organizations. I once heard it said that CEO should stand for Chief Evolved Officer. Our workplaces would certainly be more soul-focused if this were the case.

In Part I we discovered the differences between our personality and soul and looked at how we need to work with both in harmony in order to become a soul-infused personality. The more we do this, the more we seek meaningful high road work and the less we are contented by just money or job security. Taking our soul to work is a rapidly growing trend in the developed world, illustrated by the increasing numbers of people who are engaged in the path of personal and professional transformation. Although our ultimate goal is to be able to transform our work environment and our world, which we will discuss in Part III, we must start by transforming and aligning ourselves to our soul's goals and Part II will assist us in doing that.

II

Inner Transformation: The Soul-Infused Personality

Although attempting to bring about world peace through the internal transformation of individuals is difficult, it is the only way.

H.H. THE DALAI LAMA

Developing the Soul-Infused Personality

The Essence of the individual soul art Thou,
and Thou art the five elements as well.

MATA AMRITANANDAMAYI

In Part I, we examined the process of interdependence whereby the soul and personality join to create a soul-infused individual who is able to take their soul to work. Part II gives you the tools you'll need to do this so that you will be more successful in manifesting your gifts in the world. Specifically, this section of the book includes exercises to assist you in determining your personality and soul goals and ways to achieve those goals. Some methods include reprogramming yourself for success and offer solutions to overcoming fears that may sabotage your effectiveness. You will also learn about various kinds of intelligence and discover in what ways you are gifted so that you can work consciously with your talents. A variety of ways to strengthen your soul connection in your day-to-day reality will also be discussed.

Four months after his first e-mail, Dan wrote again to tell me about the decisions he had made in his life. He had found a way to satisfy both his short- and long-term personality and soul goals, while staying healthy and happy in the meantime. In committing to his soul's journey, Dan accelerated his inner transformation. Although each person's journey is unique, there are certain predictable questions and answers that each of us will face. I'd like to share Dan's next steps in his journey with you.

Dan's Story Continues

Dear Tanis,

I wanted to drop you a note and let you know how things are progressing regarding my four-month agreement with my higher self. My spirits have gone slightly up and down, but are mostly very good. Achieving a balance as my life focus changes has taken a little time, but has settled out quite nicely. I've taken the approach of, "What's the most I can get out of these four months?" rather than "How can I get through these four months?" I'm planning my trip (a two-year world tour...a spiritual and personal development pilgrimage), progressing on schedule to a summer departure, but closing no doors yet. I've established a balance of keeping busy with things that are important to me, but not overextending myself as I was initially.

I am taking yoga every Monday night and meditation every Wednesday. Both are wonderful practices that I wish I'd become involved in years ago. You spoke of the value of meditation during your class, which I fully agree with. I'd been trying for years to advance my practice of meditation, but found it hard to establish the habit of the necessary regular practice. The support of a structured weekly class and the skill and knowledge of an excellent teacher has made progress very effective. I would recommend this route for anyone starting into the practice of meditation. Yoga and meditation are both overlapping and complementary.

The main benefits of yoga I have noticed so far are the releasing of tension and general body awareness, as well as becoming very aware and conscious of my breath.

It's funny how true it is that "the teacher will appear when the student is ready." In the last few months, many teachers have appeared or emerged, mainly from people who were already in my life. For example, a good friend's fiancée and I have grown closer and established an ongoing discussion. Shadow issues are our most recent topic. The same topic came up at meditation class last night, a concept that was foreign to me a month ago. Thank you again for being one of my teachers, in helping me to learn about myself, trust in myself and my intuition, and to have the courage to act on it. I'll continue to keep you updated and will send postcards from my trip.

Best regards, Dan

Once we commit to the process of transformation, the soul gives us lots of encouragement to continue. This encouragement could come in the forms of people who have the expertise we need, and practices such as meditation or yoga. We may also begin to make different friends—fellow travelers on the path. These friends share our concerns, and even our fears, as we encounter the shadow parts of our personality that we are afraid to change. We may also notice a synchronicity in events. We hear the same message in different forms and places until we have fully understood and integrated new soulful behavior.

The Five Bodies That House the Soul

In order for you to become a soul-infused personality, and able to take your soul to work, it is essential that you understand how your personality functions. It is the vehicle that works with the soul in the world. According to metaphysical science and various eastern religions, the personality is composed of five "bodies," each with a specific function in your personal and work life. There are other higher spiritual bodies, but a discussion of these lies outside the range of this book. The five personality bodies include the physical, etheric, emotional, mental and spiritual.

The physical body incorporates genetic strengths, weaknesses, gender and race. The etheric body contains both the ancestral and *collective* memories of your gender and race, as well as the *individual* memories you have gathered through your parents, education and society. The third body, the emotional, is associated with your temperament, your likes and dislikes; while the fourth body—the mental body—deals with your skills and talents. And the spiritual body houses the *part* of your soul that works with the other four bodies of the personality to serve the specific purpose for which you came into this life.

Together, these five bodies make up the vessel that we inhabit. To become conscious creators we must understand the workings of these bodies as they affect our life in everyday reality. Each body has a talent and a function. As we progress from the physical towards the spiritual realm and from youth to adulthood, there is a tendency to move from being personality-centered to soul-centered.

Just as a baby first learns to control its physical world, most of us first learn to control our physical body. The child then learns habits that keep her safe in the world, such as not touching a hot stove. Learned habits and stored memories are the realm of the second, the etheric, body. At this stage, the child is still engaged in discovering which repeated behaviors, such as crying or laughing, will get her what she wants. These initial behaviors have a reflexive, rote aspect to them, but gradually the child develops a range of feeling beyond pleasure and pain that allows her to anticipate and hope. This realm of feeling is connected to the third, the emotional body. The cognitive function of the fourth, the mental body, develops next. Awareness allows the child to make connections between seemingly unrelated things—eventually over greater and greater time spans. For example, the child might decide that if she wants a cookie in two hours, she'd better behave now. The fifth body, the spiritual, becomes active as the child desires to please others for their sake and not only for herself. At this stage, the child learns self-sacrifice as well as interdependence as she begins to realize that through benefitting another, she benefits herself.

Activation of these five bodies in childhood is learned in the same order as the stages of individual evolution I discussed in Chapter 3. It could be argued that there are individual exceptions where development occurs in a different order and that some bodies are never activated. This is true, for example, of psychotics who are unable to empathize with the pain of others. However, in general, the awakening of these bodies tends to happen in the order given and this progression extends into our adult life as we gradually learn to fully control each body.

Once all five bodies are functioning, they work together like this: the spiritual body, the realm of the soul, directs the mental body into certain ways of thinking that will cause it to grow in consciousness. The mental body begins to develop ideas and thoughts based on its observations both of the outer and inner worlds. The mental body offers these ideas to the emotional body, which responds with feelings. Based on these feelings and on the past history associated with these kinds of feelings, recorded in the etheric body, the personality decides to take action in the world of the physical body.

Initially in our development, the physical, emotional and mental bodies are more concerned with the needs of the personality than with those of the soul. Our spiritual body houses the part of our soul that works with us in this life and, as we evolve into soul-infused beings, the soul incorporates itself more and more into our other bodies. The etheric body, or body consciousness, has a somewhat different function—it is in contact with the soul and knows the soul's purpose, while at the same time it is a servant to the personality. It's caught between these two sometimes diverging forces and has the power to make us sick if we don't pay it and our soul enough heed. The goal of the etheric body—working in conjunction with the other bodies—is self-consciousness and to work in partnership with the soul.

The Five Bodies at Work

At work, we seek first to satisfy the needs of our physical body, then our etheric, followed by our emotional and mental needs—all before meeting the needs of our spiritual body. During this progression, we move from being other-directed and desiring only what society has taught us to want, to being self-directed and making choices for ourselves. When we are other-directed, we might encounter thousands of potentially satisfying experiences and not appreciate them. Our etheric body is programmed by our culture and parents to recognize and value what they value. Yet, when we achieve these things—a house, an attractive spouse, money, status—we remain discontented unless these achievements are in accord with our soul. Only by aligning ourselves to our soul's purpose will we find joy and happiness. The two places where this is most likely to occur are in our work and in personal relationships. Let's examine how we move from being directed by our personality and culture to being soul-directed as it affects us in our work.

Physical Body

Our physical body is concerned with safety. On first entering the workforce in our teens or early twenties, our major concerns are having a roof over our heads and enough food in our bellies. There are few people in the workforce who have not met these basic needs to some extent. But there are many others considered unemployable by society—because of lack of motivation, social skills or intelligence—who are still attempting to satisfy these

The Five Bodies and Their Major Concerns at Work

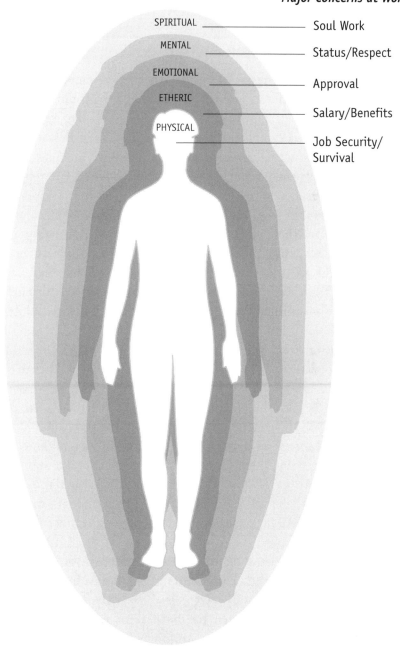

Major Concerns at Work

SPIRITUAL —————————— Soul Work

MENTAL —————————— Status/Respect

EMOTIONAL —————————— Approval

ETHERIC —————————— Salary/Benefits

PHYSICAL —————————— Job Security/
Survival

physical needs. These individuals will not be interested in soulful work until the lower needs are met.

Etheric Body

After the basic, physical needs have been met, a more subtle craving asserts itself—an interest in money and what money can buy. This is the stage that many young people find themselves in before they have established themselves financially. Because money is associated with learned needs, it is actually related more to the etheric body than to the physical. Although it's a natural first step in our attitude towards work to want to secure ourselves financially, some individuals get stuck in this stage. Their major concern is that their work provide a good salary, plus retirement, health and dental plans. Many people work only for these reasons and are too fearful to give up what they perceive to be "safe" work to do soul work. This is especially true during times of economic difficulty. I often hear, "I'm lucky to have a job," as a rationale.

The etheric body is the one most closely associated with the body soul as described by the Fox tribe I spoke of earlier (page 29). This body soul, working through the etheric body, built our five bodies with the blueprint it was given when we were incarnated. With the genetic history, it formed the physical body; cultural and ancestral history, the etheric body; temperament, the emotional body; talents and gifts, the mental body; and values, the spiritual body. As well as recording these original memories in the body, the etheric body also records ongoing memories, such as all the injuries suffered and the joys experienced throughout life.

Because the etheric body's talent is memory, it has a preference for familiar rather than unfamiliar things. Individuals with a dominant etheric body have a need for structure and order. For instance, they are shaken by the present insecurity in the job world. As we know, there is no longer such a thing as a "safe" job, and just because you have done a good job for twenty years and have been a loyal, reliable employee, there is no guarantee that the job will be there even in another six months. If you are driven by habits and patterns, as you could be when the etheric body is strong, you might find it difficult to let go of outmoded ideas in order to try something new.

I remember the president of a large corporation saying, "I cannot guarantee employment but I can guarantee employability." He understood his responsibility to keep the skills of his employees current so that, if he did have to let them go, they would have skills that could be transferred to a job elsewhere. Although I celebrate organizations that have this policy, it is also our individual responsibility to keep our skills current, and not depend on employers to do it for us. This erases negative programming of scarcity and loss, which sometimes plague the etheric body, and embraces positive attitudes that will allow us to thrive in the present and future.

Emotional Body

The third body—the emotional body—seeks love and belonging. This means that you need to like the people you work with and to feel accepted, and even loved, by them. Individuals with this motivation like to express their love and caring for others and like to help others in their work. I recently saw a movie called *Marvin's Room*. In it, the younger sister, who left home years ago, is talking with the older sister, who stayed home to look after their parents and is now dying of cancer. The older sister says, "I'm so lucky I've had so much love in my life," to which the younger sister replies, "Yes, so many people have loved you."

"No," replies the older sister, "you don't understand; I've been lucky to have been able to love so many people."

Although it may be desirable to work with people you like, this in itself does not guarantee that you'll like your job. Still, if you do what you love, you attract people with similar values and it is possible—as it was for the older sister—to have both pleasant people to work with and meaningful work. It is not an either/or choice.

When the emotional body is dominant, there may be a tendency to feel things too deeply and become incapacitated by our emotions. We may be hurt easily if someone is brusque with us, or feel taken for granted if others don't pay attention to us. The emotional body is like a child looking for approval until we learn to place it under the restraining hand of the soul on the path to becoming soul- and not personality-directed.

Mental Body

The mental body is commonly associated with intelligence and it does have this function and more. By using your talents and gifts, you'll succeed in the external world. This creates self-esteem and a sense of achievement, both of which are important to the mental body. However, the need to achieve status, power and respect—concerns of an overdeveloped mental body—have caused serious problems in the world when this need transforms into a desire for power over others and the environment. It is important that we use our power to help the world rather than for self-aggrandizement, greed or control.

Spiritual Body

As all the bodies commit to an interdependent marriage with the soul, the person becomes what Abraham Maslow refers to in his book *Motivation and Personality* as self-actualized. At this time, all the bodies can start working in conjunction with each other. He says, "Even if all these [other] needs are satisfied, we may still often (if not always) expect that a new discontent and restlessness will soon develop, unless the individual is doing what *he* individually is fitted for. What a man *can* be, he *must* be."

Self-actualized, soul-infused people are joyful, creative, courageous, truthful and concerned with the greater good. Their work and lives are a blend of both being and doing. When we are soul-infused in our work, there is nothing we would rather do than what we are doing. It may be difficult for others to tell if we are soul-infused, because it is an internal, not external, measurement.

For instance, I have two friends who are craftspeople. They live on less than ten thousand dollars a year, have an organic garden and live in the country, where they have time to read as much as they like. They are soul-infused, but someone who does not know them might mistakenly think they are simply trying to meet their basic, physical needs. The key to being soul-infused is that we are self-directed, not other-directed. Our motivation is to work at what we love. Money, and being liked or being respected are not our main motivators for working.

When we are taking our souls to work, retirement is a non-issue. We prefer to continue working at what we love and others will still find us effective. I remember one day being in an elevator with one of my clients on the way to give a customer service seminar for a large retail chain. An elderly gentleman got on and I wondered what he was doing in an office tower. After he got off my companion asked me if I knew who that gentleman was. I replied that I didn't and was told, "He's the founder and president of our company. He's eighty-two and comes to work every day. He has an afternoon nap for two hours in his office and still makes the final decisions on all major policies for the company."

There are certain characteristics that Maslow discovered in self-actualized people which I, likewise, have found in individuals with soul-infused personalities. They have an unusual ability to detect the fake and the dishonest, and to judge people correctly and efficiently. They accept themselves and their own natures without apology or complaint, and their behavior is marked by simplicity, naturalness and lack of artificiality.

At work, self-actualizers—because they are led by the soul—are interested in solving problems, focusing in general on tasks that are non-personal or unselfish and concerned rather with the good of humanity. They positively *like* solitude and privacy, make up their own minds, are self-starters and are responsible for themselves and their own destinies. Soul-infused individuals have the wonderful ability to appreciate again and again, freshly and naively, the basic goods of life, with awe, pleasure, wonder and even ecstasy. They have more than an average amount of peak experiences, where they feel connected to their souls, simultaneously feeling more powerful and more helpless.

Soul-infused people have a deep feeling of sympathy and affection for human beings in general and have a genuine desire to help the human race. They have humility, respect others and can be friendly with anyone of *suitable* character, regardless of class, education, political belief or race. They have deeper and more profound interpersonal relationships than any other adults, but these are likely to be with relatively few individuals who are also soul-infused personalities.

The sense of humor of soul-infused personalities is not of the ordinary type and consists of poking fun at themselves—and human beings in general—when they are foolish or forget their place in the universe. They are strongly ethical, but their notions of right and wrong, of good and evil, are often not the conventional ones. They have a special kind of creativeness or originality akin to the naive and universal creativeness of unspoiled children. Soul-infused people resist enculturation and maintain a certain inner detachment from the culture in which they are immersed. All of this is not to say they are "perfect." They may be boring, stubborn, irritating, cold or have temper tantrums. Paradoxically, they are fully human in their failings, while at the same time representing the potential to which all humans can aspire.

Meeting Your Needs at Work

Our five bodies are motivated by needs and by satisfying these needs, the personality feels full and comfortable enough to wish to enter into partnership with the soul. If the needs of the four lower bodies have never been met, it is difficult to have the self-esteem and self-knowledge necessary to sacrifice these needs to the soul. Not that sacrifice is always necessary. Often it's not, but what is necessary is the *willingness* of the personality to sacrifice its independence for interdependence as it unites with the soul. Not all bodies are at the same level of development simultaneously. For example, someone could have a well-developed mental body that knows in theory that marriage with the soul is desirable. Unfortunately, his or her emotional body, being underdeveloped, resists. The process to get all bodies working together to commit to the soul is ongoing and takes years. However, in general, as the needs of the five bodies are met, the personality becomes more eager to unite with the soul.

To determine if your needs are being met at work, try the following exercise. Ask yourself this question: What percentage of my physical, financial, etheric, emotional, mental and spiritual needs are being met in my present job?

❖ Physical needs include having pleasant surroundings, such as a private office, windows that open, plants, nice colors, healthy lighting.

❖ Financial needs include making enough money to live comfortably. This may or may not include dental, medical or retirement plans.

❖ Etheric needs include stability and consistency in leadership and policy and even rituals that comfort you, such as being able to sit in the same chair in meetings.

❖ Emotional needs include working with pleasant people, having no conflict, liking people you work with and having them like you.

❖ Mental needs include having interesting work where you are challenged—in a positive way—to grow.

❖ Spiritual needs include doing meaningful work that has intrinsic value for yourself, for others, and which is in keeping with your purpose in life.

Using the following chart, record your needs and what percentage of them are being met presently in each area. For example, under physical you might put, "window with view, good hours and 75 percent of my physical needs are met."

Does Your Work Meet Your Needs ?		
	Needs	Percentage Met
Physical		
Financial		
Etheric		
Emotional		
Mental		
Spiritual		

What patterns do you see in your chart? Are all, or only some, of your personality or soul needs being met? The amount that your needs are *not* met is directly proportional to the amount of discontent and frustration you may feel with your job. If the majority of your needs are not being met, you might want to consider changing jobs and will do this more readily if you have high self-esteem and career goals. The more you meet the combined needs of the personality and the soul, the happier you'll be.

Most of us, even when self-actualized, still have goals that interest us and things we want to do in the world. These goals will change continuously and new ones will replace those we have achieved. Conscious goal-setting is an act that calls on the twin resources of the soul and the personality because only the personality knows how to implement the soul's goals in the physical world. By learning to create and act on goals, we learn to control our physical reality and to take our first steps in becoming a soul-infused personality.

Answering Your Soul's Call

If you follow your bliss, you put yourself on a track that has been there all the while, waiting for you.

JOSEPH CAMPBELL

Personality and Soul Dreams

Happiness results from achieving our dreams or hopes for our life. There are two main types of dreams—the personality dream and the soul dream—and both need to be satisfied if we are to become a soul-infused personality. The personality dream often involves getting an education, buying a house and/or marrying and having children. At work, the personality dream might entail securing a solid job with a good company.

The soul dream often revolves around what we feel *called* to do. Just as Mohandas Gandhi was called from practicing law in South Africa to obtaining home rule for India, our soul might have plans for us that are totally unforeseen by our personality. When Terry Fox had his leg amputated because of cancer in his early twenties, he was called by his soul to run across Canada to raise money for cancer research. Fox's "Marathon of Hope" is still run by thousands of people each year, a fitting tribute to a young man whose soul's purpose stirred so many. I am not suggesting that our soul will call us into as challenging circumstances as did Gandhi's or Fox's, but the call is often unpredictable and unsought by the personality.

To make the personality an ally, the soul must satisfy its needs. If we satisfy only our soul dream by doing the work we love, we may lack money to buy what we want. This will frustrate our personality and make us unhappy. However, unhappiness more often results from pursuing the dreams of the personality, while remaining oblivious or afraid to heed the dreams of the soul.

Soul dreams, like those of the personality, are anchored in physical reality and it takes concrete, practical skills to manifest them. By following our soul dream, we may achieve extrinsic rewards of recognition, money, power and status, that are important to our personality. However, extrinsic rewards are not the main motivation of a soul. Individuals motivated by their soul dreams feel called to *do* something, regardless of what society or others think of it. If they don't do what their soul wants, they may become depressed, unhappy and frustrated with the rest of their life. We can often satisfy our personality by satisfying our soul dreams, but will never be able to satisfy the soul by satisfying our personality.

Christine Silverberg, Chief of the Calgary Police Service, is a wonderful example of someone who has managed to fulfill both her soul and personality dreams. When Silverberg first entered the police service twenty-six years ago, she was not allowed to carry a gun and, unlike male co-workers, was denied a pension plan because she was not considered to be a breadwinner, even though she was supporting her husband through university. She now heads a seventeen hundred-member police service with one thousand experienced volunteers and is well respected for her community crime prevention and policing policies. Chief Silverberg is married with two children and has worked hard to maintain life balance. She is an example for all women who do not wish to sacrifice female priorities in order to succeed in a male-dominated world.

Silverberg says, "Our destinies differ as our dreams. And our dreams are as distinct as are each and every one of us. No matter where we may be in our lives, we fall or rise with our thoughts, our visions, our imaginations, and once we know the power of visioning, it invades our senses, no matter what form it takes, and becomes an enticement. It becomes a desirable search. But it is not the endpoint that matters for me—it is the process of getting there. For I know only too well that our achievements today may very well be the beginning of yet another journey."

To make her point, Silverberg likes to use the metaphor of the goldfish that grows to the size of its environment. A goldfish in a bowl in a child's bedroom may be only two inches long, but placed in a pond will grow to the size of a small dog. "And the advantage that we have over goldfish," Silverberg says, "is that we get to choose the size of our bowls. I believe we can either enhance or diminish our potential by our belief systems. If we believe we can, we are capable of achieving new heights because we remain limited by only our self-imposed bowl size. The trick to achieving majestic heights is, I believe, to limit ourselves only to expectations of greatness."

There are two main steps to achieving the soul dream. First, identify what it is and, second, commit to achieving it. The remainder of this chapter will be devoted to helping you begin. I say "begin" for a couple of reasons. The first is that listening to your soul is an evolving process. Stephen Covey, author of *The 7 Habits of Highly Effective People*, once said that it took him ten years to write his own personal mission statement. And he is an expert on this topic! The second is that following our soul's voice is often accompanied by pit-stops and setbacks in physical reality that we may not have anticipated. We need to be committed to the process over the long term and be determined, persistent and willing to reformulate ourselves and our lives in accordance with our soul. This is not easy work, as we will meet with resistance from our personality, *but* the goal is achievable for all of us.

I have developed the tools and techniques over twenty years that are outlined in this book, and they work for those willing to try them. To achieve our soul's goals, we need to anchor them in the concrete, practical reality of the physical world. By doing so, we learn how to weave the spiritual and physical worlds and bodies together.

Manifesting Your Soul Dream in the World

Identifying Your Soul Dream

Identifying your soul dream is the first step in anchoring the soul in the vessel of your personality. Each individual's soul dream is unique, but here are a few examples to start your creative juices flowing.

- ❖ I have a strong desire to write a book about my family.
- ❖ My soul dream is to create a hospice for dying children.
- ❖ My greatest wish is to sail around the world in my own boat.
- ❖ I feel called to create a healing center where people of all disciplines can work together.
- ❖ My life's purpose is to bring joy to people through singing.
- ❖ I would like to stop working for others and start my own business (e.g., accounting, computer programming, counseling, graphic design, retail, travel, fitness).

In the following diagram, write down your soul's dream. What do you think your life's purpose is? Feel free to add or delete any personality dream items.

My Soul Dream

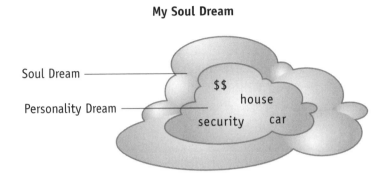

Some of you already know your soul's mission, while others may be unclear, making this exercise more difficult. But you need to flow from this first step of determining your soul's goal. It is better to take a step towards a fuzzy, foggy soul dream than to continue setting goals for the personality that are ultimately unfulfilling. By taking the first step in the soul's direction, the other steps reveal themselves in time. This exercise will help you eliminate what you *don't* want, thereby making it clearer what you do want.

Some of you may be able to better understand your soul's purpose through a guided visualization than by writing a list. Visualization is a potent tool in receiving information from your soul. It also informs your soul that you want changes to occur. Below, I have provided a guided visualization to assist you in hearing your soul more easily. You can either ask a friend to talk you through this visualization, or you can record it yourself and play it back on a tape recorder. If you choose to do it yourself, play it back with your eyes closed, while sitting or lying in a quiet place. Record the words in a *slow*, gentle voice. Allow *spaces* at the end of each

> *The Image I am born with not only pushes from the beginning; it also pulls toward an end.*
>
> JAMES HILLMAN

sentence to give you time to follow the directions. This exercise will take approximately fifteen minutes.

Guided Visualization to Discover My Soul's Purpose

Close your eyes and begin breathing deeply. The secret of deep breathing is all in the exhalation. Completely exhale all the air in your lungs and you will naturally and easily reach for the next breath. Starting with your feet, visualize all the muscles in your feet and toes. See and feel them relax. Moving into your calves and thighs, see and feel them relax. Moving into your stomach and buttocks, see and feel all the muscles relax. The relaxation travels up your chest and, as you take a deep breath and exhale, see and feel all the muscles in your chest completely relax. Visualize a pair of soothing hands massaging the muscles in your neck, shoulders and back until all these muscles relax. The relaxation drains into your upper arms, lower arms and hands. See and feel all these muscles completely relax. The relaxation now moves into your forehead and drains down into your eyes. Relax. Down into your jaw. Relax. All your muscles are completely relaxed.

Now, visualize yourself going to your favorite place in nature, somewhere you can feel totally relaxed and at peace. It may be by the ocean, in a forest, or in an open field. See and feel yourself in this favorite place. It's a beautiful day. The sky is blue with white clouds floating by. The sun is warm and there is a slight breeze. Breathe in the smells and listen to the sounds of your favorite place. Find a comfortable place and sit down. [Longer Pause] Ask your soul to explain your purpose in this life. Don't censure or judge what you receive. Just allow any images, feelings or thoughts to come to mind. What images arise? Notice where you are and what you are doing. Are you alone or with other people? If you're with others, do you know them? What kind of work are you doing? Notice everything in great detail. [Longer Pause] What words come to mind when you think of your work?

Does this look like you today? If not, how many years is it in the future? [Longer Pause] Imagine your personal life. What are you doing and who is with you? [Longer Pause] How is this life different from your life today? How is it similar?

Now, imagine that you can step into the life that you are visualizing. See a beam of light completely surround you and let it extend out and encompass the future you. Feel your present atoms joining with the future you. Allow the energy from your future vision to completely fill you, until you are that person having that life. Continue seeing and feeling yourself filled both personally and professionally with your soul dream. [Longer Pause]

When you have completely become that person, feel the energy gently returning to your body and start to return to consciousness. Do not move quickly. Open your eyes very gradually. [Longer Pause]

After you have opened your eyes, write down your soul dream and everything that you can remember from the visualization. Visualization is an incredibly powerful tool to help you become what you wish to be. I recommend that you devote time every day to visualizing yourself living your soul dream. To make sure that you have actually written down your soul desires and not your personality desires, ask yourself the following question. "If I were to do/have/be in the physical world what I have written down, would I feel that I had achieved my life's purpose?" If your answer is "yes," this is likely to be your soul's dream or the part of it that you can access presently. If your answer is "no," ask yourself what you could do that would make you feel that you had achieved your soul's purpose and write down your answer. Is this closer to your life's purpose? Also, remember that soul dreams can change. We may achieve one part of the soul's purpose in our twenties, another part in our thirties, and another in our fifties. As we grow, we learn how to manifest our potential and talents more fully, but more often than not there is a common thread weaving through our soul dreams at all ages. Writing down the soul's mission will not, by itself, guarantee success. To achieve the soul's purpose we need to establish goals and an action plan. This is the process whereby we strengthen the connection between our spiritual and physical worlds.

Identifying Ten Goals for Your Life

Whatever you can do or dream you can do, begin it.
Boldness has genius, power and magic.

GOETHE

 Now that you know your soul's purpose—or at least as much of it as you understand at this moment—it is time to set goals to help you to achieve it. You may choose to commit to a combination of personality and soul goals—which is fine—but don't set only personality goals at the expense of your soul. By committing to *some* personality goals each year, your personality becomes an ally in helping you achieve your soul's goals. If you only work towards soul goals, your personality may resist the journey because it sees no benefit for itself. As interdependent partners, the soul and personality fertilize each other. When the personality assists the soul in achieving its goals, it opens up to allow the soul more fully into its vessel. Through this process, the soul uplifts the personality to higher, more spiritual, levels. By encouraging them to work together as interdependent partners, you quicken your own spiritual transformation.

The following goal-setting exercise is one that I have done for over a decade. Each year, I set aside January 1 to write down both personality and soul goals, including any actions I'm committing to take in the coming year to either achieve these goals completely or to move them forward a step or two. What I decide to do on January 1 determines my path for the following twelve months.

After writing down my goals, I review my goal list from the previous year to reflect on which goals I've accomplished and to either recommit to or let go of goals that I have not yet achieved. Some years I have accomplished almost half of my goals. These are goals like "I want to move to Vancouver and buy a house." Sometimes I will carry a goal on my list for several years until I find the momentum to finish it. For example, writing this book was on my list for two years before I was ready to submit it for publication. And not all goals result in a final achievement that you can easily measure. Some goals, such as doing loving things for my family and friends or walking every day in nature, are dearly loved perennial goals that will probably continue to be on my list year after year. These are "evolving goals" and I hope to continue to grow in my love for these people and the natural world. I also have goals that I dutifully write down every year and don't act on. My big "non-goal" is doing daily exercise. This is an area of my life where *as yet* I have no discipline. In the future I believe that I will commit to daily exercising, but I don't beat myself up for not doing it at present.

Goal-Setting Exercise

Now, back to your goal-setting exercise. First, set the stage. This exercise, as with meditation, is more effective on an empty stomach, so, after either fasting or eating a light breakfast, sit quietly with your journal near you. If you don't normally write in a journal, use some special paper and a nice pen. Setting the stage is important because it sends a signal to the higher self that a significant event is about to take place.

Close your eyes, or keep them open—whatever works for you—but wait until you reach a calm, detached place before proceeding. In this calm state, ask your higher self, "What are ten things I want to do or be in my life?" Do not censor yourself, but allow your higher self to ask for what you really want. Write down your answers.

Ten Goals for My Life
1.
2.
3.
4.
5.
6.
7.
8.
9.
10.

When no more items come easily to mind, stop writing regardless of the number. Force nothing. Look at what you have written. Are there any patterns? Is anything or anyone conspicuously absent? Does your list include items that will help you to achieve your soul's purpose in life? For example, if your soul's call is to help the poor, have you written down a specific goal here to do it?

How many of your soul's goals are work-related and how many are related to your personal life? I have done this exercise with thousands of people and have found repeatedly that people have only one or two, and sometimes no work goals on their list of ten. Why? Because they associate work with pain and they don't want goals that will give them more pain. We need to realize that this pain is most often caused because we are *not* doing our soul's work.

Reality Checks

Having established your life goals, it is essential to examine them to see if they are possible and, in many cases, probable. By doing this you eliminate any goals that will not work, while at the same time strengthening the threads between your soul dream and the physical world. What follows are a series of questions to assist you in focusing your attention on your goals.

Are Your Goals within Your Control?

First, examine your goals to make sure they are within your power to enact. Perhaps they will take a long time, and you might have to give up something to get them. Are you willing to do this? If you are, the chances are fairly good that you will succeed. This exercise will help you to eliminate goals that are not within your control, such as, "I want to win the lottery." (By the way, winning the lottery is a personality, not a soul, goal. It's not the money people want, but the freedom money buys.) Instead of having a goal of making or receiving money, think of what would give your life meaning. Then create an action plan to do this and the money will come, if, as I've said before, you are prepared to work for it.

Are Your Goals Concrete, Specific and Balanced?

Next, examine your goals to see if they are concrete and specific. If you keep the wording and image of your goals too vague, you won't be able to work towards them. For example, instead of saying, "I want my family to be happy," it would be better to say, "I am going to spend two hours daily with my son." By doing this, you make your goals both specific and within your power.

I am mentioning personal, as well as work, goals because the soul thinks in terms of the whole life. Your soul seeks balance in all areas of life—physical, emotional, mental and spiritual. Look at your list. Do you have goals in all of these areas? It's possible that you have not included goals in one or two areas because you already feel balanced in these areas. For example, perhaps you have not included any emotional goals because you have wonderful relationships with your family and friends and feel that this is not your area of growth presently. That's great and means you are already working on it. This question was designed to help you identify the areas where you lack balance so you can determine goals to help you restore it.

Are Your Goals Unrealistic Fantasies?

Having unrealistic fantasies often prevents us from finding fulfillment in life. When thinking of soulful work, therefore, guard against idealizing it. To do so keeps the soul ungrounded in reality so that the personality learns not to trust the soul's judgment. For instance, you may have an idealized image of doctors making $200,000 a year and all their patients adoring them. This is not the reality of that profession. Most doctors work very long, stressful hours—much more than the forty which you might like to work—and often on weekends and at night. The combination of both long hours and the ongoing stress of working with people in pain can lead to strained family relationships and sometimes to substance abuse. So the fantasy and the reality of that profession—like so many others—are worlds apart. Idealized fantasies and daydreaming indicate a lack of rigor in the spiritual body. To manifest our dreams we must use down-to-earth strategies governed by the physical body.

Let's explore a goal common to many spiritual people. Numerous men and women have mentioned to me that they would like to have a healing practice or center in a quiet, natural environment. Currently, there is a growing demand in North America for alternative forms of healing, such as aromatherapy, acupuncture or Reiki, so this goal works in their favor. However, if this is your goal, before quitting your job at IBM you should do some hard research. You might want to visit the small communities that interest you to see how many healing practitioners work there already. How many people would require your particular treatment? How would they pay? Perhaps some clients would prefer to barter than to pay cash and, if so, could they barter with something you need? If you could not fully support yourself working in that small community, is there a large center nearby where you could work a few days a week? If not, do you have other skills that might be needed where you'll be living? Do you like gardening? Would you enjoy growing your own food? Do you enjoy building? Could you build your own home?

Asking probing questions will not destroy your dream, but help you bring it into concrete, practical reality. Your soul's work will pass the test of most of these questions. It is especially important for idealistic dreamers—the Don Quixotes of this world — to employ these reality checks or their life could be a series of chases after dreams that don't work out.

Prioritizing Your Goals

Sometimes we have many goals that we would like to achieve but become confused about where to start. Prioritizing our goals helps us to focus on which ones are the most important and releases our energy to take action in the physical world to achieve them. It's easier to manifest one, two or even three goals at a time, than ten. As we develop self-confidence that we can achieve our goals and the determined focus that makes it possible, we can increase the number of goals on which we are working. This process will likely take many years. It's better not to overload ourselves until we've mastered the prototype for goal-setting. Then we can repeat it to attain more goals.

So, back to you. Decide which goals are your top three priorities for this year. Make sure that at least one of these prioritized goals is devoted to attaining your soul's dream. While you are examining your goals, ask yourself, "How could I turn some of these soul goals into work?" Don't think exclusively of a nine-to-five job, but open up to the possibility of doing many kinds of work simultaneously. For example, my soul's purpose is to help people develop their potential. Some form of this purpose has been with me my entire life and has really not changed. However, my annual goals and actions to achieve this purpose have changed. When I was in my twenties, I worked as a high school teacher/counselor to help teenagers develop their potential. As I grew older, and more mature in my own spiritual practice, my goal became to help adults, which I did through leading spiritual retreats. Then I realized that by helping individuals to develop their potential in large- and medium-sized organizations, I could help thousands of people in their everyday lives. To do this I became a corporate consultant. Consulting was difficult and sometimes draining and I found that I needed more play time to recuperate and rejuvenate. So, I decided to take people on tours to the sacred sites of the world. This would—you've got it—open people up to developing their potential, while at the same time I would be able to play with others from, and in, foreign lands. Overall I have one soul dream but many ways of achieving it.

Sometimes personality and soul goals are synonymous. When we have a soul-infused personality, our work *is* often play. But we must not think that soul's work is always exciting or glamorous. The soul's work may be to raise a family, open our home to foster children, look after invalid parents or support a spouse in their work.

Driving and Restraining Forces

To manifest our goals in the world, we move step by step from spiritual to physical realms, becoming more specific as we do so. In doing this you will experience both driving and restraining forces. You started this process by visualizing your soul's dream and then made it more concrete by examining how the dream could be turned into goals. The next step after prioritizing your goals is to select *one* goal to analyze. Doing this increases your focus, which is necessary to manifest your dream in the physical world.

Choose a goal that is soul-oriented and, if possible, one that is linked to work. Make a list of what pushes you forward to obtain your goal, the *driving forces*, and what holds you back from getting it, the *restraining forces*. Driving forces might include emotional support from others, money, ambition, talent and experience. Examples of restraining forces might include fear, being too old or too young, and lack of time, money and necessary education.

Driving and Restraining Forces

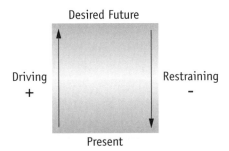

The stronger the driving forces and the weaker the restraining forces, the better the chances of achieving your goals. If the driving and restraining forces are equal in strength, you might give yourself a lot of stress going nowhere. To increase the chances of reaching your goal, you need to increase the driving forces and decrease the restraining forces.

Let's say your soul dream includes *both* having your own "soulful" business and being a good parent. However, this is difficult to achieve because you are a single parent with young children. You have what Alan Lakein calls, in *How to Get Control of Your Time and Your Life*, an overwhelming "A priority." Lakein recommends that to achieve your goal, bite off small chunks and do them one or two at a time. For example, take steps to achieve your work goal by researching the business, working part-time in a similar kind of store to learn the trade, taking a small business management course, searching for business partners, writing up a business plan and speaking to your bank manager about your plan. All of these things move you towards your goal. At some point, you will have filled in many of the little bites and it will be time to take the leap, quit your job and open your own business. Because you are doing this gradually, you increase your chances of success without jeopardizing the security of your family.

A word of caution: if your restraining forces are greater than 70 percent, you might wish to postpone that particular goal and focus on another soul goal for the time being. It requires great effort to achieve your goal if you have only a few driving forces supporting it. Take on a long-term, A-priority goal only if you are serious about it. When we have unrealistic goals we sabotage ourselves in life. Our soul can be happy doing any number of things. (Mine has been equally happy being a high school teacher, spiritual retreat leader, corporate consultant, guide to sacred sites and writer.) If you're not prepared to work towards one of your goals because it's too high a risk, or if you cannot reduce the restraining forces and increase the driving forces, find another soul goal to which you can commit.

Many years ago I was teaching a career and life planning course one night a week. A woman named Leslie was one of the participants. Leslie was in her early fifties and had raised two families. She had a B.A. and was charming, articulate and well groomed. For the first three weeks of the course, Leslie spoke passionately, and at length, of her life's ambition to become a lawyer. However, when it came time to commit to action, she was unable to do so and missed the next two classes. Concerned about her, I was relieved when she reappeared the following week.

"How have you been?" I asked.

"I've been in mourning for what I will never be," she replied. "I now realize that at my age I'm not prepared to give up everything I've achieved to go back to school to become a lawyer. I've been mourning the death of my dream, and I'm now here to see what my new dream will become."

What a woman! I celebrate her courage to let go of one dream and to find another. And she did. Everyone in the group commented on her poise, style and professional presentation. This was one of Leslie's talents and, before long, she decided to teach others how to achieve "the professional look" and to develop self-esteem. She discovered a new career.

We, like Leslie, must be ready to burst the balloons of our career illusions. As I've said before, soul work can be anything, but we must look at the *reality* and not the *illusion* of the work before we commit to it. My mother's unfulfilled dream was to be a flight attendant so she encouraged me to do this. At first it sounded interesting because I wanted to visit other countries and learn about other people. I even went so far as to apply for a job as a flight attendant, but was turned down because I was too short and near-sighted. My physical vessel did not fit that job. Later, I realized that being a flight attendant was not in keeping with my soul's purpose. I had wanted the illusion but not the reality of that job. So I began looking for other ways to travel while still doing my soul's work.

Achieving Your Soul's #1 Goal

> *Success is measured not so much by the position*
> *that one has reached in life as by the obstacles*
> *which he has overcome while trying to succeed.*
>
> BOOKER T. WASHINGTON

Commitment to Action

Now that you have committed to your soul's goal, you will need an action plan to achieve it. With a plan,

followed by implementation, of course, your dreams have a much greater chance of happening. A plan is the final step needed to anchor the soul's dream in the world. The personality must completely support the soul's dream or it will not act—thereby sabotaging the soul. Only with the support of the personality will it be possible to achieve your goals.

The action plan anchors the spiritual seed even more firmly in the physical body. There are really two goals, not one, and both goals teach you mastery of the physical world. The first goal is that you accomplish whatever objective you have set for yourself. The second and equally important goal is that you do all that you can to achieve your objective. The first goal may sometimes elude your grasp but the second one never will. It is totally within your control and it is the actual striving that gives life meaning and that transforms you into a soul-infused personality.

So let's look at what you can do. Action plans consist of writing down several steps that move you from where you are now to attaining the goal. It is necessary to write two dates: a date to start and a date to accomplish your goal. This step is a commitment to action. Making lists is the first step in achieving a goal, but only through action will you achieve it. Starting is the hard part. Once the first few steps are accomplished you often find that you gain momentum and it becomes easier to reach your goal than not to reach it.

There are two kinds of actions that help with this process. The first actions are those which increase the driving forces. For example, if your goal is to become a healing practitioner, your action steps might include studying various kinds of healing and gaining experience by working for someone who has a practice similar to the one you want. The second kind of actions are just as important as the first. They help to remove restraining influences in your life, such as reducing or eliminating the amount of time you spend with unhelpful or even toxic people. You might also include eliminating your personal time-wasters such as spending time on low priorities as well as stabilizing yourself financially. Your action plan should include both types of actions.

Action Plan to Achieve My Soul's Goal
My soul's goal is:
Date start:
Date achieve it:
Action steps:
1.
2.
3.
4.
5.

When you examine your action steps, ask yourself the following questions: Am I prepared to do all the steps that I've listed? Am I being realistic with the time frame? Are these steps within my control? If not, will others support or hinder my actions? The more these steps are within your control, the greater the chances of reaching your goal. If you are not prepared to do one, or more, of these steps, change the step to something you are prepared to do.

Visualize Yourself Attaining Your Soul's Goal

> *Success is not the result of spontaneous combustion.*
> *You must set yourself on fire.*

REGGIE LEACH

Earlier we employed a visualization technique to see what our soul's goal was. Now, we use visualization again to strengthen the soul's message to the personality. This has two results. First, the goal materializes more quickly. Second, the personality and soul learn to trust their relationship as interdependent partners.

This visualization, which consists of continually creating a mental image of yourself achieving your goal, is a key factor in success. What we see is what we draw towards us, so if we visualize ourselves living the soul's goal, we draw it to us. Visualization is not pie in the sky stuff; it can greatly influence our physical reality, as evidenced by a well-known study of basketball players at an American university. The players were tested to see how many baskets they could shoot on average and then were divided into three groups. The first group was instructed to practice for an hour a day for a month. At the end of the month, they were re-tested and found to have improved by 24 percent. The second group didn't practice physically but spent an hour each day visualizing sinking baskets. This group managed to improve their basket-sinking skills by a dramatic 23 percent. However, the performance of the third group—who neither practiced nor visualized—declined.

So it's important to follow through with *both* visualization and the concrete steps of our action plan, like the first two groups of basketball players, to attain our goal. By doing this we weave together more of the strands of our spiritual and physical bodies, which increases the speed at which we manifest our goals.

The way to do this is to dedicate five minutes each morning to visualizing your goal. Do this daily and, if possible, several times a day. This technique is more effective when you visualize only one goal at a time. Repeating the visualization creates a strong thoughtform and draws your soul's goal towards you. Feel excited and energized by the thought of living your chosen goal. If you feel anxious, doubtful or confused in your visualization, it will be harder to manifest the goal and you might want to reassess whether or not it is achievable at this moment in your life.

I use the word "visualize" inclusively. There are actually three main "senses" that can be used to increase your chances of reaching your goal, and my definition of visualization embodies all of them. About 80 percent of people have a preference for visualization—actually seeing an image of their goal in the mind's eye. A second group of people are more kinesthetic and experience a "gut feeling" in their bodies that they will be successful. A third group are auditory and actually "hear" their inner voice talk to them and say, "You will reach your goal." Some people use all three senses; they visualize, feel and hear. It doesn't matter in which form you receive information. What is important is that you are convinced of the rightness of your soul's goal for you. But visualization by itself is not enough—you also must continually take the concrete steps you have listed on your action plan.

One Soul Has Multiple Personalities

Visualization is one way that the personality and soul can learn to work together for maximum effectiveness. Another important way is for the soul to use not one, but many, aspects of the personality. No one aspect of an individual's personality—mother, daughter, career woman, artist—is enough to house the soul and satisfy its needs. During our period of inner transformation, we learn to know and work with all aspects of ourselves.

For instance, we might have different kinds of soul work that run either sequentially or consecutively throughout our lives. In the first part of life our soul work might be to raise a family and in the second part to work as an accountant in a large organization. Or vice versa. Soul work might just as easily entail balancing three careers at once, all of which we love. How does the soul manage to fulfill so many roles in one life? It does it through the many vehicles which are our sub-personalities.

You will recall that the word personality is derived from the Greek word "persona," meaning mask. The personality is a construct that we use in the physical world to accomplish our goals and we employ many "personas" to do this. The soul chooses various sub-personalities to express itself in the physical world and, like facets of a diamond, they reflect different aspects of our true essence. Identifying these sub-personalities is important because they can either help or sabotage us in achieving our goals. For example, if your soul's goal is to develop human potential within the corporate setting, you must dress and act in a certain way that will allow you to fit in. If you don't don this mask, you won't get the job—pure and simple.

But this "business" mask is not all of you. You have many roles in your life that require different aspects of your personality—parent, lover and child—and they all wish to find expression in the physical world. Not expressing or acknowledging them may lead to their surfacing in inappropriate ways that can undermine you. For example, if you allow your "career" personality to control your "good parent" personality, you will have little time for your children, resulting in feelings of guilt and frustration. Or a man whose "lover" personality is not nourished in his marriage may make inappropriate sexual advances to a colleague at work and end up being fired.

In a soul-infused personality, the soul acts like a control station, deciding which personality to bring forward at what time. The more conscious we become of the needs of our various personalities, the more we can fulfill their needs in a positive way in our life. By doing so, we work with the soul's design.

Sometimes, one or more of our personalities may actually revise history to suit the soul's purposes. This is a nice way of saying that we occasionally lie so that our life story better fits our soul's destiny. Jungian analyst James Hillman, in *The Soul's Code*, recounts the story of how Leonard Bernstein insisted that his childhood had been one of absolute poverty with no music whatsoever, whereas in reality he grew up in a house with maids, sang in his private school's choir and was piano soloist for its orchestra. Likewise, John Wayne often claimed that his parents owned a drugstore in a town called Glendale. This was denied by a longtime resident who knew the family well. Isadora Duncan, born Dora Angela, changed her name, continually lost her passports and changed her age as it suited her. Even Carl Jung was not exempt. He believed—with no factual basis—that he was the result of one of Goethe's illegitimate liaisons.

The point I'd like to make is that these "fictions" may be more in accord with these people's souls than if they told the real facts. Goethe's work deeply influenced Jung's own. Duncan's gift was to bring mystery, grace and beauty into this world—all of which have a timeless quality. Wayne's persona was founded on his "man of the people" image, and Bernstein might well have needed to believe that his childhood was impoverished and constrained to be able to transcend it. The hero rising to greatness from humble beginnings is a common myth, much more common and heartwarming than stories of a little rich boy with everything getting more. So, the soul sometimes does not confine itself to the literal truth as much as to the metaphorical truth.

There are a host of personalities that our soul uses to find partial expression. These personalities are the soul's tools for exploring and mastering the physical world. No single aspect of the personality is complete enough to house the soul's diversity. We can all think of people who have not developed the various facets of their personalities. They seem one-dimensional, flat and uninteresting. Many of us are on too tight a rein and could use encouragement or a push to explore our many facets. Exploring our various personalities would increase our joy in life, while allowing our soul to merge more easily with our physical vessel.

There are a wide range of personalities inside us that we must understand if we are to get them to cooperate in meeting our goals. Some of the dominant ones I've noticed are: an ambitious career person we could call the Boss; a soft, caring, motherly type I'll call Mom; a lusty lover called Cheri or Handsome; and a big kid called Sissy or Sonny. Perhaps, part of you is a performer, the Star, a recluse called Garbo or the Hermit, or a masked persona who no one knows much about—the Lone Ranger. These personalities are often gender neutral; a man could have a Mom personality and a woman a Boss personality. Multiple personas is one of the ways the soul has of balancing our male and female characteristics so that we can learn interdependence.

Some of these personalities find expression more easily than others in a work setting, but all of them can express themselves to some extent. At work Mom likes to nurture others in countless ways, from birthday cards to thank you letters and notes of commendation. Cheri or Handsome are interested in creating beauty, so take them shopping when you want to update your wardrobe, or ask for their help in decorating your office. Sissy or Sonny are often the big kid part of you that wants to play, so turn them loose telling jokes to brighten your co-workers' day, or enlist their assistance in organizing original marketing strategies for the company's products. The Star seeks recognition and visibility, so find a corporate venue to support this, such as becoming an in-house trainer or MC of the Christmas party. The Lone Ranger wants to do good in the world, so find a cause for your office to support. And the Boss likes to organize, so make sure that you're giving him enough to coordinate.

The following exercise will assist you in discovering the qualities, needs and names of your various personalities. By completing it, you will have a much better idea of the various parts of yourself and how to work with them, not against, to achieve your soul's goals. List your various personalities. What are their qualities, talents and liabilities? Give a name to each one. What does each personality require to make it happy, and how can you meet its needs in constructive ways? How do these personalities either assist or sabotage you in achieving your soul's or personality's goals? Record your answers.

After you have completed the chart, think of ways of meeting the needs of your *various* personalities so they'll cooperate with your soul. Some of this can take place at work, as I've discussed, but some might need to happen in your personal life. If you have a strong "big kid" personality, for example, and have not decided, like Robin Williams, to become a full-time actor, perhaps you could join a little theatre, do amateur stand-up comedy or become a scout leader. We are only limited by our imagination! Your personalities are the way in which your soul has fun and learns in the physical reality. Being spiritual and soul-

My Personalities		
Name	Qualities	What It Wants

infused does not mean being one-dimensional. It means being fully who you are in the vehicle you have chosen in this life. By exploring the multiplicity of who you are, you become fully who you are. I am in agreement with Jack Kornfield, who writes in his book *A Path with Heart*:

> Who am I? When we begin to answer [this question], we are filled with images and ideals—the negative images of ourselves that we wish to change and perfect and the positive images of some great spiritual potential—yet the spiritual path is not so much about changing ourselves as it is about listening to the fundamentals of our being.

Reprogramming Yourself for Success

Whenever we try to pick out anything by itself, we find it hitched to everything else in the universe.

DEEPAK CHOPRA

In the preceding chapter you discovered your personality and soul goals and created action plans to achieve them. This process involved weaving the spiritual body together with the physical body in order to anchor your dreams in the material world. The physical vessel that houses your personality has now been created; the next step is to activate that vessel on a cellular level so that your entire personality is programmed to succeed. This entails working with the etheric body, which interpenetrates the other four bodies of the vessel and which has its own consciousness as the body soul. The etheric body holds all your memories, both positive and negative. To erase negative cultural, familial, learned and self-imposed memories—in order to reprogram yourself for success—you must unlock the secrets of this body. This journey, by necessity, takes you into the realms of both science and metaphysics.

The beginning of each stage in humanity's evolution is heralded by an invention or discovery that renders the belief system of the previous cycle obsolete. This happened, for example, during the Iron Age, when iron replaced bronze in weapons manufacturing, allowing the warlords to be more efficient in their conquests. Now, at the culmination of the third stage of human evolution, we have learned to use science and technology largely to support, for the most part, our personality desires. Today, an even more wide-ranging change is occurring—one that will affect all of us. As we enter the fourth stage of evolution, we will discover and learn to work with the spiritual laws that create the material world. This is happening even now as our science and technology removes the barriers between what we can actually see in the physical world and what we can only infer.

Subatomic Physics

To better understand how our thoughts determine our reality, we must examine the unseen realm of the etheric body. In recent years, we have discovered that matter is composed of much more space than was previously thought. Many of us have heard it said that humans are 70 percent water. For me, this conjures up an image of a human balloon filled with water swishing from side to side! Humans, in reality, are composed of 70 percent water *atoms* and like all atoms, water atoms consist of approximately 99.999 percent space and .001 percent matter. Fritjof Capra, in *The Tao of Physics*, says that if we visualize the nucleus of an atom as a grain of salt, the electrons moving around it would be hundreds of feet away. What lies between them is space. This means that *we are mostly space.* Space or ether, whichever you prefer, is non-visible to current scientific measurements and yet it is not without life. This ether is the etheric body.

But how many of us are able to visualize ourselves as space or ether, and not as solid? It's very difficult; but this scientific fact has far-reaching consequences as to how we relate to ourselves, others and our world. Science has proven that we are mostly space and yet we persist in seeing ourselves as solid. Our atoms are continually interacting with the atoms of chairs and trees, as well as with the atoms of other humans, and yet we continue to believe that we are isolated beings. This is to our detriment. Accepting ourselves as part of the whole of life—which is what we are—gives new meaning to both what our work is and how we do it. Everything we do impacts on the world. This means that *all* work matters. Even routine and less than satisfying jobs can create something for the good of the organization or the Earth as a whole. This is an empowering concept and increases our responsibility for the choices we make. Consequently, living up to our potential affects not only us but all humanity. By using our gifts and developing our potential, we can change our environment for the better, for others as well as for ourselves.

As we update our view of reality, we realize that we are totally interconnected with everything on the planet. The violent television program that we watch is not "out there"; it is also "in us." Jesus' words, "What you do for the smallest of creatures, you do for me," are literally true. Harming another is harming ourselves, and helping another is helping ourselves. The fourth cycle of human consciousness is one of interdependence, based on the interconnection of all life. So seen in the light of recent scientific discoveries, the importance of doing the soul's work becomes overwhelmingly important.

Science has not only proven that we are interdependent with everything else, but also that *our thoughts actually create our physical reality*. What yogis and metaphysics have taught for centuries, physicists have now discovered to be true. One of the founding fathers of quantum physics, Danish scientist Niels Bohr, pointed out that subatomic particles can come into existence because of the presence of the observer. Bohr and other physicists have discovered that they can—merely by their thoughts—make subatomic particles change form and move in the direction that they wish.

This means that by physically directing matter with our thoughts, we can work with our etheric body to do or be whatever we envision. Many of us find this concept frightening because it means that, to a large extent, we literally control our destiny. We are creators of our own reality. Rather than putting our heads in the sand and hoping that this idea will go away if we ignore it, we must become conscious creators. We can limit our dream to what our society or parents think are possible for us, or we can determine a dream for ourselves and turn it into reality. In order to do this, we might need to *reprogram* our view of what is possible for us. Reprogramming ourselves takes us into the realm of the body soul, its etheric body and its headquarters—the pineal gland. Examining the function of the pineal will assist us in understanding how the process of creating our reality in life and work actually occurs.

The Pineal Gland

Three and a half centuries ago, Descartes speaking of the pineal gland said, "I have clearly ascertained that the part of the body in which the soul exercises its functions is neither the heart nor the brain as a whole but is only the innermost part of the brain, which is a certain very small gland, situated in the middle of its substance."

One way of describing this gland, and its director—the body soul—is to say that the pineal contains the soul's master codes for us. It receives information from the divine source and then tells the body how to feel, act and respond. And how does it do this? We know scientifically that the pineal contains crystalline structures and, as we age, these crystals increase in number. Crystals are among the Earth's most complex minerals. Dhyani Ywahoo, a crystal medicine elder of the Tsalagi—the Cherokee people— teaches that "the quartz crystal is neither solid nor liquid; it vibrates at 786,000 pulses per millisecond, its continuum moving faster than light." Describing how our mind works with these crystals in our pineal, Ywahoo says, "[Our] mind flowing along the superstructure of intention, as expressed in crystal forms, precipitates the form."

Western science is now discovering what the Tsalagi and other aboriginal and spiritual traditions have known for hundreds, even thousands, of years—that our thoughts work with crystalline forms in the body to create our physical reality. By choosing to let the soul direct our thoughts—through the pineal gland—we create a physical, emotional and mental body aligned with the soul's purpose. This process is a more sophisticated version of how we use crystals in technology.

Our industries employ crystals in telecommunications equipment to relay and store large amounts of information, and in laser technology to create holographic images. In the same way, I believe that the pineal gland uses its crystals both to store and relay complex information throughout the body—but it does more than that. The pineal can also be programmed to *send* information. Just as crystals in our communications equipment can be programmed with new information, so we can direct the body soul and etheric body to reprogram our pineal to send healthy, positive messages to the body. Viewed this way, the human body is like a sophisticated holographic image that is programmed by our thoughts. Deepak Chopra supports this opinion in *Ageless Body—Timeless Mind*:

> Your body is a 3-D projection of your state of mind. Your slightest shift of mood is picked up by every cell, which means that you do not think with your brain alone—all fifty million cells in your body actively share your thoughts.

Science, through these recent discoveries, is moving closer to comprehending the spiritual mysteries that control our universe. In the ancient Vedic teachings of India, it is written that man is a dream that is dreamt by God. If this is so, then we, by controlling our own thoughts and holographic projections, are creators in the making. This is an awesome responsibility and one that we can participate in either consciously or unconsciously, positively or negatively.

Negative Self-Talk Versus Optimism

We are what we think.
All that we are arises in our thoughts.
With our thoughts we make the world.

DHAMMAPADA

Each of us has approximately forty-five thousand thoughts a day. Most of us cannot go more than eleven seconds without talking to ourselves. But is our self-talk positive or negative? All self-talk reinforces the pattern in the etheric body so it's essential that we consciously decide what program we want to give it. There's no sense setting positive goals if we're undermining ourselves with negative self-talk. It's like planting weeds in our own garden. We may be giving ourselves conflicting messages. The conscious message is that we want to achieve our goals; the unconscious message is that we are unable to do so for one reason or another. If we are sabotaging ourselves with negative self-talk, it is usually because of our fears.

Where does negative self-talk originate? It usually begins in childhood. Daniel Goleman, author of *Emotional Intelligence*, writes of a study conducted on farms in Iowa. For three weeks researchers observed children between the ages of two and twelve to see how many positive and negative comments were said to them. When the responses were tallied, researchers made the staggering discovery that each child, on average, received 32 positives and 431 negatives from their parents during that three-week period.

Children are particularly vulnerable to being programmed and I'm sure that the parents of these children would be horrified to hear these results. Many of us are simply unaware of how many negative comments we make to our co-workers, spouses and children. After a while, we continue to run this negtive program internally, which influences the way we talk to ourselves even when others say positive things about us.

So how do we reprogram ourselves and let go of negative self-talk? We do it through visualization and affirmations, through doing what we most fear and performing rituals to let go of old thinking. Information about subatomic physics, the pineal gland and body cell replacement show us how to reprogram ourselves. Granted, not everything changes overnight. We are in a continual process of becoming. However, the more consistent and persistent we are about reprogramming ourselves, the deeper and more lasting the impact on us. We can choose to attribute behaviors to genetics or environment—be these our boss, company or parents; *but* we make choices every moment in how we think. Thoughts determine feelings and feelings determine actions. Choices determine our reality.

Dr. David Schweitzer, a professor in humoral pathology at the Nu Health Clinic in London, England, photographs thought-forms in the body to determine the health and well-being of his patients. These thought clusters are found in the body fluids and act as a liquid tape recorder, capable of storing information. Schweitzer has also discovered that the solid particles in the blood combine with electromagnetic forces to form particular structures that can be called "memory clusters." These memory clusters are the physical manifestation of how the body soul and etheric body work in the world of form. Every thought we think is impregnated in the blood, so it's critical to good health—physically, mentally and spiritually—that we keep our thoughts positive.

Optimists have a strong belief that everything will turn out for the best in their lives. They see pain, frustration, loss and setbacks as opportunities to re-examine direction, to build character and to develop qualities such as patience, compassion and persistence. Optimists do not blame others for their situation, but take responsibility for themselves and look at how they could do something differently. Optimism is also a predictor of success.

One researcher studied insurance salesman for the Metlife company. He discovered that optimistic salesmen sold 37 percent more insurance in their first two years than pessimistic ones and quit only half as often. Optimism at work translates into more success, which means more promotions and more money. Because they are also more pleasant to be around, optimists attract people and opportunities to themselves. Optimists have more physical, emotional and mental resilience than pessimists. They do not take failure personally and believe that, ultimately they will succeed.

Both positive and negative emotions also affect our physical well-being. People who experience chronic anxiety, long periods of sadness and pessimism, tension and incessant hostility, cynicism and suspicion double their risk of asthma, arthritis, headaches, ulcers and heart disease. It's obvious, therefore, that our mind affects our emotions, which in turn create physical health or disease—and ultimately success or failure in achieving our goals.

Strengthening Positive Thoughtforms

We create thoughtforms for everything we do. By capitalizing on positive thoughtforms that our etheric body—directed by us—has created and strengthened through repetition, we work with the flow. It's more difficult to create something for the first time than it is to modify or improve it. You know the first report you write is more difficult than the next and the next, and the first budget you balance takes longer than the tenth. Not only is it easier for us to build on our own positive thoughts and actions, but also it's easier to build on others' discoveries. Let me give you an example to illustrate this point.

Deer—like most animals—have favorite watering places. The first deer to discover a watering place may bruise and scratch itself by making its way past scrubs and trees. The next deer sees the broken twigs and smells the scent of the first deer and, by slowly following the path of the first one, also finds the water. As more deer do this, the path becomes wider, until all deer can easily walk to the water.

Humans—like deer—find it easier to repeat established patterns. We find it simpler to apply an idea that has already been created than to think a new thought or find a new way to perform a task. Balance in work—for many of us—would be a combination of creating new products and services and improving on existing ones. If we do nothing new, we are in danger of rusting out from boredom and if we do only new things, we risk the possibility of burning out from stress.

We can work with the etheric body to strengthen an existing thoughtform through daily affirmation and prayer. Our prayers and affirmations can take two forms. We can pray for what we want; we can also give thanks for what we have received. Ideally, these two practices will be in balance so that we give equally to the universe and to others as we also open ourselves to receive abundance from the universe and from others. This interdependent balance renews both body and mind.

It is important to create an affirmation that has a positive focus without negatives. It is preferable to say, "Every day I am more loving to others" than to say, "I'm *not* as impatient as I was." Affirmations, prayers, and chants align sound to vision and so increase the speed with which we can change our old programming. We must remember to combine affirmations with gratitude, lest we become too tight and needy. Gratitude is expansive and relaxed. It allows our cells to trust the universe and the process to provide us with all we need to accomplish our soul's task.

Rewards That Work

The secret of success is to fall down seven times and get up eight.

CHINESE PROVERB

Having a vision of our purpose in life, setting goals and establishing action plans builds a template—a thoughtform in the etheric body—to help us to take our soul to work; but this alone is not enough. It is through willpower, enthusiasm and persistence to succeed that we activate and reinforce this thoughtform. What separates successful people from unsuccessful ones is not the ability to dream. Almost all of us have dreams of what we want to do and be in life. What separates those who attain their soul's dreams from those who fail is taking action. If we reward ourselves along the way, it is easier to take action to achieve our goals.

I learned this important lesson as a teenager. At school, I disliked many subjects and hated homework and studying. Because I enjoyed English, I did that homework first. Next was history and then—way down the list—math and French. My marks reflected my preferences and I barely scraped by in the last two subjects. So much did I dislike studying for exams that I became a crammer. I'd put off studying until the last possible minute and then cram the key points, sit the exam and promptly forget all the information. The further I progressed in school, the less this system worked. Out of desperation I decided to try something else.

If homework and studying felt unpleasant and undesirable, then I had to find a reward for doing them. I loved to play, so I made many different kinds of play—watching TV, reading science fiction books, visiting friends—my rewards. Enlisting my parents' assistance, I informed them that I was going to my room to do my homework and that they were not to let me watch television or phone my friends until I had finished. My parents were not disciplinarians and would never have motivated me this way, but they laughed good-naturedly and agreed to do their part. If I came out of my room to go to the toilet or to get a drink, my parents asked me how I was doing. I'd give them a progress report, and they'd congratulate me on my determination.

I learned two things at that young age. The first was not to wait for someone else to motivate me; the second was that having support from others increased my chances of success. I don't think that I would have made it through three degrees and seven years of university if I'd never discovered this reward system. In fact, I still use it.

My present equivalent to doing homework is preparing seminars and keynotes. I love giving the seminars and that is the reward; but the preparation is often not enjoyable for me. Still, it is necessary for the seminar to be successful. My system for writing books is similar. Although I feel a strong soul need to share my ideas with the world, writing them down requires discipline. I write for five to seven hours early in the day, and then reward myself with a late afternoon walk or socializing with friends in the evening. By giving myself ongoing small rewards I can delay gratification for the larger reward (i.e., publishing a book) for long periods of time. In this way I am very productive, and both my soul and personality are satisfied.

Daniel Goleman and others have documented a study conducted by Walter Mischel on "impulse control" in determining success in one's entire life. Four-year-olds were offered a choice: they could have either one marshmallow immediately or two if they waited until the researcher had run an errand. The children were then tracked until they graduated from high school, and the results were dramatic. The four-year-olds who had no impulse control—those who ate the one marshmallow immediately— turned out to do far less well in school than those who had waited until the researcher returned.

Those who resisted temptation at age four were twelve to fourteen years later more socially competent, personally effective, self-assertive, self-reliant, trustworthy, and better able to cope with frustration and take initiative and were still able to delay gratification in pursuit of their goals. The children who were unable to delay gratification and grabbed the one marshmallow immediately were more likely to be stubborn, indecisive, easily upset, mistrustful, resentful of not "getting enough," prone to jealousy and envy, more irritable and still unable to put off gratification.

Delayed gratification is essential in both life and work. The personality, in the form of the physical, emotional and mental bodies, often wants things—food, sex, approval, respect—*now*. As we gain more control of these bodies, we can delay gratification for longer periods of time until ultimately these things, although nice to have, are not our main motivators. Impulse control brings our etheric body under the control of the soul and thereby increases our effectiveness. Working consciously with our body soul and etheric body allows us to program, to a great extent, the reality we wish for ourselves. We do this by creating a vision of what we want and then strengthening that image by thinking of it often. This brings the vision into form. Optimism strengthens this vision and fear weakens it.

Overcoming Fear

Life is either a daring adventure or it is nothing.

HELEN KELLER

How Fear Affects You

Fear is a concern of the emotional body. Having a healthy emotional body is essential to the soul, as the soul wants the qualities of hope, enthusiasm, determination, joy and love that reside there. It is not in the divine plan to do away with emotions, but to free positive emotions suppressed by fear. If we are to learn to work positively with the emotional body, we need to address the fears that hold us back from achieving our goals.

Fear is the personality's way of resisting the soul call, not wanting to lose control of itself and possibly die. Psychiatrist Sigmund Freud said that the cause of much psychological illness is the fear of knowledge of one's self—of one's emotions, memories, talents and destiny. I believe we fear both that we are worse than we know and that we are greater. Both fears, of weakness and greatness, keep us from fulfilling our potential. The personality is not stupid; it is correct in its belief that by listening to the soul it will lose its autonomy. It is not correct, however, in assuming that this will diminish it. In fact, the personality's union with the soul leads to both of them being able to accomplish more than either by themselves.

So what is fear? Fear is an uneasy feeling that something we don't want may occur. There are various levels of fear, starting with mild anxiety, moving through increased nervousness towards hysterical terror. One of the insidious characteristics of fear is that even irrational fears appear rational. Fear has a clinging quality that covers everything we look at in a murky gray. When fearful, we see the glass as half empty, instead of half full, and seek supporting evidence for why we can't have what we want. Fear is a negative force that decreases our chances of reaching our goals, whereas motivation is a positive force that increases our chances of attaining them. When we are afraid, the movement of energy, which we would normally turn outward into manifesting our dreams, is turned inward. With motivation we expand; with fear we contract. Holding ourselves back from doing what we really want to do leads to feelings of constraint, frustration, resentment and envy of others. Moving towards our goals, on the other hand, leads to feelings of optimism, self-confidence and joy. Overcoming our fears causes the emotional body to stabilize and expand so that we are better able to take actions asked of us by the soul. Starting with small steps, we can learn to take larger and larger ones as our personality learns to trust the soul not to harm it.

To achieve the soul's goals, we must give up the safe, known place where we are and enter the unknown. This causes fear. We must give up our independence to raise children, or quit a secure, but meaningless, job in order to do our soul's work. Living is a process of continual change. We cannot remain static. We are either growing or diminishing, depending on

> *There is a tide in the affairs of men Which, taken at the flood, leads on to fortune; Omitted, all the voyage of life is bound in shallows and in miseries.*
>
> JULIUS CAESAR,
> WILLIAM
> SHAKESPEARE

whether we meet life's challenges or back away from them. If we deny the soul's goals, we will never be truly happy.

Fear affects us physically in much the same way stress does, because fear is often the underlying cause of stress. When fearful, we prepare physically for either fight or flight. Blood pressure is raised, heart rate increased, sex drive reduced and digestive processes turned off. Sustained fear exhausts the immune system so that we are unable to ward off real viruses and disease. In effect, we wear ourselves out with wanting to act but being afraid to act. We go nowhere and feel defeated, depressed and exhausted—hardly a state to be successful at taking your soul to work.

Scarcity mentality is the root cause of most fear. This mentality is characterized by such thoughts as, "There's not enough love, success, money, happiness for everyone." This thought leads naturally to the next one, "There are winners and losers." In making that connection, we put ourselves into one of these two categories, based on our self-esteem and life experience. When we think of ourselves as "winners," we may become aggressive and greedy and try to hold on to what we've got and to keep others from getting any. We say to ourselves, "There's only so much to go around, so I'd better look after myself." If we consider ourselves "losers," we may fall into depression or escapism and avoid taking risks. We waste time doing low priority work because we don't dare go after what we really want. Many people even vacillate back and forth between thinking of themselves as winners or losers, depending on feedback they receive on any given day.

The emotional body is striving ultimately for equanimity so that—regardless of outside forces—we can maintain an emotional detachment. Remember that the soul is already detached and it views our emotional fears and traumas with a kind of objective neutrality. At the same time, the soul needs the passion and zeal of the personality in order to accomplish goals. Without this we'd be so much into "being" and not "doing" that there would be little reason to accomplish anything. The soul's dilemma is to foster the passion and enthusiasm of the emotional body, while not allowing it to sink into fear. Not an easy exercise, but certainly achievable as attested to by the lives of many spiritual leaders. The Dalai Lama and Thich Nhat Hanh are two of many role models who show the way to maintain equanimity and joy in the face of immense difficulties.

To eliminate scarcity mentality, we need to remember that we are interdependent and all in this together, and that what we do for another we do for ourselves. By reminding ourselves of this, we lose our fear of others because we are not separate from them.

Adhering to the scarcity mentality is a resignation of our responsibility to fulfill our soul's destiny in our life and work. Neither an inflated nor a deflated view of who we are is accurate. By accurately assessing our skills and doing the best we can to create a better world, we reduce scarcity thinking. Why? Because by believing and acting as if there is abundance—enough money, friends, interesting work, joy—in our lives, we actually attract these things to us. By doing this, we reclaim mastery of our emotional body and commit it to marriage and partnership with the soul. I believe the percentage of people leading soul-infused lives is increasing and that, as a race, humans are moving towards self-actualization. My perception is based, as I mentioned before, on the increase in the entire area of spirituality in mainstream North America.

> *Who sees all beings in his own Self, and his own Self in all beings, loses all fear.*
>
> ISA UPANISHAD

This evolving paradigm is one of courage. Some time ago, I heard business writer and consultant Tom Peters say, "If you haven't been fired by age thirty, you're not pushing your boundaries." I agree with Peters that in the past, organizations have preferred "yes" people. In such places, getting fired or quitting might very well be a sign of personal growth. But this is changing. Emotionally mature, self-confident organizations are seeking employees who take risks, ask challenging questions and work interdependently to find the best answers, regardless of whether they or someone else thought of it.

This is a time for individuals to push their boundaries and move beyond fear to ask for what they want and need. Not only will they be much happier and healthier, but leading a cautious life is no longer an option. There isn't any job security today and not engaging in life-long learning is a recipe for personal disaster.

Self-Actualized Life	Cautious Life
❖ work congruent with life purpose	❖ job security
❖ continuous learning	❖ comfortable routine
❖ soul-directed	❖ personality-directed
❖ working at something we value	❖ money is our main reason for work
❖ pushing our boundaries	❖ working repetitively

I know few, if any, totally fearless people. However, I do know many people who act even when they are afraid. That's all we need to do in order to embrace our goals and our potential. Scared or not, this is a time for us to commit to manifesting our goals and doing the best we can. As we do this, we will regain control of our emotional body and learn to work in partnership with our emotions rather than being victimized by them.

Major Fears and Solutions

I said earlier that fear is the concern of the emotional body. Our five bodies, however, are not separate, but interpenetrate and affect each other. Each of the five bodies has a specific fear and in mastering this fear we learn control of that body, which in turn helps the other bodies. This offers the soul a stable vessel for its work in the world. The physical body fears the unknown; the etheric body fears change. The emotional body fears rejection, while the mental body fears failure, and the spiritual body is afraid of losing its independence. These fears adversely control people's behavior and are not mutually exclusive. More than one, or possibly all, may be operating at any given time.

Even self-actualized people have fear, because they fear losing the lifestyle and work they love. However, the closer one becomes to being soul-directed, the less these fears control one's behavior. This is not to say that one is totally without fear, just that one can act even when afraid. Also, our fears change as we evolve. Fears that controlled our behavior when we were twenty may be different from those that control us at fifty. Most of us have combinations of all these fears—I know I do—but some may be stronger than others. To deduce your major fear, ask yourself the question, "Which fear is my Achilles heel—the one that holds me back from doing what I most want to do?" That is your most vulnerable place.

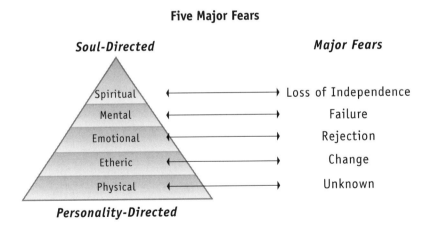

Fear of the Unknown

Fear of the unknown is common, resulting from our disconnection from the Earth and from our physical body, which is fed by the air, plants and minerals of the planet. When we are not connected to the Earth, we are not grounded, which leads to a free-floating anxiety. Through continual movement from one job to another and one home to another, eating foods not of our environment and living and working inside sealed buildings, we disconnect from our roots. As a result, we spend much of our time being anxious and worried, without even knowing the reason. We could have an exciting job that we love, enough money, great friends and a loving family but we are still anxious. By losing touch with our planet and the very earth on which we stand, we can come to regard everything outside of ourselves as suspect.

We have two primary bonds: we are an Earth being—connected to the physical world of our planet—and a Spirit being—connected to God, the Creator. If we trust neither God nor the Earth that supports our life, we fear the unknown. This results from being disconnected from spiritual and natural laws. This lack of trust carries over into our relationships with others and even with ourselves. When we are ungrounded, we don't trust that we can survive all that we encounter in our path. Without roots, any breeze can blow us over. We must establish a relationship with both parts of ourselves—our Spirit and Earth selves—in order to reside without fear in this world.

To help overcome fear of the unknown, try this simple and enjoyable solution. Like a tree, we need to root ourselves in the soil of the natural world. As we do this, our emotions stabilize and the fear of the unknown will subside. Devote time daily to reconnecting with the Earth; go for walks in nature, grow plants, breathe through the soles of your feet and with every step become conscious that you are walking on a living being whose life sustains you. This is cause for celebration and as you do this, you will notice that your anxiety dissipates and peace and joy replace it.

Fear of Change

Fear of change is caused by lack of a good relationship with the etheric body. Remember, the etheric body is in charge of creating all your programmings and memories—both inherited and learned. One could say that the etheric body has a tendency to be "set in its ways," which means that its strength is in maintaining continuity. It needs this quality to control the autonomic nervous systems in the body so that you don't have to devote time to thinking about breathing or keeping your heart beating—time that could be better spent working consciously in the world.

Fears in the workplace related to etheric body issues include adapting to changing organizational policies and procedures, getting a new boss or having to learn a new job or a new skill. Downsizing is a major trauma for individuals who fear change because everything changes at once—people, policies and jobs. Sometimes, their fear is so great that these individuals actually become immobilized. These men and women might still go to work, but they are numb and in a state of shock. They cannot concentrate and, like an ostrich hoping not to be noticed, they keep their heads down and hope the danger will pass.

To build up your tolerance for change and to stabilize the etheric body, I suggest that you introduce change gradually by doing one new thing every day. At work this could be trying out a new meal in the lunchroom, sitting in a different chair during meetings or driving a different route home from work. By doing this you will expand the amount of change that you can handle. As you become comfortable with small, ongoing changes, you will be able to make greater ones, such as reorganizing your office, creating new products and services or adopting a new marketing strategy for your company.

On a daily basis you might adopt a technique that I've found makes a positive difference in people's lives. If you have a tendency to say "no" when others ask you to try something new, you might practice saying "yes." I understand this might cause more fear initially, but it is a necessary first step in developing a working relationship with the etheric body. The etheric body will take direction from you if you ask it. It resorts to old behavior patterns only when there's no one steering the ship. Finally, change the way you talk to yourself. Here's an affirmation that when repeated daily reprograms the etheric body to relate to change as a friend and not as an enemy: "Nothing in life is constant but change. Gratefully, I rise to meet life's challenges."

Fear of Rejection

The emotional body is concerned with all fears—because all fear is emotional—but the fear of rejection is particularly strong in someone who is not balanced in this body. When we have a strong need to be liked, to fit in and to be accepted by others, we fear rejection. In order to prevent rejection, we deny our needs while assisting others to meet theirs. This denial leads to feelings of frustration and martyrdom.

The emotional body is associated with the element of water, and because water is formless, people with the fear of rejection often have difficulties with boundaries. This means that they have difficulty assessing how much to request for themselves and how much they should give to others. Exhibiting passive-aggressive behavior—being passive and not standing up for themselves when they want to say "no" and then becoming aggressive and inappropriately dumping their frustration on someone else—can happen when the emotional body is out of balance. Some people will be so repressed that they are unable to ask others for anything and, by couching themselves as a victim in the drama of life, dump their frustration on themselves.

Mary is a woman who has difficulty with the fear of rejection. She has led a very traditional life, raising a family and supporting her husband in his work. As a younger woman, in addition to having three children of her own, she also adopted a difficult child and cooked meals for twenty men in a remote construction camp run by her husband. Mary's soul work is service and, after the children grew up, she continued this role by opening a bed and breakfast that was always packed because of her loving care of guests.

Mary questioned neither her life nor its meaning and was content with serving others without asking for anything for herself until her body sent her a wake-up call. Over a period of months, Mary, now in her early sixties, found her energy diminishing. At first she was not concerned; she thought this was a natural part of aging. However, fatigue soon became exhaustion accompanied by acute memory loss. She was diagnosed with a severe thyroid condition. In metaphysics, the thyroid and throat have to do with the ability to speak up for oneself—something Mary had never done. When surgery was recommended, she decided to pursue an alternative route and gradually, by following her own inner guidance, she improved.

But her body was not through with its lessons for her. The next year, during a routine medical examination, a lump was discovered in her breast. Cancer. Part of her breast was removed and doctors advised both radiation and chemotherapy. Once again Mary was faced with the decision to accept what "the authorities" thought was the best course of action or to follow her own inner guidance. Meanwhile, her husband was not handling the situation well and went into a depression with his concern about losing her. Mary, as she had done for years, put her own needs second and started looking after his. She lost confidence in her own inner guidance, which advised her to treat her cancer by minor surgery, change of diet and homeopathic means, and commenced the more radical suggested medical treatment, which her husband also advocated.

Mary's gift was love and her soul work was to love others—but not at the expense of her own needs. Ignoring herself this way indicated an imbalance in her emotional body and a fear of rejection, common in many people who have caring, open hearts. But often our soul will put extreme pressure on us and make our lives miserable until we learn our lesson. During the cancer treatment Mary became very ill—yet she continued to try to meet the emotional demands being made by her husband.

Mary was living in the city temporarily while she underwent treatment. One day her husband said that he was coming to visit her and she went into internal distress. Her soul demanded that she focus on getting well and not on looking after him. After a lifetime of saying "yes" to him, she was able to say "no" for herself. This was a hard thing for Mary to do for fear of hurting his feelings and appearing not to care. Yet this was exactly what she needed to do for herself and, by this practice, she both physically recovered and made great strides in overcoming her fear of rejection.

As with most fears, the cure to overcoming them is to do what we fear most. I appreciate that this is very difficult to implement in reality, but it is the fastest, longest-lasting solution that I know. If you have a fear of rejection, what you probably fear most is telling others what you really think, feel and desire. So start doing this in lower-risk situations. Assert yourself with strangers who butt into line in front of you at the grocery store and ask people who are talking in a movie to be quiet. It's easier to be assertive and risk rejection with strangers than it is with the people we live and work with every day. As you build up your self-confidence you can take on even bigger risks.

A small action at work might consist of saying "no" to ongoing overtime. From there you might move on to renegotiating work responsibilities. To become more assertive, you might find it easier to move ahead one small step at a time. But the important thing is not to try a new behavior once and then drop it. If you do, you'll never retrain your etheric body and will continue to experience a fear of rejection.

Another tip that works in reclaiming control of the emotional body is to associate with people who encourage you to be "real," and decrease time with those who want a "yes" person. And be as nice to yourself as you would like others to be to you. To put this into practice, watch the way you talk to yourself and use the affirmation, "I am wonderful just the way I am." Finally, visualize yourself doing the behaviors that you most fear and see yourself succeeding. *This is a solution that works well for all fears.*

Fear of Failure

The fear of failure is due to an imbalance in the mental body. Sometimes our most active body is the body where we also have the most fear, because a strength overdone often becomes a weakness. Individuals, for example, with an active mental body might be able to out-think most people and do things more quickly, but quantity is not always quality, and more is sometimes less. They think rapidly because the mental body and thoughts are under the auspices of the air element, which is very quick and darts from one idea to another.

High achievers often have a strong need to receive recognition and respect from others, accompanied by an equally strong fear of failure. They might believe that no one can do things as quickly, efficiently or as well as they can. These thoughts lead to the erroneous belief that they must be strong at all times and not let others see their mistakes, uncertainty or need for support. High achievers might fear losing control and even believe that they can't trust anyone but themselves. They can also find lots of "evidence" to support these thoughts. Sometimes a lack of balance in the mental body is indicative of an over-development in the head and a need to return to the world of the heart.

I'd like to share with you an example of how one man did this. Ken's story begins while he was still employed as a senior manager at a manufacturing company. He and two of the other managers became increasingly frustrated as they realized that the power supply section in which they worked was undervalued by management and would probably cease to exist within a few years. So they decided to buy out that section and start their own business. Fortunately, they had the right combination of talents to do this. Ken's specialty was electronics, a second partner's was mechanical design and manufacturing and the third partner specialized in finance. Their business did very well initially and increased from the original eight employees in 1983 to approximately fifty people seven years later.

"Our relationship worked well because we were co-dependent," says Ken. "We were all control freaks and if you own your company, you have ultimate control. Each of us had ultimate control of our area and it was an unspoken agreement that we would not question each other's authority. I think it's a normal drive in human beings to control their world and to create what they desire. But we were obsessive about control and there are some things that are not rightfully controllable. For example, I was obsessive about technology and used it as an intellectual distraction to get away from relationships. If you spend lots of time with one thing you get really good at it so I had lots of payoffs with my work because I was sacrificing a normal life by working nights and weekends. Actually, I think a lot of men have these qualities of obsession and desire to control."

Two things happened that changed the co-dependent relationship among the partners. The first was that Ken, through therapy and pursuing metaphysics in search of his connection to the transcendent, commenced his own inner work to explore his lack of balance. We often overcome a problem in a lower body by seeking to develop a higher body. That is the route Ken took. In searching for his soul, he was at the same time dealing with the incorrect thinking in his mental body, and his process of transformation accelerated.

At the same time as this was happening, the company had reached a size where the old way of working was no longer effective. When Ken started to discuss the areas in which he felt the organization was failing, he broke the code of silence by which the three partners had lived. His partners found this very difficult to accept. The finance officer eventually retired and unfortunately died within a few years; the other partner continued to work in his former fashion until his and Ken's differing management philosophies became too far apart for either them or the company to bridge.

Their major difference was based on how they treated staff and what the staff was expected to do. "Self-motivation was my thing," says Ken, "whereas my partner believed people couldn't be productive unless they were under enough pressure to perform. Part of my personal growth work was in letting go of control, and I came to appreciate the incredible promise people carry within themselves. I went from a place of 'I'm the only one who can do it right' to 'most people have the skills to do the job.'"

An uneasy impasse in how Ken and his partner viewed the world was creating difficulty not only for them, but for their organization as well. Ken was moving towards a practice of interdependence. His partner, on the other hand, wanted to keep the employees dependent while maintaining his own independence. Unable to resolve their differing approaches, Ken started looking for an exit strategy that would not adversely affect the fortunes of the company. He hired a consultant to help the company change its limited strategy and, as a result, employees became engaged in the process of moving in a different direction. Even though Ken had been prepared to leave, it was no longer necessary because it was his partner who no longer fit the new thinking and made the decision to leave the company. This often happens when we confront our fears of failure and of losing control—as Ken did, by being prepared to leave—the universe knows that we've learned our lesson and supports our new behavior.

When I asked Ken how he felt about his current place with the company, he replied, "I'm only doing technology now because I'm familiar with it. I have gone through a fundamental shift from interest in technology to interest in relationships. It's been hard, but that is where my learning is. I've struggled with sticking with a team until together we can push forward into new areas and gain ground. These jewels are much more precious to me than what I can do by myself. Before, I found meaning from things I did alone and now if I'm not working in concert with someone, it doesn't have much meaning."

"I've found," continued Ken, "that the key ingredient for survival in a growing company is to realize that companies are dynamic, ever-changing organisms. We have to change our mindset to grow and that might take us into uncomfortable, unfamiliar territory. The challenge is to accept this change gracefully,

Life shrinks or expands in proportion to one's courage.

ANAÏS NIN

understand its relevance and then step out of the way. I now listen to the whispers of my soul and things tend to be easier, more enjoyable and full of wonder. If you ignore the whispers, they turn to shouts—so now I've become sensitive to the whispers. The possibilities are vastly greater if you seek and embrace transformation than if you don't."

In learning to overcome his fear of failure, Ken became interdependent—a characteristic of a soul-infused person. By following his example, we too could learn to delegate duties, surrender control and ask others for help. Also, we could admit when we don't know something and trust others not to hurt us when we're vulnerable. This will help move the focus from our head to our heart, as will practicing the affirmation, "I do unto others as I would have them do unto me." Real strength, as Ken discovered, comes from mastering ourselves and by learning this, we have less desire to master others.

Fear of Loss of Independence

Soul-infused individuals can still have fear. The fears that other people face might not control these individuals, who more often fear losing their independence. For example, soul-infused individuals gravitate towards jobs and relationships that give them joy and happiness. They appear—on the surface—to be fearless and self-actualized. Because of their spiritual fire, these men and women often have charismatic personalities and others are uplifted and catalyzed by them. They are committed to their soul's purpose, but sometimes fear that if they also commit to a material life with home and intimate relationships, they will lose their spiritual autonomy and independence. Their fear, therefore, is not of merging with the soul, but of merging with the personality, which they view as being the lesser partner. To complete the transformation to becoming a soul-infused personality who is taking their soul to work, it is necessary to love and work with both the soul and personality.

There are many paths to consciousness and so far I've been discussing only one. A second path is exhibited by the young knight Galahad, whose story is found in yet another version of the myth of the quest for the Holy Grail. Galahad was a pure knight, a "virgin," untouched by the world of form. In his spiritual purity he found the Grail and ascended into heaven. This is the path chosen by many yogis who live ascetic lives, abstaining from the physical world through extreme fasting, celibacy and little sleep. Some of these yogis are so unconscious of the physical world that they seldom talk and need to be fed by others to stay alive. These God-realized beings often transform others by their very presence, but this is a path very few Westerners are able to embark upon. Most of us are more comfortable with Perceval's path: living thoroughly in the world while at the same time becoming a soul-infused personality.

A gifted spiritual teacher and colleague of mine walked Galahad's path before switching to Perceval's. For years he led a celibate life and devoted himself to meditation, his own spiritual unfoldment and commitment to world service. After following Galahad's path for many years, he was called by his soul to relinquish his spiritual heights and re-enter the world of form. He met and fell in love with a woman who already had children and he became both a husband and a father. He faced his greatest fear, losing his spiritual independence and, by doing so, he became interdependent. He merged the world of soul and body, spiritual and physical, and returned to the place he had started and now lived in a different way.

If you fear the loss of your spiritual independence, it might help to remember that wholeness and unity come from depth as well as breadth of experience. You must learn to carry out all duties, regardless of how small or large, with equal joy. Because you might fear losing your connection to spirit, you might need to risk losing this connection by fully committing to someone or something in the physical world. In doing this, your heart will open in a new way and you will lose the cool detachment of the soul that may have been there before. An affirmation to help with the fear of losing your independence is, "Not my will but thy will be done." As you say these words, trust that your soul is giving you opportunities to learn something that will help you walk in the world as a soul-infused personality.

Leading a Fearless Life

> *There are people who shape their lives by the fear of death and others who shape their lives by the joy of life.*

CHARLES HANDY

As children we are fearless. We learn to fear based on our own life's woundings, teachings and by letting our parents' and family's fears become ours. The quickest way to master fear is to face it, walk through it and take the action you fear taking. It is helpful to engage simultaneously our physical, etheric, emotional, mental and spiritual bodies in the process. The more we are able to do this, the quicker we master our fear.

Thai meditation master Achaan Chah called this path "facing into one's difficulties." To help his students overcome their worst fears or problems, Achaan Chah made them experience them. For example, he had his frightened monks meditate in the cemetery at night and had his sleepy monks ring the 3 a.m. wake-up bell in the monastery.

Tantric techniques like these—called the quick path to enlightenment—have been used for centuries by Hindus and Buddhists. These techniques could be anything that pushes your buttons to make you face and overcome your fears or change behaviors that victimize you. We might not have to sit in cemeteries at night, but we need to do what we most fear, or we will always be controlled by it. I know it's easy to say, but hard to do and, worse still, the process is ongoing. It does not stop. Having overcome one fear, you may find another one waiting. Sometimes we might think that we are not up to the test, but when we rise to overcome the fear, we wonder why we haven't acted sooner. Unfortunately, we might forget this lesson when encountering the next trial on life's path. By passing the tests repeatedly, we do become more fearless. Through this process we manifest our soul's purpose in the world.

Realistic Versus Unrealistic Fears

> *The problem is not that we aim too high and fail. It is that we aim too low and succeed.*
>
> ANONYMOUS

Often what we fear is not real, but we act as if it is. Most of what we worry about never comes to pass. We must differentiate between fears that are realistic and those that are unrealistic, so that we are not immobilized by things that won't happen. The following technique helps in overcoming unrealistic fear.

1. This technique will work with any personality or soul goal but for the purpose of this exercise, you may wish to choose a goal concerned with your soul's work. Using the chart that follows, write down your soul's goal. For example, one person might say, "I want to start my own business in ___ ."
2. In the negative numbers section, under -10, write the worst imaginable thing that could happen if you try for your goal. For example, "I go bankrupt, lose my house, my wife leaves me and I never recover." Now, write down a fear that's not as bad as -10 but is still bad and give it a -7 or a -5. This might be, "My business fails. I lose some money, but retain my house."

3. The next step is to write down beside 0 a neutral statement, one that is neither bad nor good. For example, "I'm doing okay in my business, but I'm neither happier nor sadder than I was in my previous work." When afraid, people tend to focus on the negatives and don't consider the positives. They think of everything they might lose, but not of what they might gain by taking action. For a more realistic picture of outcomes, and to offset the negative fears with positive possibilities, writing down the positives is important.

4. Turn to the plus section. Think of a +3 or +5 positive achievement that could happen if you decided to do your soul's work. For example, you might put, "I'm doing better than I did in my last job. I'm happier, like my work better and have enough money." When fearful, we hardly ever think of the *best* possible outcome. Remember, a +10 positive achievement is at least as likely to happen as a -10. A +10 achievement might be, "I've found my soul's work and my entire life is blessed. It exceeds my wildest expectations." Write down your +10.

Eliminating Unrealistic Fears	
Goal: I want to	
+10	
+7	
+5	
+3	
0	
-3	
-5	
-7	
-10	

Now that you have completed the chart from -10 to +10, draw a line separating your unrealistic fears from your realistic fears. For example, if your -10 is that you become a bag lady and never get another job if you quit your present one, you need to realize that this is extremely unlikely. If you remain well motivated, there are many opportunities available for you in life. However, a -5—that you end up failing initially in what you want to do—may be possible. Remember, you do not need to worry about unrealistic fears, only realistic ones. If you let unrealistic fears control you, you will never achieve your goals.

Next, examine your realistic fears. If your worst realistic fear were to happen, could you handle it? Would you be able to cope with the realities of that outcome? If the answer is "yes," take action to do your soul's work. If the answer is "no," re-think your goal. The more we are able to risk, the greater our chances of achieving our goal. Choose the risk level that best suits your desire and ability to cope with risk.

Discussing your fears with others will help you to discover if they are unrealistic or realistic. Sometimes you might think your fear is realistic, but a neutral observer would consider it unrealistic. This is exactly what happened to a woman attending one of my workshops. Pearl's goal was to retire and live half the year in Florida and the other half in a cottage in northern Canada. She was fifty-five years old, her husband also wanted to retire, and they owned their cottage and house outright. Pearl believed that her goal was impossible because she did not have enough money to retire. I asked her if we could examine her financial situation in front of the other participants and she replied, "Of course, but I know I don't have enough money." Her mind was made up.

Together, we examined her finances, and it became obvious to every participant that Pearl had enough money to retire and fly back and forth from Florida seven times a year if she wished. The strange thing was that Pearl was still unable to believe this. She had an unrealistic fear and no amount of reason and fact could change her mind. She might have had deep programmings in her life that she would have to confront and eliminate, through the techniques I've discussed, in order to see that achieving her goal was possible. Although at that moment Pearl was unable to believe that her fears were unrealistic, she helped every person in the workshop realize that they also might be blind to their unrealistic fears.

Dangers of Being Unrealistically Positive

This fear assessment exercise may also be of use to individuals who see their dreams and goals in an "unrealistically" positive light with rose-colored glasses. These people have the opposite problem to that of the people I've just described. They have no difficulty envisioning the positive outcomes of their goal—a +10 or +7—but they have great difficulty foreseeing negative outcomes, such as a -5 or -7.

I once knew a teacher who dreamt of owning a professional baseball team. Roger called it "a challenge of destiny" and formed an alliance with several other men—all of whom had the same dream…but little money. Together they raised enough money to hire and outfit players. The success of the venture hinged on two crucial factors—corporate sponsorship and large numbers of people attending games. Roger and his partners did not make contingency plans should these two factors not materialize. When they did not receive the sponsorship they had hoped for, they continued in the optimistic belief that they would get large attendances. Game after game, they continued to lose money, but still they plowed on until by the end of the season they were hundreds of thousands of dollars in debt.

It was an unrealistic dream that didn't pass the reality check and Roger ended up paying off the debt for many years. The danger for an idealist like Roger is not the lack of dreaming, but the lack of grounding the dream in reality. However, the majority of us have the opposite problem. We don't commit to *realistic* dreams—dreams that have every chance of success—because we are fearful. This is what some Native Americans refer to as being "two-hearted." Cherokee medicine woman Dhyani Ywahoo says that this is the worst kind of illness and describes being two-hearted in this way:

> You want to do and have the ability to do but you don't do, and you argue with yourself about it.... [It is] good to be of one mind, one heart, and to see the ifs, ands, buts and possibilities only as thoughts, without attachment, keeping clear your goal of being all that you can be.

Becoming a soul-infused personality is ongoing and as we engage in this process we become increasingly fearless. We do this by overcoming the fears in each of our bodies and by learning to recognize the differences between realistic and unrealistic fears. We need to see the world as it is, neither in an overly positive or overly negative way. In doing this, we learn detachment from it, which is necessary to maintain emotional stability. Then we can choose how best to use our talents in the world.

There are four key ingredients that all of us need in order to consciously work with our five bodies so that we can take our soul to work. The first three I have already described. One, we must *align* our soul's goal with our personality, connecting the spiritual body of the soul with the physical body. Two, we need to *reprogram* ourselves for achieving our goals by employing positive thoughts of success, leading to mastery of the etheric body. Three, we have to *overcome* our fears by actually changing the way we act. This reinforces the new positive programming. By doing so, we stabilize the emotional body to support the positive actions we want to take. In the next chapter, *How Are You Smart?*, we will examine the fourth key to our inner transformation: *identifying* our unique gifts, talents and intelligence. This process allows us to strengthen our mental body, which in turn reinforces our chances of achieving our goals.

How Are You Smart?

This above all, to thine own self be true,
And it must follow, as the night the day,
Thou canst not then be false to any man.

HAMLET, WILLIAM SHAKESPEARE

Soul and Talents

If you ask someone, "Who are you?" they will often answer "I'm a retailer" or "I'm a bank manager." We become so closely identified with our work that we seldom step beyond them to examine who we *really* are. In this chapter we will examine how our gifts and talents—as well as our "call" in life—can combine to help us to discover our real Selves. Our talents are the ways in which we are smart and our conception of this lies within the realm of the mental body. By learning how we excel, we gain mastery over this body.

In the last chapter of *The Republic*, Plato discusses the soul's descent into the world. Plato says that each time we reincarnate we choose a "lot," a purpose or a destiny to fulfill. The soul remembers the lot although the personality forgets it upon incarnating. Plato states that the soul "grows down" and anchors itself into the world in four ways—via the body, the parents, the place and the circumstances of birth. To become conscious of the soul's purpose, we need to fully inhabit the body as a vehicle for the soul and discover why we chose our parents and our birth-place. Also, our life circumstances—being born rich or poor, with or without access to education or stimulating people, whether joyful or painful—have a way of catalyzing our soul's purpose.

I am convinced that the soul *intentionally* chooses the personality and talents to help it manifest its destiny. Therefore, by acknowledging and developing our talents, we cooperate with the soul's purpose. Many exceptionally talented individuals do not rise to their soul's call and live rather unexceptional lives, while some individuals with average talents rise to greatness through sheer persistence and force of will. Thomas Edison once said, "Genius is 1% inspiration and 99% perspiration." Whether we consider ourselves a genius or not, our obvious talents often give us clues to the soul's purpose.

How Are You Smart?

In our North American culture, we have a limited view of what talent, or genius, is. We must expand this if we are to see our own, and everyone else's, unique gifts. In his book *Frames of Mind*, Howard Gardner, a psychologist at the Harvard School of Education, discussed what he believed to be the seven major talents of individuals: linguistic, mathematical-logical, spatial, kinesthetic, musical, interpersonal and intrapersonal. Recently, Gardner has added naturalistic intelligence to his list and I am told he is soon to add spiritual intelligence as well.

Gardner says that "these intelligences typically work in harmony" and that our conventional school system teaches and rewards mostly logical-mathematical, intrapersonal and, to some extent, linguistic intelligence. This means that people who have other kinds of intelligence receive little positive reinforcement or development of their talent in school, to the detriment of both the individual and society. An IQ test measures only these three kinds of intelligence and even in these areas such tests are not predictive of general intelligence. Gardner's words illustrate this point:

> [These tests] reveal little about an individual's potential for further growth. Two individuals can receive the same IQ score; yet one may turn out to be capable of a tremendous spurt of intellectual attainment, while another may be displaying the very height of his intellectual powers.

Gardner does much to stretch our notion of intelligence past the tight grip in which IQ has held us. But he didn't, nor could he have grappled with *all* the unique gifts, and combination of gifts, that we can make into meaningful life and work. To work consciously with the mental body, it is up to each of us to identify our own gifts and discover how to make them work for us.

So how do we start looking for these talents? How we performed in school is not necessarily the best place to find the answer to the question "How am I smart?" The book *Cradles of Eminence* by Mildred and Victor Goertzel describes how three-fifths of four hundred famous modern people performed less than brilliantly in school. We know that Gandhi, Einstein, John Lennon, George Patton, Robert Browning, Pearl Buck, Isadora Duncan and Gertrude Stein—to name a few—all had problems conforming to a system into which they did not fit. All of these people had a unique brilliance that didn't surface until they had left school.

In my work, I have identified three main models of what we might call smartness, brilliance or genius. These models—the prodigy, the renaissance person and the gifted one—shed light on how our talents work with the soul.

The Prodigy

Be not afraid of greatness: some men are born great,
some achieve greatness, and some have greatness
thrust upon them.

Twelfth Night, William Shakespeare

A prodigy discovers their unique talent and is recognized for it early in life. This person could be a musical genius like Mozart or Glenn Gould, or someone with an obvious talent in mathematics or computers. Prodigies discover their life work in childhood or their teens and spend the next thirty, or more, years honing that work. Prodigies have very focused gifts and *might* be quite backward in developing what the rest of us consider to be normal life skills. For example, they might not know how to cook for themselves, do laundry or drive a car. They may not have well-rounded personalities, but prefer instead to focus their time and energy on the perfection of their particular skill.

Prodigies are born great. They inherit more of a particular gift from the soul than the rest of us. Their path ascends rapidly from the realm of physical form to the realm of spirit. They are connected more to the soul than to the personality. As they travel on the wings of their gift, they act as "way-showers," shedding light on future possibilities in consciousness for the rest of humanity. However, their gift comes with a price. They never totally descend into the five bodies of their personalities. As a result, they are susceptible to burn-out, as witnessed by the early deaths of Mozart, Byron, Keats, Sylvia Plath, Shelley, Emily Brontë and Gould. Often they are split between the world of spirit and the world of form and are both saint and hedonist. Not wishing to be limited by the physical body, they explore its pleasures in sex, alcohol and drugs in much the same way that they receive ecstasy from the soul. This lack of restraint and balance makes it hard for prodigies to live within societal norms. They often shatter the necessary conformity that the personality demands.

This is not to say that all prodigies have a pattern of substance abuse or early death. But ones who live to ripe old ages usually do so by becoming more "average," their exceptional talents, to some extent, spent. If they do live longer lives, it is often because someone has looked after them and shown them how to live in the physical world. "Normal life" is as difficult for the prodigy to learn as writing a symphony or creating a new mathematical theorem is for the rest of us.

The following diagram illustrates how a prodigy or genius develops. The outer circle encompasses the total potential of an individual including all of their talents. The musical prodigy starts to develop one unique talent early in life, until by middle age, they have filled in a great deal of this circle. This process is true for all prodigies.

The Prodigy

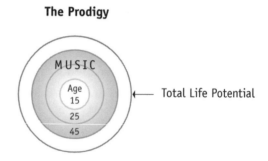

The Renaissance Person

> *I always wanted to be someone. I wish I'd been more specific.*

LILY TOMLIN

In discovering our talents, the majority of us walk a different path than that of the prodigy. The prodigy's path ascends to spiritual realms, while the renaissance person's path descends into the material world. The prodigy is an expert in macrocosmic existence, while the renaissance person is an expert in the micro-cosmic world of their own lives. Unlike the prodigy, renaissance men and women excel in mastering all of the five bodies—but the process of revealing their specific talent usually takes four or five decades. But because their path is one of descent into form, renaissance individuals are more removed from the spiritual world and have a harder time hearing the call of the soul.

Unlike the prodigy, renaissance people usually do not find their talent in their early years and might not discover it until middle age. This is because these individuals have many different interests. For example, a renaissance person might have talents with people, business, music, writing and speaking, but does not excel in any one of them enough to make them exclusive careers. The renaissance individual explores all these areas—either simul-taneously or sometimes sequentially—so it takes much longer to achieve a high level in one of them than it does for the prodigy, who focuses on only one. It might take a renaissance person many years to see a pattern encompassing all these interests and be able to turn it into meaningful work.

One example of such a person is Hildegard of Bingen, born in 1098, who rose to greatness in middle age. She was a nun who had seen visions from an early age, but had kept silent because they would not have been accepted from a woman. In her forties, Hildegard's visions and voices became so demanding that she took to her bed with illness and could not rise until she had committed to doing her soul's work. Hildegard then found the courage to tell others of her visions and was cross-examined by her bishop. She asked to found her own order—something un-heard of for a woman. At first her request was denied, but when it appeared as if Hildegard would die, her abbot agreed. For the next forty years, she recorded her visions, wrote music and po-etry and corresponded with the Pope and other learned people of the time.

The scientist-painter-inventor Leonardo da Vinci is another example of renaissance intelligence. Today he would probably have ended up in a special class for the learning disabled. His writing was atrocious, he had trouble reading some of the basic texts of his time and he made simple mistakes in arithmetic! Yet he became a musician, anatomist, poet, engineer, geologist, astronomer, philosopher, inventor and creator of some of the world's most beautiful paintings. More of da Vinci's paintings would be with us today if he hadn't experimented with new painting materials that have not lasted through time. His masterpiece *The Last Supper* would be almost unrecognizable today if it weren't for its careful restoration by the art community over the years. However, that same quality of continually trying to improve was also part of da Vinci's greatest gift. He is a role model for our age because he continually pushed his boundaries to know and learn, while applying his unlimited curiosity in diverse directions. However, on his deathbed he expressed regrets that he had not lived up to his potential.

The Renaissance Person

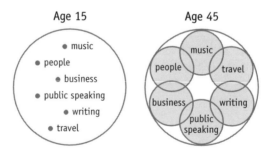

Typically, renaissance people appear unfocused in early life and don't find their true work until their various interests intersect in their late thirties or forties. One renaissance man I know has many interests: music, people, business, public speaking, writing and travel. At the age of fifteen, John's talents in each area were very small and he found himself unable to decide on a career, as nothing stood out as an obvious fit. During his twenties and thirties he pursued these interests through a series of jobs as newspaper writer, adventurer, raconteur and part-time musician. He was successful at whatever he did because he had a good business sense that helped him market himself. Over the years he honed his assortment of talents until by the time he was forty-five, they had combined to form a unique set of skills that were his own genius.

Unlike the narrowly focused prodigy, the renaissance person has many career paths from which to choose. John is presently faced with two career choices. One is to become a writer of travel articles about interesting people and the other is to both write and speak on the subject of business. The choice is his to make; he'll likely be successful in either career. Sometimes I hear renaissance people bewail that—unlike prodigies—they don't have one major talent and that this makes their choice of work more difficult. Rather than seeing this as an obstacle, why not consider the benefits of being offered a variety of work options that can satisfy your soul at different times in your life?

The Gifted One

> *I've always had this thing of him and me; he goes on stage, he's famous, and then me; I'm just some kid from Liverpool.*
>
> PAUL MCCARTNEY

There is a third alternative to these two paths. Instead of being either the conventional prodigy or the renaissance person, we could be a gifted one, a combination of the two. Albert Einstein, physicist, concert-level violinist and mystic, is an example of someone who walked this third path. Like the renaissance person, Einstein was cross-fertilized by his various interests but, like the conventional genius, he focused the majority of his time on one talent—physics.

Like Einstein, gifted ones may develop their primary talent early in life. However, as they age, they develop other talents which allow their soul to find greater expression. Prodigies can become one-dimensional human beings. Gifted ones avoid this;

they are well-rounded individuals, simultaneously remarkable for their dominant talent.

The Gifted One

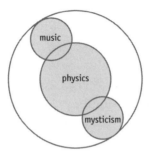

Gifted ones are called on to balance the two paths of ascent and descent. When they ascend into the world of the spirit they feel special, and when they descend into the world of form they feel ordinary. This can be a painful practice of expansion and contraction, which may cause gifted ones to feel split in two. However, as they continue to engage in this process, the body and soul gradually begin to tolerate each other.

Jean Houston, a teacher and role model for me, is a gifted one. Jean is one of the world's foremost thinkers in the area of human potential, and her talents, like those of prodigies, were recognized early in life. As a child living in New York, Jean was befriended by the Catholic philosopher and priest Teilhard de Chardin. Then, as a young adult, Jean was mentored by Margaret Mead, who nurtured Jean's love for indigenous cultures. Later, Jean became a friend and colleague of Joseph Campbell, who stimulated her interest in the importance of myth in each of our lives. None of these brilliant thinkers were in her life by accident. They were called by Jean's soul to catalyze her own brilliance, which is as broad as it is deep.

Today, in her late fifties, Jean Houston is considered by many to be a "teacher of teachers." She conducts a Mystery School in upstate New York and has written sixteen books on topics ranging from expanding our mind power, to the hero and the goddess, to her own autobiography. And she still has time to be a riveting speaker at countless conferences, advise the Clintons at the White House and cook gourmet meals.

I think of Jean as a gifted one rather than a renaissance person because her one gift—that of developing human potential—is so large that it overshadows her others. Also, she rose to prominence early in life because of this one gift. A renaissance person usually does not rise to prominence until middle age. One of Jean's favorite sayings to people who moan about their hard lives is, "Don't pathologize, mythologize!" This saying is consistent with her gift to encourage others to ascend to their soul's dream, their myth, and not to descend into their personality's pain.

Another example of a gifted one is Ann Mortifee, a Canadian singer whose first musical score, written at age eighteen, *The Ecstasy of Rita Joe*, was performed by the Royal Winnipeg Ballet. In her early fifties now, Ann continues to be active both in singing and writing music, her major gift, but her work has broadened over the years to include conducting workshops, writing poetry, parenting and writing songs for the dying.

Ann's road of bringing the paths of ascent and descent together has not been easy. As she said to me, "When I'm singing, I feel totally connected to the world, the divine and all beings. I'm filled with love. And when I return to the ordinary world, I often feel lonely and cut off from the transcendent. But I've had to learn to run an office and be a mother. These have been difficult lessons, but I don't regret learning them because I think that's what my life is about. Still, when I'm writing songs I can go on for eighteen-hour days and feel energized, yet four hours in my office exhausts me."

Ann has often told me that her struggle is to bring Ann Mortifee "the gifted one" together with Ann the ordinary person, and to know that both are her. In her early years, they were more separate but in middle age they are merging.

None of these three paths is better than the others; ultimately all of them lead to union with the soul. The prodigy is born more comfortable in the soul's world. The gifted one is split initially between the divine and material worlds and must learn to bring them together. The renaissance person is fragmented into many personality talents that need to be brought together to create a vessel for the soul. Only when the vessel is complete can the soul fully enter.

How Are You Smart?

The three models I discussed illustrate different ways of being smart. To learn more about *your* unique talents, you might wish to complete the following circle by drawing and labeling your various talents. Of the three models—prodigy, renaissance person and gifted one—choose the one that is most like you and draw circles for your major talents. Make sure to include both work and personal life interests. Your gifts might reflect interests you've had since childhood; likewise it is possible that some of them are more recent.

My Talents

When these talents combine does a pattern emerge that indicates the direction for your soul's work? Try not to limit yourself to concerns about money, or what others will think. Your pattern might indicate one career in particular. It could also point to several simultaneous careers. Fewer and fewer careers fit into the one nine-to-five job that has been associated with work in the past.

Which Workplaces Suit Your Talents?

Prodigies seldom work within organizations. They break new ground and often don't have personalities that thrive when confined by systems and policies of organizations. In those rare instances when prodigies do work in organizations, they are most likely to be in research and development, science, or in some area where they are given a great deal of freedom to explore independently.

Gifted ones, however, are often stars in their chosen vocation. In the business world, they have a brilliance that sets them apart from their fellow employees and moves them into visibility at an early age. Reflecting the more well-rounded personality of the renaissance person, gifted ones thrive—although sometimes with compromise—in fast-paced, innovative organizations. Gifted ones might also make good entrepreneurs and choose self-employment because this allows them the freedom to develop their gifts quicker than is possible within a traditional organizational structure.

Renaissance people often fit better into the existing workplaces than the other two types. This is especially true when they are younger, more flexible and still developing their talents. Existing jobs give renaissance people a way to do this that is beneficial both for them and their organization. However, in middle age, as renaissance people become clearer about their life path, they may find the traditional workplace a forced fit. At that time, they are more likely to leave to work within smaller organizations, from home or start their own business.

Organizations range widely in the amount of innovation and diversity they can embrace comfortably. The greater their ability to do so, the more all three types of people can work within them. The emerging model of interdependence is desirable for many organizations who seek to attract talented people of many types—especially organizations involving new technologies, medicine, science or education.

If we are to shine, we must find a workplace where our talents are recognized and promoted. Otherwise, we go against the grain and will never develop our talents fully. Organizations have a "corporate soul" just as each of us has an individual one. When I walk into an organization, I immediately have a gut feeling about whether I fit there or not. If I were to dissect this feeling into observable parts, I'd first examine how easy it is to get into the building. Is it locked? Are there security codes? Next, I notice how I'm greeted. Is it warm and welcoming or cool and efficient? Are people dressed in a casual or formal style? All these things send me messages about how I should conduct myself within that organization. Occasionally, I might decide that the organizational style is too rigid for me. Its vibration is not conducive to my particular talents, which need a certain degree of trust, warmth and openness to shine.

It takes courage to seek work situations where we can fully use our talents, and the desire to do so is one of the greatest reasons for seeking self-employment. But regardless of whether our path is that of prodigy, renaissance person or gifted one, all paths are ways of developing our own particular soul talents and giving them to the world. We will be able to achieve this only if we can understand what our soul wants us to do and this entails strengthening the fifth—the spiritual—body.

Ways to Access Your Soul

The man or woman who possesses no awe or sense of mystery is a candle without a wick.

ALBERT EINSTEIN

Priest and Celtic scholar Father John O'Donahue says that it is important to think of the body residing in the soul rather than the soul residing in the body. The spiritual body, where the soul resides, is the most subtle of all five of the bodies that have been discussed. The soul surrounds and interpenetrates the physical, etheric, emotional and mental bodies, although we may not be aware of this until we increase our sensitivity to feel and hear our soul. The soul, like a conductor, cannot play beautiful music unless the bodily instruments are tuned and paying attention to it.

The vessel of our personality is continually embraced and filled to overflowing by the divine love of the spirit. We need only to open ourselves to receive this gift. To fulfill our purpose and create our own unique music, we must be able to understand what the soul wants us to do. Its message is often subtle—barely heard in the whisper of the wind and felt only in the space between the ebb and flow of a wave. If, in our busy life, we do not take the time to listen, we cannot manifest our true purpose. There are many ways to open ourselves to listen, feel, see and know the soul. Our preferences will differ, but the following are some of the most effective means for strengthening our spiritual body.

Cultivating Awe and Mysticism

One way to cultivate the soul, and through it the spiritual body, is by developing the qualities of awe and mysticism. Mystics see and hear things not in three-dimensional reality. They hear the voice of angels, of other spiritual beings, and of the souls of both others and themselves. Mystics, shamans and prophets have existed in all cultures and at all times. Teresa of Avila, Black Elk and Mohammed, for example, were at the center of the religious life in their times. Mystics have been persecuted as witches, praised as seers and venerated as poets and scientists.

Nikola Tesla—like many scientists and inventors—experienced mystical visions that led him to his scientific breakthroughs. Often called "the man who invented the twentieth century," Tesla discovered the alternating electrical current, the AC motor and AC generator—three inventions that power the electrical system of modern technology. His visions of these inventions were so vivid that he had to put his hand through the visions to make sure they weren't real. Albert Einstein, a mystic as well as a physicist, discovered the theory of relativity by seeing himself traveling on a beam of light. Speaking of the importance of this mystical quality, Einstein said, "The most beautiful thing we can experience is the mysterious. It is the source of all true art and science."

We can all cultivate this quality of mysticism by listening to our inner voice, and by following our intuition and gut hunches. However, this ability comes more naturally to some than others. By reading spiritual poetry and stories about mystics, we become attuned to our soul—our higher self—as we do when we associate with people who have this gift. It does rub off. Most of us have had a mystical experience, although we may call it by a different name, such as our inner voice or God's voice. The 18th-century writer Madame de Staël said, "The voice of conscience is so delicate that it is easy to stifle; but it is also so clear that it is impossible to mistake it."

We need to both listen and act upon the instructions of the soul. By acting for the good of ourselves and others, we strengthen our relationship with the soul and bring more of it into the personality. Only psychopaths lack the morality to know good, although the rest of us can *choose* to ignore good at great cost to the soul. Dag Hammarskjold, Swedish statesman and secretary-general of the United Nations between 1953 and 1961, summarized these consequences:

> You cannot play with the animal in you without becoming wholly animal, play with falsehood without forfeiting your right to truth, play with cruelty without losing your sensitivity of mind. He who wants to keep his garden tidy doesn't reserve a plot for weeds.

Meditation and Retreats

Under thy great sky in solitude and silence, with
humble heart I shall stand before thee face to face.

RABINDRANATH TAGORE

Another way to learn to communicate with your soul more clearly is through meditation. Through meditation you increase your ability to access the spiritual realm both of the soul and of the Creator so that you can realize your own divinity. The goal of enlightenment is both a means and an end in itself. Through practicing meditation you will increase the number of little enlightenments or "ahas" that you experience. This process is cumulative and leads to a quantum change in understanding and consciousness. Most meditation techniques have one thing in common: they calm the mind. Like a good spring cleaning, they get rid of habitual clutter while restoring a harmonious vibration to all the bodies.

There are three main types of meditation practices that do this. The first is called Mahayana in the Buddhist tradition and is a heart path where you dedicate yourself and your work in service for the happiness of all sentient beings. Mahayana meditation is essentially a practice of action, not contemplation. The information found in this book gives you tools and techniques to follow this kind of meditation in the world.

A second meditation practice engages the body in the spiritual journey and includes ritualized movement patterns that help you to balance the spiritual and earth energies in order to create a strong physical vessel to house the soul. Examples of this practice are Tai Chi and Chi Gong. These more active kinds of meditations might be helpful either if you have difficulty sitting still or if you need to re-establish your connection to the earth under your feet and to the energy moving through your body.

The third kind of meditation is a sitting meditation, like Vipassana, where the goal is to see reality clearly. This involves sitting in silence in a state of open and choiceless awareness of the arising and passing away of experience. Another example is Transcendental Meditation (TM), where you chant a mantra—a Sanskrit word—and allow thoughts to surface. The purpose of TM is to eliminate and move beyond thought. St. John of the Cross, the great Christian mystic, said that the key to union with the soul is silence and work. Work we have; it's silence we lack. Sitting meditations take you into the silence where God and the soul's voice can more easily be heard.

Practicing these types of meditations for half an hour to an hour every morning before breakfast and/or before dinner helps many individuals to hear the soul. Dr. Herbert Benson, author of *The Relaxation Response* and originally skeptical of TM, studied its benefits and found that it lowered blood pressure and heart beats per minute. As well, meditators entered a restful state that was deeper than sleep, in which their brain patterns were more coherent and integrated than during the waking state.

Most of us in the Western world are in need of some form of regular meditation. Working too intensely and for too many hours, we often return home at night to television, where we are bombarded with more stimulation. On weekends—when we could rest—we race here and there shopping for things we don't need. There is little time for peaceful contemplation and it is difficult—even impossible—to hear the soul during the frenzy of activity. Creating a space for contemplation on a daily, weekly and yearly basis is essential.

Some of us need more meditation time than we can find in daily routines and find annual retreats helpful. Most retreats emphasize silence and prayer, although often a spiritual adviser assists us—either personally or through group talks—in focusing our meditation. Retreats can be days, weeks or even years in duration and could have a Christian, Buddhist, Hindu or non-religious focus. Daily meditation opens us to listening more closely to the voice of our soul, while retreats help us to let go of any attachments we have to things of this world, such as relationships, pride or material possessions.

> *Activity and reflection should ideally complement and support each other. Action by itself is blind, reflection impotent.*
>
> MIHALY
> CSIKSZENTMIHALYI

Some retreats focus on the denial of the bodies and we might choose to forgo sleep, food, interaction with others or any external stimulation that could distract us from higher consciousness. Buddha taught that our attachment to these things is the cause of our pain and misery and that letting go of our attachment is the path to enlightenment. Jesus also taught a path of non-attachment. As he said, "Be in the world but not of it." Both Buddha and Jesus were active participants in the world. Their lives are examples of how balance of the three kinds of meditation practice as well as retreats can aid us on our journey towards conscious life and work.

Prayer and Affirmation

Words lead to deeds.... They prepare the soul, make it ready, and move it to tenderness.

SAINT TERESA OF AVILA

There is a fundamental difference between meditation and prayer. The telephone is a helpful metaphor to explain this difference. We put the earpiece to our ear to listen to what someone is telling us and we speak into the mouthpiece to express our thoughts to the listener. Both parts are necessary for total communication. Meditation is like the earpiece of the phone, where we listen to what the soul wants to communicate to us, and prayer and affirmation are like the mouthpiece, where our personality communicates to the soul what it wants. Both ingredients are necessary for developing a working partnership between the soul and personality so that we can fully manifest our gifts in the world.

Prayers and affirmations are similar in that both tell the soul what you want it to give you. Whether you pray, "God, please help me to be a better parent," or affirm "Every day I am a better parent," the outcome will be the same if you put loving energy behind your thoughts and words. The *Zohar* says, "Prayer without intention is like a body without a soul." The power of prayer or affirmation is so great that we need to make sure that we always intend the highest good when we pray because we're likely to get it.

Laury Hammel, founder of The Longfellows Clubs—three tennis clubs and a holistic health center—in Wayland and Natick,

Massachusetts, has had years of experience with the positive results of prayer. Eighteen years ago, Laury bought his first tennis club with just $633 of his own money and borrowed the rest. The business now grosses over $7 million annually, has ten thousand members and employs three hundred people. The journey has been very difficult for Laury and he firmly believes that without prayer, his business would not have succeeded.

For many years Laury's clubs have been recognized as the best of their kind in New England, but because he had very little starting capital of his own, he experienced ongoing difficulties paying the bills. Many times along the way it looked as if his business would fold, but through a combination of hard work and prayer, Laury and the businesses survived. At one time, Laury was totally broke and in default to the bank. He had applied to the Small Business Administration for a loan but his partner, understanding their precarious financial situation, would not co-sign it and without his signature the deal could not go through. Laury had done everything he could to raise the money, but it wasn't enough. In order to survive, three separate things outside his control had to happen. On New Year's Eve—after months of prayer combined with emotional agony—all three things occurred simultaneously. Laury's partner agreed to be bought out; a friend lent him $200,000 with only Laury's word and signed note as guarantees; and the SBA approved the loan.

> *Prayer obviously produces results, otherwise millions wouldn't pray.*
>
> J. KRISHNAMURTI

And why would so many people be willing to do so much for Laury? It's because he's given so much. He has five children—all of whom were born with special needs—so for many years he has been active in his community looking for ways to help such people. As early as 1977, he created a Handi-Racket Tennis Program for children with physical, emotional and mental difficulties. This program has expanded to include hosting Special Olympics and social clubs for the same disabled people who are now adults.

Laury also founded the New England Business for Social Responsibility in 1988, which grew into the national Business for Social Responsibility.

Laury shared with me that his prayers are not always answered in the way he anticipated and that sometimes he just prays that God will help him to do the greatest good rather than making a specific prayer. In this way, Laury trusts that God knows better than he the path Laury should take. But Laury doesn't just pray and wait for God to give him what he wants; he works hard at his business so his clubs will thrive in the material world.

Like Laury, I've found that the combination of working hard to improve my business, while allowing God room to work magic has brought tremendous benefit and joy to my life. Many people have difficulty trusting that they will be provided for by the universe. Affirmations, as well as prayers, can help us to learn to trust and wait on the will of heaven. I practiced one for many years that helped me to learn these qualities.

Start by tapping lightly on the thymus gland, located in the center of the chest about four inches below the throat. Dr. Jack Diamond, in *Your Body Doesn't Lie*, states that a healthy thymus gland strengthens the immune system because it produces the white blood cells that are so critical in fighting disease. I think of the thymus as the higher heart and tapping it lightly signals the heart to open and be receptive to the chant.

While tapping on the thymus, chant the word "*Allow*." When chanting *Allow*, feel the "ah" opening your heart. Visualize yourself receiving whatever the universe wants. "Ah" is used in many cultures as a heart sound. It is the "Ah" of the Christian "Amen" and the Islam "Allah." Both of these words may stem from the Egyptian Gnostic creation myth that says that God laughed seven times to create the world and each laugh was a "Ha." The "Ha" sound is also found in an ancient Cherokee chant.

Here is another affirmation that you might find equally helpful. Every morning say out loud, "I am more loving and relaxed every day" or "I trust God/the Creator to give me what I need in my life." While repeating these words, imagine yourself being loving and relaxed in your dealings with others and welcoming all opportunities to learn. At the end of the day, just before retiring for the night, review the day and remember all the times you did well or were loving and relaxed. Forgive yourself and others for the times that either you or others behaved as less than you could have been. Visualize all these difficult times as if they were now perfect and in harmony. Remember how you're never supposed to go to bed angry at anyone? This folk wisdom is the basis of this powerful affirmation.

Nature

> *To see a world in a grain of sand*
> *And a heaven in a wild flower,*
> *Hold infinity in the palm of your hand*
> *And eternity in an hour.*

"AUGURIES OF INNOCENCE," WILLIAM BLAKE

Some people connect with their soul more easily in their community and within buildings designed for that purpose, while others find their soul through solitude in nature. Many poets—Wordsworth, Coleridge and Blake come to mind—have written of the transcending power of nature to link us with the eternal. The Greeks and Romans actually set aside sacred places in nature for people to meditate. These usually contained groves of trees and springs where the nature spirits could help to heal a person. It was forbidden to fish there, cut down trees or disturb the area in any way. We need to reintroduce this concept of sacred natural places today. Cultivated parks in cities are all very well, but untamed nature often contains the greatest powers of soulful rejuvenation. Nature helps us to re-establish a balanced, calm vibration—necessary to access the soul.

Preferred physical environments differ from person to person, but often reflect the specific natural element that individuals most need to balance themselves. Some people need more of the earth element, which anchors them to the physical body. Walking through forests and connecting with trees, herbs and flowers is healing for these people. Others feel better when they live near water, which affects their emotional body. The rhythm of ocean waves, which resembles the ebb and flow of the blood pumping through our bodies, can have a hypnotic, calming effect. Streams and small rivers can ease depression and lift our spirits. Others are drawn to mountains, whose raw power and clear air uplift the mind and facilitate clear thinking. Mountains can also strengthen our power and our aspiration to the highest spiritual life. Finally, there are those who are drawn to the desert. Many older people feel this attraction when heat—the fire element—decreases in their physical body. They naturally prefer to retire to Florida, Arizona, the Caribbean and other warm places.

Incorporating nature into the work environment nourishes our soul for everyone. In some workplaces, this means inner courtyards with fountains and trees, where people can eat and relax. Office buildings need windows that open so that employees can breathe fresh air and see the sun and clouds in the sky. Plants in offices and flowers in central locations uplift the spirits of employees. If people are working in one location for 60 percent of their waking hours, they need environments that are conducive to their health.

Home and Work Environments

The *appropriate* home and work environment required to support and nurture our soul is different for each of us. Some of us need the peaceful setting of country life, while others feel more in harmony with the bustle of a large city. Still others need a combination of both these settings. Even the kind of house or apartment we live in is important. Are we drawn to old houses or modern ones? Do we prefer small, cozy rooms or high ceilings and skylights? Do we want a bedroom in the attic or on the ground floor? We need to make these choices consciously, both at home and at work.

We also require the right colors in our work environment to evoke creativity—but not over-stimulation. Too many offices are painted gray, beige or stark white—colors that can be depressing to the soul. Colors, like the four elements, create atmospheres that are either conducive or harmful to us. Cooling blues evoke waters and sky, and violets and purples conjure up the darker night sky. Yellows and golds are colors of the sun and add an up-lifting sunniness to a room. Reds and oranges are more fiery and stimulating. Green, like fuschia and burgundy, is a color of heal-ing and is a balance between the cool and warm colors.

Even traveling to work affects people in different ways. Some men and women find it beneficial to their soul to live in the coun-try and, to do this, have accepted a daily commute that can take hours out of their day. Some people use commuting time to read on the train, listen to music on the radio or drive in complete silence to think new ideas. Working at home suits others because no traveling is involved and they can create the atmosphere that best suits them. However, there are some individuals who would be lonely if they didn't have other people for company during the day.

Some parents with young children prefer to place their chil-dren in daycare and go to work undistracted, while other parents love to work at home to spend more time with their kids. Each of us is unique. At this time in our evolution we are searching for workplaces with an environment that supports our unique needs.

Introverts and Extroverts

Introverts need silence and space in order to hear their soul. They require a lot of time alone—definitely more than extroverts. Mar-garet is an introvert and her path, like that of many introverts, entails reading books about philosophy, religion and poetry, as well as autobiographies of individuals with great souls. Soul cultivation for her is a quiet evening at home, listening to music and reading. When Margaret's soul resonates with what she reads, she glimpses what she must do in her own life. Margaret, like most introverts, prefers to form her ideas alone and tell others when her process of creation—or revelation—is complete.

While introverts are more reflective, extroverts are more experiential. George is an extrovert and he, like Margaret, enjoys reading and music, but unlike Margaret, George finds that only by discussing his ideas with others does he have revelations about his soul's purpose. Extroverts, like George, prefer to talk to others during each step of their thinking process and refine their thoughts and ideas based on the feedback they receive. It's as if extroverts—like George—need someone else as a mirror to show them more clearly who they are and what they think, while introverts—like Margaret—have their own inner person with whom to have a dialogue.

Margaret and George are married. It's not uncommon for introverts and extroverts to marry, because each learns from being in a relationship to his or her opposite. But this only works when there is mutual respect for each other's learning preferences. To be effective in our personal and work relationships, we need to appreciate what style works best for us and to honor other people's preferred style.

Extroverts will thrive in environments based on teams and partnerships where there is a great deal of interaction with people. Professions that draw them are sales, marketing, training, education, personnel, social service, retail businesses and community work. Introverts, conversely, thrive in atmospheres where they are allowed time to think and reflect. They dislike having to come up with answers to important questions on the spot and prefer to go away and think before responding. Introverts gravitate towards such careers as accounting, research, science, strategic planning, urban planning, architecture, writing and editing.

The soul finds it easier to work with us when we are engaged in work that suits our temperament. Otherwise, it's a kind of forced fit making ourselves do something that goes against our disposition. However, many introverts, such as Albert Schweitzer, have been called into very public arenas and have risen to the occasion because of their higher need to serve humanity. Conversely, it's not uncommon for extroverts to lead, to some extent, an introverted life because they find it necessary to write books— an introverted activity—in order to reach more people with their ideas.

Way-Showers and Teaching Tyrants

Regardless of whether we are introverts or extroverts, forming a conscious connection with our soul is often not easy. Some of us find it helpful to have a role model, mentor or what I call a way-shower to show us the way on this spiritual journey. In India, these gurus become personal teachers for life, but in North America it is more usual to study with many people with expertise in our various interests. If we choose our way-showers well, both Eastern and Western paths can be ones to help find the soul. Some of these way-showers may be a joy to be around and when we are in their presence we feel peace or even ecstasy. Other way-showers, who can be referred to as teaching tyrants, may cause us considerable distress by pricking our weak areas. Both kinds of spiritual teachers might be necessary in our journey to consciousness. Teachers do not need to be perfect, but they must be able to help us access our souls better than we can do ourselves.

One such teacher is Namgyal Rinpoche, author of *Glimmerings of the Mystical Life*. When he was younger, and over a period of twenty years, Namgyal took his students on journeys around the globe. One of these students, Nobuo, accompanied him to South America in the seventies and recalled the experience. "There was a tendency for a lot of his students to cling to him," says Nobuo, "and Namgyal wanted to teach us detachment. One day we woke up to find he had gone and had left no message for us. Most of us were pretty upset. Some wanted to try to find him and others wanted to stay where we were to wait for him to return. Namgyal didn't come back for days. During that time most of us learned that we could manage quite well without him.

"Another time we were in a restaurant that served Western food and we were all looking forward to Western meals after all the South American food we'd been eating. Namgyal asked each of us what we wanted. I ordered wieners and beans because I connected that food to happy memories in Canada. When the food finally came, Namgyal gave each of our orders to someone else. This certainly taught us quickly to expect nothing and to be detached from results."

As you can see, the process of working with a teacher is not necessarily pain-free. Teaching tyrants—as the Cherokee call such spiritual teachers—prick our weak areas, so that we can develop soul consciousness. Teaching tyrants might get angry at us, be stern or elicit guilt, but if all is done consciously and with the right motivation, we learn our lessons.

Everyday life offers us the same learning opportunity. We interact with people on a daily basis who elicit a wide range of both positive and negative responses in us. We work with some people more easily because our temperaments complement each other and our values and ways of thinking are similar. However, it is not always with these people that we grow the most. It is often working with people we don't like, or with whom we have a fundamental difference in opinion, that affords us the greatest opportunity for growth. Perhaps this occurs by learning to appreciate their point of view, or perhaps it is because they teach us patience, humility, forgiveness and other important qualities that arise through the difficulties of working with them. We must learn not to be triggered, and to react appropriately, in each situation.

Engaging in meditation and prayer are only a small part of our day—most of our time is spent with others, often including teaching tyrants. Even when it is difficult, we need to be able to both hear and act on our soul's wishes.

Of course, there are many other ways to access the soul than the ones mentioned. Many people encounter transformative experiences through singing, dancing, painting, or writing. Others find a path to the soul that lies through the senses and find that sexual activity or even food can give them great pleasure and a sense of awe and wonder. Still others use drugs, such as alcohol, Ecstasy and LSD to reach a temporary state of bliss. The goal—regardless of the path that one takes—should not be to expect continual bliss, but to become a fully conscious person living and working in the world. When the soul is able to work consciously with the five bodies that constitute the personality, we achieve this.

Part II of this book has been designed to offer tools and techniques that assist with this process. First, we weave together our spiritual and physical bodies by examining our soul's goal and then anchoring that goal in the physical world in a concrete, practical way. We can do this by setting action steps that are achievable. Second, we need to eliminate negative programmings that sabotage us from achieving our goal and re-program ourselves for success. This is accomplished by working with the etheric body. Third, we must examine the fears that hold us back from achieving our goal and learn to overcome them by taking action to reduce their control over us. By doing this we strengthen the emotional body. Fourth, in order to strengthen our mental body, we must discover the ways in which we are smart and find workplaces and work that best utilize these talents. This is an essential step because we can never excel by doing something that lies outside the realm of our true gifts. Lastly, we need to establish an ongoing link with our spiritual body by daily practice so that the threads between our soul and personality become stronger.

Our five bodies are usually not equal in strength, so some of us must spend more time focusing on grounding our soul's goal in the physical world, while others will need to focus on overcoming fear. It is necessary to strengthen our weaker bodies in order to become a soul-infused personality. But while we work on our weaknesses, we need to continue practicing our strengths. By doing this we maintain our self-confidence and become an example to others.

Our inner transformation is a lifelong process. However, we can make it productive by putting our knowledge and goals into practice in the outer world. Work and interpersonal relationships are two areas that help to develop a soul-infused personality while at the same time allowing us to make a positive difference for others and the world around us. Transforming our outer world, as with our inner transformation, is a lifelong journey.

Outer Transformation: Taking Your Soul to Work

There is no such thing as an enlightened person; there is only enlightened activity.

SUZUKI ROSHI

Manifesting Your Full Potential

A new center—presently dormant in the average man and woman—has to be activated and a more powerful stream of psychic energy must rise into the head from the base of the spine to enable human consciousness to transcend the normal limits.

Gopi Krishna

Part II was concerned with the process of inner transformation that each of us needs to undergo in order to become a soul-infused personality. To do this I examined the five personality bodies—physical, etheric, emotional, mental and spiritual—that create a vessel to house the soul. In Part III, you will discover how to mesh the needs of your personality and your soul with your work.

Some of you might feel that you are already doing your soul's work and are interested in learning to do this more fully either where you are working presently or in a similar job. Others might realize that there is a poor match between your soul's dream and the work that you are doing. Whether you believe that your current occupation is your soul's work or not, there are many ways to bring more soul to your present work in order to create a healthier environment in which both you and others can thrive.

Part III examines seven topics that are crucial for developing this life energy in order for you to manifest your full potential in the world:

- ❖ increasing your life energy
- ❖ cultivating people who feed your soul
- ❖ mastering the material world
- ❖ walking the path of heart
- ❖ creating organizations with soul
- ❖ activating your intuition, and
- ❖ working in harmony with natural cycles.

These techniques are concrete and practical and yet are founded on eternal spiritual principles. By practicing them regularly, you can integrate both soul and personality in your life and work.

Although each of our journeys is unique, mastering these areas is a necessary and predictable part of our process of transformation. Recently, I received another e-mail from Dan, whom we met earlier. He is still working for the same company but is planning to travel around the world on a spiritual pilgrimage. While he waits for the right time to travel, he continues to work as an engineer and has been able to find joy in his current work.

Dan's ongoing journey at work

Dear Tanis,

The past months have been an incredible journey. I am currently feeling very optimistic, centered and energetic, while still working at the job I had described as my "prison" only a short time ago. The main reasons for these positive changes in my life are: learning to use an optimistic, exploratory style, focusing on my circle of control, learning to love the world as it is, coming to know my true Self and living in the present. I firmly believe these all have led to very positive results in my life.

I realized that since I have chosen to remain in my current situation for the time being, I might as well get the most out of my time at work. Therefore, I chose to conduct my job with pride, interest and even a degree of enthusiasm. Having put this extra energy into my job, I am receiving positive results which makes work more pleasant and builds, rather than diminishes, my self-esteem. I am enjoying the job much more every day, thanks to the positive energy I am putting into it.

The world is a crazy place at times, but it is a wonderful place and I am very glad to be a part of it. I am quickly learning to cherish all the little things, and to sweat only the big ones. I used to find myself worrying about a multitude of little things, many of which were inconsequential or out of my control. I had been denying and blocking out the reality of my undesirable present by continually being busy, always on the go, never allowing myself to be truly in the present. It is very difficult to come to know yourself when your mind is so busy that intuitive and self-realizing thoughts can't find their way into your conscious mind. But my busy mind is calming and I can now feel myself walking with more confidence in a much more relaxed way. I find myself much more able to deal with life events, now that I am leading my life in a more mindful manner. I am also less worried about what others think of me, and am more willing to openly be myself.

Now that I feel myself radiating a contented, enthusiastic confidence, I find myself attracting and choosing to be with certain people. My new-found enthusiasm and joy for living is catching. I notice the people around me changing in many areas as well. I believe it is true that to change the world, you have to start by changing yourself. I avoid people who are continually negative and complaining. I don't need to fuel their destructive fires or to allow myself to be brought

*down by them. This wonderfully happy and positive way
of being cannot be maintained without effort and support
and I require and thoroughly enjoy the company of joyous,
positive, encouraging and enlightened people.*

*What I find most exciting is that I have learned to be
happy in my current job, which makes this the best time for
a career and/or life change. I am no longer running away
from something I dislike, rather I will be leaving something
I am happy with for something which is more in line with
how I want to spend my life. There are likely going to be
many challenges along the way, but I am confident that I
have created success for myself so far in life and will continue to have even greater success in my future endeavors.*

Best regards, Dan

As we observe in Dan's story, there is no clear distinction between one's inner and outer transformation. Both processes are
ongoing and the two fertilize each other. The deeper our understanding of ourselves, the more we have to offer *potentially* to the
world. I say potentially because it's possible—unlike Dan—to be
out of balance in the process of inner and outer transformation.
Some individuals do very little inner work, have little consciousness of their soul or the souls of others, and yet put their energy
fully into working in the outer world. These individuals will most
likely be personality-dominated and might make choices for themselves and others that do not serve the world in the long run—and
possibly not even in the short run. Other individuals spend years,
perhaps decades, engaged in their own inner spiritual process, but
never integrate this knowledge into their outer work. In neglect-
ing to do so, the world does not benefit from their wisdom.

Dan is balancing the time and energy he devotes to his inner
work with that of his outer work, and he is applying what he is
learning in his personal journey to his workplace. For Dan, inner
and outer work are no longer separate. This attitude is the key in
taking our soul to work; it typifies the interdependent mind-set

that we need in the coming cycle of human evolution. The path of outer work, by itself, exaggerates the importance of independence and serves the personality at the expense of the soul. The path of inner work, by itself, is one of dependence where we wait for God or our soul to direct our every thought or action. Neither of these separate paths are indicative of a soul-infused personality working in partnership in the world.

As we hear in Dan's own words, this journey, although sometimes difficult, brings great joy, optimism and self-confidence. As Dan rises to the challenge of living fully in the present moment—while still keeping his ultimate goal in mind—his life energy increases and makes him more effective in all aspects of his life. Maintaining and cultivating our life energy contributes to our happiness and our ability to achieve our life's goals.

Your Seven Chakras

To manifest our potential, we need to understand and learn how to use the laws of energy. In this book I refer to the intangible force that keeps us alive as life energy, but it is also referred to as *chi* in China and *prana* in India. It is not within the sphere of this book to do a thorough investigation of *how* this life energy works in the body. However, it is essential to your inner and outer transformation that you have a basic understanding of how to utilize this chi/prana in both your personal and work lives. Your energy is your life force. It is an invisible current that moves around and within each one of us like electrified air. By living a physically healthy life, surrounding yourself with emotionally supportive people, thinking positive thoughts and doing what you feel called to do in life, you can dramatically increase your energy in all five personality bodies.

Life energy is either increasing or decreasing depending on two things. The first depends on your home and work environment being conducive to growth; the second depends on how well you make use of these environments in order to grow. We will examine what you can do within your circle of influence to increase and use your energy more effectively in both of these ways. By doing this, you will feel better about yourself and others and increase both your chances and the speed at which you attain your goals.

One of the first recorded sources of this circulation of life energy in our bodies is found in the *Upanishads*, written about 600 A.D. in India. This system of knowledge is now well established in the East both in Hindu and Buddhist spiritual traditions and also as the basis for Eastern science and medicine. It was introduced to the Western world in the 1920s through Theosophists and their study of metaphysics.

According to this Eastern science, life energy circulates in the body by way of three channels, like electrical wires located along the spine in the etheric body. The first channel—the solar channel—is more masculine, yang and positively charged, and descends into the body from the universal spiritual life force. The second channel—the earth channel—is more feminine, yin and negatively charged, and ascends from the Earth. These positive and negative energy channels merge with a third central channel at seven centers along the spine, called *chakras*, a Sanskrit word, meaning wheels. These wheels are like computer disks that receive information from two programmers—God (or whatever you choose to call this universal intelligence) and the Earth. The chakras decode this information and transmit it through the mind and body, spirit and matter, soul and personality.

The amount of energy we are able to circulate is determined by the width and openness of the three channels, similar to how a thick electrical wire can conduct more electrical energy than a thin one. The chakras, like computer disks, receive the energy from the channels and translate it for use in the bodies. If our chakras are open and effectively using the energy coming to them, obviously we have more energy available for the other bodies. Lack of energy is usually caused by negative thoughts, actions and feelings, such as fear, that keep the chakras from functioning properly.

The seven chakras are like battery chargers boosting and re-fining our energy for use in the bodies as the energy ascends and descends. To accomplish this task, the chakras alternate between holding a more masculine or feminine current. The first chakra at the base of the spine is more masculine and yang; the second chakra found below the navel is more feminine and yin; the third center located in the solar plexus is more yang; the fourth center near the heart is more yin; the fifth center in the throat is more yang; then these two currents of energy eventually unite in both the sixth and seventh centers—the third eye located in the fore-head and the crown at the top of the head.

The Qualities of the Seven Chakras

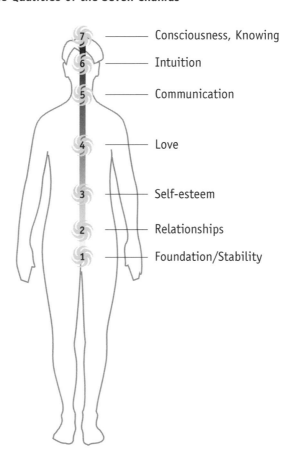

7 ——— Consciousness, Knowing

6 ——— Intuition

5 ——— Communication

4 ——— Love

3 ——— Self-esteem

2 ——— Relationships

1 ——— Foundation/Stability

To develop our energy fully we must be open and functioning in all seven chakras. And we must be able to move back and forth from the more masculine chakras of action—first, third and fifth—to the more feminine chakras of receptivity—second and fourth. We should feel equally comfortable with the qualities of independence and dependence and the ability to exercise our own will or surrender to the will of others and the universal divine will to be able to practice the quality of interdependence. Neither the more masculine or feminine path alone will allow us to become an interdependent soul-infused personality.

The first chakra at the base of the spine opens fully when an individual is at home in his or her physical body and lives in connection with nature and trusts it for support. Having a secure foundation with the physical body and the planet is necessary for this first chakra to flourish. The second chakra, located below the navel, opens when our relationships with others are in balance and when we both give and receive equally. The third chakra in the solar plexus expands more fully when we use our power of choice and free will to transform ourselves and to manifest our gifts in the world. The fourth chakra in the heart expands when we love others as ourselves. The fifth chakra, the center of communication and creativity in the throat, increases when we realize our power to birth what we envision and step forward to do it. The sixth chakra, the third eye located in the center of the forehead, is associated with intuition and clairvoyance. It opens more fully when we see what would be good for us to do in the world long term. Lastly, the crown chakra opens when we become a soul-infused personality dedicated to serving others in the world. At that time, we understand that this is the only real choice and commit to do it willingly because our soul and personality are no longer separate. Jesus spoke as a soul-infused personality when he said, "My father and I are One."

The chakras do not always open or expand in the order mentioned. Often, we learn the functions of some of the lower and higher centers before finally moving to the heart chakra, which will be the major focus for humanity in the approaching fourth cycle of our evolution. For instance, we might first learn to use the intuition of the sixth chakra and the creativity and communication skills found in the fifth chakra combined with the ability to master the material world and relationships, found in the lower three chakras. We might even have an enlightening breakthrough in the crown chakra and experience the divinity of all beings before opening the heart chakra to serve others in the world.

We all have different talents and fears and therefore some chakras are more active than others. When our personality develops its talents and overcomes its weaknesses and fears, all chakras align and the soul's energy is able to work more fully in the body. It takes both a strong personality and bodily vessel to hold the soul's energy and it is for this reason we devote the earlier part of our life to developing the vessel. As the personality matures, the chakras open like flowers to receive the soul's energy. The five bodies—physical, etheric, emotional, mental and spiritual—are able to accommodate the increased current of the merged soul and body energy. This is a continually evolving process. If we have too much Solar, yang energy, we are too active, too hot and tend to burn ourselves up. With too much Earth, yin energy, we are too passive and don't exert enough will to manifest anything in the world.

There are certain predictable steps to consciousness connected to the workings of these chakras that all of us undergo. During the first stage of human development—both individually and collectively—we must learn to control our passions and emotions. We open the dependent and harmonious feminine aspect of the life force. In the next stage, we strengthen the vessel by developing independence and control of the mind—the more masculine aspect of the life force. In order to become a soul-infused personality these feminine and masculine—Earth and Solar—energies need to be balanced, and when this occurs, they merge and ascend. In metaphysical science this merging is called the "divine marriage." When this marriage takes place, the seven chakras are awakened to a higher state of consciousness so that we will more fully know what our work is in the world and be able to do it.

The process of the marrying of these two energies does not happen overnight. Some people are overdeveloped in either their feminine or masculine natures and therefore are open in some chakras but blocked in others. There are many ways, including meditation, affirmation, bodily postures, diet and psychotherapy, to open these seven centers. But one of the most potent methods is to change our behavior and the way we interact with ourselves and others. Becoming conscious of our motivations, feelings and thoughts, as well as taking responsibility for our actions are effective and direct paths to consciousness. Seen this way, work is not a distraction from our spiritual journey, but a place where we can apply ourselves and become conscious creators.

As we engage in both our inner and outer transformations, the amount of energy we have grows. If we are needy or underdeveloped in one of these seven areas, the chakra concerned with that function might take energy from others and the environment. Conversely, when we are comfortable and confident in one of these seven areas, that chakra is energized and actually radiates energy to others and the environment. The amount of energy available to us to manifest our gifts in the world is therefore dependent both on the degree to which we have undergone our own inner transformation and the degree to which we are acting and applying our talents in the outside world.

How Organizations Use Their Chakras and Energy Fields

Organizations, like human beings, create a certain energy field based on how well they function in each of their seven energy centers. Just as chakras cannot be seen by our physical eyes, so the chakras of organizations are not physically visible. But we can perceive their effect on employees, executives and customers. For example, some organizations are more ego-driven—a characteristic of the third chakra—whereas some are highly visionary—a characteristic of the sixth chakra, the third eye. The energy fields in organizations—which are created through the use of some chakras and not others—are the result of many tangible and intangible factors, such as the kind of business, leadership styles, policies and procedures and employees, use of their own chakras.

Each chakra is responsible for a particular characteristic of a business. Ideally, in any human being or organization, all chakras should be open so that the energy flows freely along the channels that connect them. When this happens in a business, a clear vision is sent from the seventh chakra of the organization down to the first chakra, allowing people to produce the products and create the services that align with that vision.

Individuals often feel more comfortable working for organizations with an energy field that is the same or at least complementary to their own. For instance, an individual with a high need for security and a low desire for change might have a dominant first chakra. This person would be uncomfortable in an organization where the leaders and majority of employees have a dominant third chakra of dynamic power and fast change. The more that organizations and their employees are integrated and working with all chakras, the more flexible and tolerant they are of each other's talents. It is difficult for an individual to effect change in their organization if the leaders and majority of employees are not functioning in the same chakras. This leads to a sense of frustration and sometimes futility. However, if the organization wants to change, and sees a benefit to itself in embracing the characteristics of its underdeveloped chakras, then the individual seeking change might be acknowledged and allowed to help the organization strengthen these areas.

The first chakra is called the root chakra because it connects the person to the physical world. In business, this chakra has the same function. Businesses that excel in this energy center are down to earth, practical and good at selling the products they create. They balance how much they spend with how much they earn. The root chakra is concerned with doing, not thinking. It gives employees rituals and rules to follow that create order and security at work. This allows employees to experience a sense of being "in the flow" without thinking about what they're doing. However, the downside—if the organization is overdeveloped in this area—is a kind of rote doing which eventually numbs the minds of employees.

When a business is experiencing financial difficulties and is concerned with survival, this is communicated to its employees, who start worrying about their own survival. If a company has great visions, but doesn't put them through the test of common sense that ground them in reality, then difficulties can arise. This kind of company has its head in the clouds and often struggles to pay the bills. Mergers, downsizings and the continual dangers found in our living and working environments can cause dysfunction in the root chakra. To open this energy center, organizations need to bring their ideas into practical reality and hire solid managers who can translate the dreams of their leader into action. Creating rituals, traditions and rules that give employees a sense of safety and security can also be helpful.

The second chakra is concerned with relationships. Companies balanced in this chakra usually have happy employees because people feel personally liked, valued and that they count as individuals. Companies that treat their employees well also have happy customers, because people who are treated well pass this feeling along to others. Organizations who value the second chakra host daycare centers, hold retirement and Christmas parties, offer words of praise easily and engage only in constructive suggestions for improvement. Because of these positive actions, employees are loyal and speak well of their employers.

Conversely, organizations that experience difficulty in the second chakra—are destructively critical of employee performance, don't treat women and minorities with the same respect as men, make promises that are not kept and regard employees as replaceable parts. Employees talk behind one another's backs and sabotage each other's effectiveness. At the end of the day, they race out the door and never think of socializing with their colleagues after work or on the weekends. The pervasive negative atmosphere in such companies is often dehumanizing.

The solution for such ailing companies is to build up the second chakra by increasing nurturing and the sense of care, warmth and security. As an employee in such a company, you can help by showing an interest in your co-workers' lives and families. For instance, you might make donations to co-workers' charitable concerns or recognize their work by letters of thanks. But just as some businesses underuse the second chakra, others overuse it. Organizations who overuse the second chakra often keep their employees dependent on them by over-supervising them and not asking them to push their boundaries to try new things. They impede the growth of their employees by treating them like children.

The road to independence lies in the third chakra of will and power. Organizations exuding third chakra energy are dynamic, charismatic and have high self-esteem. Employees are encouraged to take risks and are empowered to do so. These organizations are often fast moving and fiery, and move opposition aside through the power of their personality. This driving energy is typical of businesses started by entrepreneurs, such as Microsoft or Apple, and atypical of most banks or educational institutions. There are opportunities in third chakra companies for people of talent, regardless of race, creed or sex—as long as employees can keep up the fast pace.

However, organizations that have too much third chakra activity may develop an inflated ego and a sense of superiority. They could lose the connection to the higher purpose of their work and begin engaging in stimulating projects for their own sake rather than for any intrinsic benefit to others. Third chakra energy can be over-stimulating and when people burn out or are unwilling to keep up the pace, they are quickly replaced by energetic newcomers. So, the cycle perpetuates itself.

Conversely, if there is a lack of third chakra energy, an organization might become de-energized, depressed and slow to make necessary changes. People lose joy and enthusiasm—two qualities found in organizations which abound with third chakra energy. Employees who are afraid to acknowledge their power might experience difficulty working in third chakra organizations. Power implies responsibility and some people prefer to remain dependent and have others tell them what to do; this is not possible when organizations access the energy of the higher centers.

The three lower chakras relate to the world of action and the self; the higher three chakras relate to our perception and understanding of the world. These two realms meet in the fourth chakra, the heart.

The fourth chakra is the mid-point in the chakra system—where the needs of the self are balanced with the needs of the greater whole. When organizations become aware that what they produce affects every living creature and start to make responsible decisions based on this knowledge, they work with the heart chakra.

When organizations reach a certain level of success but are unwilling to let go of their own egotistical needs, they become dysfunctional in the heart chakra. They exude a kind of stinginess and lack of generosity. Energy continually moves. Organizations, like individuals, are either evolving or devolving—it's their choice. Some organizations, such as not-for-profits, hospitals and social service agencies, might have heart-centered missions but do not practice these same qualities within their walls. This split in consciousness becomes very difficult for employees to bridge and leaves them feeling like hypocrites in their work.

The fourth cycle of human evolution is moving us away from the third chakra of independence into the fourth chakra of interdependence. Companies working in teams and partnerships with others practice, to varying degrees, a "group consciousness" typical of the heart chakra. These companies adhere to equal opportunities for women and minorities and are concerned that their products and services help the world. Deep listening occurs between employees and there is flexibility to serve other people's needs. An open heart is often based on a certain loss of ego, so companies based in this chakra think in terms of "we," rather than "I," and look for the best solutions to problems regardless of who came up with it.

The fifth chakra creates, receives, controls and transmits communication. This center is a powerful one for manifestation in the world and is related on a higher vibration to the second chakra, which, in addition to being concerned with relationships, also deals with procreation. The throat chakra births new things into the world. Everything in the world, from thoughts to feelings to material objects, is vibrating. By using the fifth chakra, businesses are able to synthesize thoughts and create specific vibrational frequencies and patterns. Organizations that use the throat chakra excel in communication and sometimes make communication—which is itself a growing industry—their business.

When we communicate well, we send other people our thoughts and thereby affect them. If leaders do not have honorable intentions, but have a strong use of the fifth chakra, they can do great damage. Charismatic leaders such as Hitler and Mussolini led millions of people down erroneous paths through their speeches. Questions concerned with the fifth chakra that you might ask include, "Does my organization tell the truth about its products and services?" and "Does it create things that are worthwhile in the world?"

It is through employing the fifth chakra that organizations stretch into the full range of their power. Organizations working with the lower three chakras might be family-run businesses affecting their community and possibly their nation, but businesses operating in the fifth chakra often have global impact. Such organizations need to learn to control their power. To work ethically, they must achieve a balance between the freedom to create new products and technologies and the benefits that ensue for others. As organizations move from lower to higher chakras, the responsibility for their choices increases because of their growing power to influence and control the entire world.

While the fifth chakra uses sound vibration, the sixth chakra works with an even faster vibration—that of light. Just as we see the flash of lightning before we hear the thunder, organizations that excel in the sixth chakra are highly visionary and can spot trends long before others do. Qualities associated with such companies are intuition, long-range planning, clarity of vision, focus and leading-edge products and resources. These businesses devote time and money to research, and employees are encouraged to be imaginative and innovative. Highly visual and spacious work environments allow the imagination to soar, but there must also be enough time for ideas to come to fruition naturally. People who work in science, medicine, new technologies, inventions, academia and health care all need this kind of innovative, non-pressured work environment to thrive.

Organizations using the sixth chakra enter a timeless dimension where space and time meet. This sounds a bit like *Star Trek*, but it is in fact what happens. Individuals and organizations with long-range vision have more time to implement their business strategies. Japan's long-range vision as to what consumers will want in ten or twenty years has given it a distinct market advantage in many industries, including automotives, computers and various other electronics, all formerly dominated by North American companies.

The last chakra is the crown, which opens when individuals and organizations become soul-infused. Organizations that work with their crown chakra feel a mission to do their work. Individual employees might see their work within the context of the evolution of humanity and might even let go of their basic needs in order to serve that mission. As with Perceval, the question that such organizations seek to answer is, "Whom does this company serve?" Companies that are balanced in all chakras are able to manifest this seventh chakra mission in the real world. However, a company with an open crown chakra, but which is ungrounded in its lower chakras might have wonderful ideals and values about serving humanity, but be unable to make or sell products that are needed in the world.

Whereas the lower chakras are related to doing, feeling, speaking and seeing, the seventh chakra is related to *knowing*— a realm that vibrates even more quickly than light. There are many kinds of knowing within the domain of the seventh chakra. Knowing incorporates and balances the dualities between the rational and intuitive, conscious and unconscious, manifest and unmanifest, objective and subjective. Companies that are able to embrace the paradox of "both/and" instead of "either/or" often have a functional knowledge of the crown chakra. Their vision and values guide their decisions in a very practical way. For example, such companies might use this chakra to decide whom to hire, what service to provide, where to locate the organization and with whom to partner. These companies, while working as co-creators with divine will, work best when they are continually assimilating new information. Information gives these companies a context for their knowing, so that their understanding becomes tangible. By becoming aware of recent findings in science, economics and environmental issues, while continuing to think of what's best for all living beings, these companies actually become better at their business.

Energy moves both up and down the chakras continuously, from inspiration in the seventh chakra to manifestation in the first chakra and back again. The more each center opens up, the more energy becomes available to the entire organism. If an organization is blocked in a certain chakra, moving its attention to the next chakra up will often unblock the lower one. For example, if your organization has an open heart chakra and wants to do something good for the world but isn't sure what, moving its attention to the creative throat chakra will likely help in finding the answer.

Energy Fields of Organizations

Organizations, like human beings, are living energy systems. Healthy organizations—like healthy individuals—have a sense of purpose; their goals are clear and they are engaged in manifesting these goals. Individuals working within such organizations align themselves with the organization's purpose. As long as their personal values and skills are in accord, there will be a harmonious relationship. Healthy organizations have a sense of flow and congruence about them because their energy is moving towards their goals. Scientists Ilya Prigogine and Rupert Sheldrake refer to this movement as an "energy field" and say the strongest energy vibration in an organization will eventually align the entire system in that frequency.

An organization, however, can lose its sense of purpose and no longer have a coherent energy field. Perhaps customers aren't buying its products, or it can't compete in a global economy or its vision is outdated. When this happens, the company often loses its market share, goes into a mid-life crisis and frantically grabs at the newest business fad in order to survive. Its behavior resembles that of a middle-aged person who jumps from fad to fad— anti-aging cremes, vitamins and a new sports car—in an attempt to restore youth. An organization with low self-esteem may begin to blame its employees just as someone suffering a mid-life crisis may become critical of loved ones. Perhaps the organization will even begin to downsize and then hire new and "better" people to save it.

Ultimately, to regain happiness, a person undergoing a mid-life crisis must find a new goal. This is also true of ailing organizations. A company must let go of its former vision of itself and embrace a new one based on the current reality. Just as a person undergoing a spiritual crisis might, an organization could develop a more open heart and desire to serve the world. Currently, there is a growing trend among large organizations to give billions of dollars annually to worthwhile causes. These organizations are measuring their value not only in financial profit, but also in how much they give back to others. As organizations are starting to work through their heart chakra, so are an increasing number of individuals.

Individuals are cells in the body of their organization and they affect their workplace just as their workplace affects them—it is an interdependent relationship. Departments are like members of an organization's family. Does the organization feed each department, like a good parent feeds each child, or does it give one department preferential treatment over another? In organizations, as with families, such behavior creates dysfunction. It's no good putting large amounts of energy—in the form of time, people and money—into developing a wonderful product if you don't do the market research to make sure that customers want that product or fully train your staff to sell it.

So what is the strongest feeling *you* have when you think of your organization? Is it excitement, inspiration, depression, fear, anxiety, warmth? If you asked your co-workers about their dominant feeling, how do you think they'd answer? Organizations that are going through, or that have gone through, massive downsizing or financial difficulties create very different energy fields from ones that are growing and thriving.

Is there anything that a single employee can do to turn around an ailing organization? As with a sick spouse or friend, you might not want to bail out of the relationship if your organization has been good to you. You might choose to stay to assist the organization in creating a new vision. If you remain focused on what you can do—within your sphere of influence—to create a healthier workplace, your presence in itself will create a positive coherent field to support the organization's future success.

Still, because of their greater sphere of influence, those that have the most impact on the organization's energy field are its CEO and directors. The role of such people is to create a vision that everyone understands and that the majority are willing to follow. This is the way to create a coherent energy field for success. This won't work, of course, if the CEO's vision is not grounded in reality, is fuzzy or is considered suspect by employees. Trust and mutual respect are key ingredients in getting employees to accept their leader's vision. In the old organizational paradigm of independence, one of the prevalent ways that CEOs created the field of energy they wanted was to fire their predecessor's senior people and bring in their own. This strategy might work in the short term but it creates an atmosphere of fear and anxiety, with employees continually looking over their shoulders wondering who will be the next to go. In interdependent organizations of the future, employees will follow leaders not out of coercion but out of respect and shared values. These leaders will epitomize the high ideals to which others aspire.

Just as organizations have a certain amount and type of energy, so do individuals. In the following chapters I will examine how personal chakras can be developed so that we can maximize our energy in everyday life and work to achieve our goals. The discussion begins with the first chakra because it is the foundation for our energy in the physical world.

Increasing Your Life Energy

It's never too late to become what you always wanted to be.

ANONYMOUS

Increasing Physical, Sexual, Emotional and Mental Orende

Energy is not static. Linked by the chakras, it flows through the five personality bodies and feeds them. Energy is drawn up from the Earth through the first chakra, which connects us to the physical world. This energy is magnetized by our thoughts and feelings. It grows when we do what we love and diminishes when we don't. It increases and decreases depending on the people with whom we associate and the environment in which we live and work. To manifest our potential, it is essential we understand the laws of energy—how to increase it and what drains it.

Many spiritual traditions contain teachings about the laws of energy, but I have chosen to discuss those of the Twisted Hairs, a group of aboriginal spiritual teachers who work with the sacred laws of the universe. They are called the Twisted Hairs because the members of this group come from many North and

South American tribes, including the Hopi, Navaho and Maya. Spiritual elders from these tribes refer to the overall energy of living beings—including that of humans, animals, plants and minerals—as *orende*. Orende is the same as the *chi* or *prana* of the Chinese and Indian energy systems I mentioned earlier. Our total life energy is made up of our physical, emotional, mental, sexual and spiritual orende levels. The higher our orende in each of these areas, the easier it is to accomplish our goals in life and the more fully we operate as a soul-infused personality.

There are many ways to increase your overall orende, but one of the simplest is to pay attention to what you enjoy. This means examining what foods make your body feel healthy, what people you like, what thoughts increase your energy, what actions feel good. Few of us have the same amount of energy in each of our bodies. For instance, your emotional orende could be stronger than your physical. If there is a large gap between your strong and weak areas of energy, you might want to focus on improving a weak area, rather than focusing on the areas in which you already excel. This will result in increasing your overall orende and establishing a better balance between the energy of your five bodies.

By answering the following questions, you will have a better understanding of the areas in which you either have or lack energy. This is not meant to be a definitive assessment, but rather a quick way to help you focus your attention on areas where you could increase your energy.

Physical Energy

Referring to the following chart, circle the number which best describes your present *physical* needs. If your energy is higher than these numbers, write down a number from 6 to 10 in the blank box, keeping in mind that Jesus or Buddha would likely have been a 10. As you are alive, do not put a "0." Circle a "1" if you are extremely low in energy in this area.

	3 meals 8+ hours sleep	2.5 meals 7–8 hours sleep	2 meals 6–7 hours sleep	1.5 meals 5–6 hours sleep	1 meal 4–5 hours sleep	
physical need for food and sleep	1	2	3	4	5	

To strengthen your physical orende, try to eat a healthy balanced diet, including, if possible, organic fresh fruits and vegetables. The Twisted Hair system recommends reducing the intake of food and sleep because they are unnecessary and make the body too sluggish. This rationale coincides with the thoughts of inventor Thomas Edison, who said, "The reason I can work eighteen hours is because I eat very little, sleep very little and wear clothes that do not pinch the blood veins in the slightest."

However, I have observed that *some* people—especially those on a strict ascetic path—actually need to increase their food intake to build up their physical body. There is a reason for my apparent contradiction. Because of Native people's affection for the Earth, they are more often grounded in the physical body. If you are too attached to the physical world, you might need to lighten your physical vessel to increase your orende. If you feel too spacey, you might need to ground yourself by feeding the physical body. Listen to your inner guidance to learn which path is correct for you to maintain balanced physical and spiritual health.

Occasionally some spiritually oriented people believe that it is preferable to avoid all aspects of the lower two chakras, because they offer sensual temptations related to food and sex. However, in turning away from such needs, these men and women might be resisting communion with their own bodies, leaving them without foundation. If these people lack a strong foundation in their first chakra, they might find it virtually impossible to obtain material goods, or have difficulty keeping jobs, being on time and paying the bills. If we are not grounded in the first chakra, we have no container, no vessel, to hold the other bodies. If we were meant to be just spiritual beings, we wouldn't have a body. We need a body to learn how to become a creator and this planet is our testing ground.

Some people fear grounding in the physical body because it implies limitation. But it can be a relief to be embraced by matter, where there are more absolutes and fewer choices. In our modern world we are overwhelmed by choice. By living closer to the land and honoring the organic cycles of the year, we simplify our lives and recover this lost balance and stability. The first chakra, because it is related to the earth element, is concerned with unity and mass. In opening our first chakra, we become more aware of physical sensations in our environment. Walking in nature will ground our energy and awaken our sense of beauty and balance, as will the taste of food, physical exercise and physical contact with another human being.

Sexual Energy

Referring to the following chart, circle the number which best describes your present *sexual* needs. This means the desire for sexual expression rather than the actual sexual act, because sexual energy can be used in a variety of ways, including healing and creative expression. If your energy is higher than these numbers, write down a number from 6 to 10 in the blank box. Do not put a "o." Circle a "1" if you are extremely low in energy in this area.

	3–6 months	1–2 months	8–14 days	3–7 days	1–2 days	
sexual desire	1	2	3	4	5	

When considering your sexual needs, you might have noticed that you have low sexual energy. There could be many reasons for this, including working too hard or suffering from burnout. If overwork is the cause, by restoring life balance your physical and sexual energy will likely return. In developing your sexual energy, remember that it may be employed for healing yourself and others or for spiritual breakthroughs, as well as for sexual pleasure. It is not frequency of orgasm that is the criterion for positive use of this energy, but level of fulfillment. Does your sexual energy open your heart to others, does it break up old patterns, does it feed your blood and cells, does it lead to heightened intuition and energy? These are the criteria for optimal use of your sexual energy. Furthermore, sometimes you might need to strengthen your sexual orende through celibacy. By not releasing this energy through orgasm, it builds up and can be employed in reaching higher spiritual levels. Sexual energy can also be harnessed to change old patterns in the etheric body by focusing your attention on the pattern you wish to change and then releasing your energy to create a new pattern. Sexual energy is the Earth aspect of the life force energy and it is especially strong in the lower two chakras.

Emotional Energy

Referring to the following chart, circle the number which best describes your present *emotional* needs. Having an emotional need means that you *need* approval and love from others. When you receive this emotional nurturing, you feel good about yourself and them. If your energy is higher than these numbers, write down a number from 6 to 10 in the blank box. Do not put a "0." Circle a "1" if you are extremely low in energy in this area.

If you need a lot of approval from others, you will receive a low score for your emotional orende. This may surprise some of you, but there is a reason for this. We increase our emotional

	several times a day	1–2 days	3–7 days	8–14 days	1–2 months	3–6 months
need for **emotional** approval from others	1	2	3	4	5	

orende as we move through three stages: *needing* love from others in order to be happy; *wanting* love; and *preferring* love but being able to live without it without suffering. Emotional energy increases when you are independent of others for the fulfillment of your emotional needs. The more self-directed you are, the higher the score. The more other-directed, the lower the score.

Do you act in accordance with your soul's wishes regardless of what others think? This is emotional independence. I am not recommending selfishness or lack of consultation with others—especially if your decisions affect them—but the ability to act appropriately even if others reject you. By doing this, you overcome the fears discussed in Chapter 8 and put yourself on the path to self-actualization.

Mental Energy

Referring to the following chart, circle the number which best describes your present *mental* needs. If your energy is higher than

	3–6 months	1–2 months	8–14 days	3–7 days	1–2 days	several times a day
need for **mental** stimulation	1	2	3	4	5	

these numbers, write down a number from 6 to 10 in the blank box. Do not put a "0." Circle a "1" if you are extremely low in energy in this area.

Mental orende increases through curiosity. You are strong in mental energy if you are curious about people, ideas and/or things such as computers and machines. What's important is the curiosity itself. You can develop your curiosity by changing old thinking and behavioral patterns, meeting new people who are also curious, reading in a variety of fields, taking a course or even driving home a different way each day.

In order to calculate your total orende, add together your physical, sexual, emotional and mental orende scores and divide the total by four. The number you obtain is your orende level in the material world: _____. The Twisted Hairs would say that most humans function at between 2.3 and 2.6 out of a possible 10 units of orende. Humans who have better mastered the laws of the world have levels of 5 or more units. The only way any of us get to 10 is if we no longer need to eat or sleep. Personally I have quite a way to go, but there are yogis in India who are reported to have achieved that.

> Few people think more than two or three times a year. I have made an international reputation for myself by thinking once or twice a week.
>
> GEORGE
> BERNARD SHAW

Often the practices we choose to increase our energy in one area help another area at the same time. For example, by engaging in counseling we learn to examine old patterns and thoughts that are holding us back from living the life we want. Erasing these old patterns is one of the most potent ways for increasing our spiritual energy because it affects so many chakras. At the same time, it leads to emotional independence from others—which increases our emotional energy. And it is mentally stimulating as we become more conscious of how and why we behave the way we do. It will likely affect our physical and sexual energy as well. As we replace negative or incorrect thoughts and feelings about ourselves and others by positive and correct ones, our energy increases because whatever is blocking the energy is removed.

Assessing Your Spiritual Energy

Each of the seven chakras is associated with a spiritual gift. By understanding each of these gifts and talents you can assess your overall spiritual energy. Some of the spiritual concepts may be unfamiliar to you. I include them because all of you have these qualities, to some extent, and they become stronger if you pay attention to them.

This questionnaire is not meant to be an in-depth assessment, but is a helpful guide for you to reflect on the spiritual gifts you have mastered, on those you are learning currently, and on where the path to consciousness will ultimately lead you. To assess your spiritual energy, circle a number from 1 to 8 in *each* of the chakra categories which best describes your present level of functioning. Please ensure that you have full use in a lower level of functioning before circling a higher score. This represents your *current* area of learning.

When you have finished, add the numbers together for *each* gift and divide by 7. This score gives you some indication of your spiritual energy: _____.

1st Chakra: Gift of Mastering the Physical World

1. I have a basic knowledge of the material world and have some success surviving in it.

2. I am connected to nature and the natural world.

3. I meet my bodily needs through appropriate diet and exercise.

4. I have good rapport with all beings and can sense real danger.

5. I am financially independent and have enough money to do as I wish.

6. I totally know my inner fears—including my sexual fears—and am able to control them.

7. I am a chameleon and can blend into any situation.

8. I am able to become invisible to others and can—with their permission—move my consciousness inside their bodies.

2nd Chakra: Gift of Clairsentience and Relationship

1. I express my emotions appropriately.

2. I have begun to understand my dreams and have "gut" feelings about others.

3. I'm sensitive, empathic and a good listener.

4. I sense the energy of others and am aware of their intentions towards me.

5. I am capable of and apply full heart-to-heart communication with others.

6. I am able to deal with and protect myself from any tyrant.

7. I have made my "enemies"—those people who didn't like me—into allies.

8. I am a lucid dreamer, am conscious in the dream state and can create the reality I want.

3rd Chakra: Gift of Manifestation

1. I glimpse my paths, talents and hurts.

2. I accept change as inevitable and necessary.

3. I understand the importance of manifesting what I want in life and of eliminating what I don't. I know it is possible to have full prosperity and abundance in my life.

4. I am able to let go of all attachments and possessions and see my illusions.

5. I am able to deal with chaos and have abundance in the material world.

6. I have good discipline, control, patience, timing, have achieved the career of my choice and live in joy and love.

7. My life moves without conscious effort and I have learned to change when everything changes.

8. I can manifest anything I need in my life.

4th Chakra: Gift of Healing and Love

1. I have long-term friendships and relationships.

2. I love myself.

3. I have a desire to help others and do so.

4. I am able to heal the symptoms of the physical, emotional and mental bodies of others.

5. I heal the root cause of all emotional, mental, physical, sexual and spiritual maladies.

6. I am able to heal someone by affecting their etheric body.

7. I create environments to help others open their hearts.

8. My heart is continually open in serving the greatest good for others.

5th Chakra: Gift of Telepathy/Clairaudience

1. I sense communication beyond the spoken word.

2. Sometimes I hear voices or my conscience.

3. I trust my inner guidance and act on it in the everyday world.

4. I hear what to do to help humans and the minerals, plants and animals.

5. I use my clairaudience in the human world at will. There is no longer a need for verification from others about what they mean. Now I seek only clarification.

6. I am able to speak a difficult or painful truth to anyone at any time.

7. I am able to communicate telepathically.

8. I am able to shift others' energy by my thoughts.

6th Chakra: Gift of Clairvoyance

1. I believe in clairvoyance but have not had a personal experience of it.

2. I have begun to practice visualization.

3. I see/feel energy around others and know when it changes.

4. I see auras—the etheric and astral energy body.

5. I can demonstrate retrocognition and precognition (past and future knowing) at least half the time.

6. I can see my illusions and misalignments and return to harmonious balance.

7. I see beings in other realities and understand how they influence our world.

8. I am able to recognize the souls and gifts of others.

7th Chakra: Gift of Enlightenment

1. I have total acceptance that a life spent in pursuit of knowledge, wisdom, love and enlightenment is the only path.

2. I actively seek and commit to my sacred path with heart.

3. I recognize the beauty of all traditions and peoples and seek to weave them together.

4. I have experienced a dark night of the soul in my physical, mental, emotional, sexual and spiritual selves.

5. I have begun the journey of transforming my workplace and surroundings.

6. I have erased all personality issues and have established new rules and laws for my life.

7. I live ethically and do what's good for the seven generations of people following me.

8. I am aligned to the universal life energy.

To develop your spiritual energy, you might start by assessing your present energy level in each of the seven chakras and then focus on strengthening your weakest areas. You can usually make more gains in improving a weak area than in focusing on an area where you are doing well. Other ways to improve your spiritual energy include meditating, dream remembrance and analysis, studying spiritual teachings by yourself or with a teacher who has spiritual gifts, performing rituals or chanting, and engaging in counseling. It's important to find a method that brings enjoyment to your life so that you'll wish to continue.

Your physical, sexual, emotional, mental and even spiritual energy levels are grounded in the world by the first chakra. Through this chakra you relate to yourself as a self-contained individual with a connection to the Earth that sustains you. It is necessary to first understand who you are before seeing how you relate to others—the realm of the second chakra.

Cultivating People Who Feed Your Soul

Keep away from people who try to belittle your ambitions. Small people always do that, but the really great make you feel that you too can become great.

MARK TWAIN

Black Holes and Shining Stars

The first chakra is related to one's self. The second chakra function deals with our relationship with others. In strengthening the first chakra we become more aware of our body and the energy it contains. But we do not exist in a vacuum. We continually interact with others and these interactions have the potential to either increase or diminish our energy. The second chakra is one of attraction, pleasure, nurturing and being nurtured. This attraction to others is personal—unlike the more objective love we feel in the heart chakra. The second chakra is associated with qualities of surrender and receptivity and the universe helps us to learn these qualities by making someone attractive and enjoyable to us. If the first chakra was "me," then the second chakra is "me and you." The first chakra is more independent and yang, while the second chakra is more dependent and yin.

Have you ever noticed that some people energize you and others drain you? An energy exchange exists in all relationships. Some individuals, like shining stars, are energy-donors, while others, like black holes, are energy-drainers. We are either increasing the energy of others, and they ours, or we are diminishing their energy, and they ours. If we are depressed, burned-out or negative, we take energy from others. If we are enthusiastic, optimistic and enjoying life, we give energy to others.

Imagine you've had a good weekend and have come to work on Monday morning full of enthusiasm. A colleague drops by your desk and proceeds to tell you about her terrible weekend in great detail. If this person is normally optimistic, you will likely be supportive and lend a sympathetic ear. However, if this colleague continually talks about the negatives in her life, you'll find this exchange exhausting.

We need to refrain from spending time with people whose favorite game is "ain't it awful." We may have concerns about being perceived as impolite or non-caring, but these black holes drain our energy. I am not recommending abandoning friends who are going through a particularly difficult time. However, associating with people whose lives are *always* difficult drains our orende, leaving us with less energy to pursue our own goals and enjoyment.

People are black holes when they are overly needy or demanding of your time. You know, the kind of person who wants to tell you about every life event that has transpired for them. Some of these people appear like victims looking for a rescuer. However, if you engage in their game, you might soon discover that they are the persecutors and you are the victim, because they hold you captive with their tales of woe. There are several ways to spot potential black holes. Are their voices whiny? Do they tell negative stories about their life? Do they like you to tell negative stories about your life? Do they associate with people who are taking action and accomplishing their goals, or with people who are sitting on life's sidelines complaining about their situation? If people have had difficult lives and have engaged in black hole behavior in the past, but you sincerely feel that they want to change, then by all means support them. You will soon witness whether they are going to change or not by their actions. Unrepentant black holes, however, can be bottomless pits. No matter how much you try to help them, it will not be enough.

You may think I'm being unnecessarily hard, but energy, like time, is a precious resource. We need to make conscious choices about how we use both of these resources. The second chakra is concerned with balance and relationship, and the kind of relationships I've just described are not in balance. Healthy relationships entail a balance in the amount of energy that you give and the amount you receive. I'm not suggesting that you do daily tallies but when you think of work colleagues or friends, you will have a good sense about the state of the energy balance between you.

To increase your life energy, cultivate energy-donors—shining stars—and at the same time be one yourself so that shining stars will wish to associate with you. There are many ways you can donate energy and feed the souls of others. Have a good sense of humor, give good hugs, be interested in others' lives and suggest good ideas to help others achieve their life purpose. Think of shining stars you know at work. In what ways do they give energy to all those who meet them? Basically, if you feel better after having been with someone, this person is a shining star. These people are gifts in your life.

The Laws of Cohesion, Adhesion and Repulsion

If we want to achieve our soul's goals, it helps to associate with people who have high energy. Friends and colleagues often mirror us, so it's important to notice whom we attract. Do we attract men and women who are successfully manifesting their soul's goal in the material world? It is important to make conscious decisions about the people we want in our support network. We only have so much time to nurture relationships and—although it is possible to love all people unconditionally—it is necessary to decide which relationships will have the best chances of bearing fruit for both parties. Maslow said that self-actualized people form strong but relatively few relationships with others and that their friends are either self-actualized or close to being so. Let's not forget that these same self-actualized people might be doing great good for the world. They would not have that energy to give to the world if they were carelessly dissipating it in their interpersonal relationships either at work or at home. Self-actualized, soul-infused personalities make conscious choices to have interpersonal relationships where the energy is balanced between them and the other person. This is a good use of second chakra energy.

I'll give you an example. Let's say that you are the manager of marketing for a mid-sized company and have three top priorities to accomplish. One is the long-range goal of creating an advertising campaign and the other two are short-range goals: hiring a design consultant and meeting with your team to get ideas about which new product would be best to promote. You are just starting your work day and are collecting your thoughts when a colleague drops by to discuss some changes that are going on in the company. You politely listen, but ultimately these changes do not concern you. After three-quarters of an hour this colleague leaves and now you have three calls to return to potential customers who want to discuss your upcoming hot products—the ones you haven't had time yet to discuss with your team. Then your boss comes in and wants you to help him with one of his projects. By the time you've helped him, it's lunch time and you've agreed to meet with a recent university graduate who is majoring in communications and wants to find out where to look for a job. The afternoon continues in much the same way as the morning did and, by the end of the day, you are frustrated and anxious because you have not had time to work on any of your three priority items.

We all have had days like this and sometimes events like these exist outside of our control. However, if we allow others to control our time, we will never achieve our goals—the goals by which our company values our contribution—and, therefore, we will never be successful. Reciprocity is important in ongoing relationships. If you help out your boss with his top-priority item today, will he help you by giving you time to do yours tomorrow? It's important to devote a certain amount of time on an ongoing basis to helping others, such as the university graduate, with no expectation of reward, but all of our time cannot be devoted to such undertakings. And the colleague who dropped in to chat, does he do that every day? Every week? Is he helpful when you want to talk to him about something that concerns you? All of these questions need to be examined so that we can channel our energy into worthwhile endeavors.

Each of us has a certain amount of life energy and we are attracted to people whose energy is the same as ours or greater. In our interactions with others, we follow the orende laws of cohesion, adhesion or repulsion, depending on the difference in energy between them and us. If the orende difference between you and another person is plus or minus one—based on your orende scores in the last chapter—the energy is cohesive. This means you have a positive attraction to each other. Both of you feel energized and stimulated by the relationship and not only like, but also respect each other. Cohesive relationships lead to growth in both individuals and are based on interdependence.

If the energy level difference between you and another person is plus or minus two, the energy is adhesive. This means that the relationship is based on dependence and is stuck in certain roles. As long as each of you conforms to specific roles—which might be parent/child or boss/subordinate—the relationship works. However, if one of you tries to change the relationship, it will either go through a difficult transition or it will end. Fortunately, if both people want to change the relationship to a cohesive one, they will most often succeed.

Repulsion is the third way in which our energy relates to others. If the difference in life force between you and the other person is greater than two, you will both experience repulsion because there is no common ground of understanding. In this event, the higher energy person experiences an energy drain and the lower energy person feels needy, angry or resentful. This often happens when one person is committed to her soul's goals and the other is still establishing the personality.

There is an exception to the rule of associating with people whose total amount of energy is similar to yours. It's possible to have a satisfying relationship with a person based on only one common interest. For instance, you might see someone on a regular basis to jog or to sing. The relationship might not work in any other area, but can be enjoyable in the one specific activity that you both enjoy.

It's unusual to find individuals who have our exact energy level in all physical, emotional, mental and spiritual areas. Often, we are attracted to people who have our "mean" orende level, but who are stronger than us in one specific area and who can teach us how to increase our energy in that area. This often happens in successful marriages and in partnerships like that of Doug and Sandy's. Doug is skilled at seeing the big picture and dreaming up marketing plans to get there. Sandy excels in managing and motivating people. Doug's strong mental energy and Sandy's strong emotional energy combine to create an effective and healthy business partnership. Both people learn to develop their weak areas by observing and practicing the strengths of the other.

Choose friends, spouses and work colleagues with no more than two degrees difference. I appreciate that this may be difficult to do at work, but most of us can decrease the time we spend at lunch and during breaks with people who are not compatible and increase our time with those who are compatible. We don't have to give people the questionnaire in order to determine their scores.

We know this answer intuitively because relationships are more harmonious and growthful when we associate with people whose orende level is similar to ours.

If our entire workplace feels disharmonious, it could be that we do not fit in with the energy there and should look for another place to work. Our work or friends might be compatible for years, but if our orende levels change, we may no longer find ourselves cohesive. This usually does not happen overnight, but is a gradual process of growing discontentment. When people say that their work or a certain person is making them sick, this is *literally* happening. Staying in relationships where our energy is drained sickens the body and the soul.

Cultivating People Who Feed Your Soul

> *Do unto others as you would have others do unto you.*
>
> MATTHEW 7:12

Why do some people have lots of wonderful relationships, while others are either alone or associating with negative people? It's not luck; it's skill. What we value we do well. Some people practice growing relationships like others practice golf and are rewarded by being well liked by others. But it's not just a matter of quantity; the quality of our relationships is of utmost importance. It's better to have two or three relationships with people who have both the desire and ability to help you achieve your soul's goals than to have ten relationships with people who are "interesting," but who distract you from your soul's purpose. The following ideas will help you develop high-quality relationships both at work and in your personal life.

Be selective when choosing new friends and associates. Is this person someone you want in your life for years? Do you share similar values and interests? Does this person know how to be a friend? Choosing relationships is like buying the correct ingredients for a special meal. You might be an excellent cook and have a great recipe, but if your ingredients are not appropriate, the meal will not turn out. So it is in life. You can have a good recipe for success—high potential and a clear soul's purpose—but if you choose friends and work associates that do not enhance that purpose, even though they might be wonderful people, you may become distracted from your goal.

Take a minute to consider your own qualities—sense of humor, specific skills, natural abilities, work experience, network, values, interesting life experience, courage or compassion. Is the person you've selected interested in what you have to offer? If not, choose someone else and don't perceive her lack of interest in you as rejection. She, like you, might be making conscious choices of how she uses her energy and might be deciding not to put her energy into nurturing another friendship right now. Her time might be devoted instead to her children, spouse, life's work and existing friends.

Still, there are ways in which we can make ourselves more attractive to a prospective friend or colleague. These ideas might seem all too obvious and feel a little stilted at first but only by being a friend do you gain friendship. Discover what the other person wants and enjoys in life. You can do this by asking them directly or by deducing this from the topics they choose to speak about. Some people just want hiking buddies, others want a network through which to expand their business, others are interested in soul friends. Invite your prospective friend or colleague for coffee or lunch to get to know her better. Cultivate this new relationship immediately and don't take it for granted. Send thank-you cards for thoughtful things she has done and refer to books, articles and people that will help her towards her goals. When she speaks of other friends and colleagues of hers who are interesting, express an interest in meeting them and show appreciation for her introduction. Reciprocate, if you can, by introducing her to people she would enjoy. Relationships are like flowers in our garden. If we fertilize and water them, they are beautiful and will grow and multiply. If we neglect them, they wither and die.

Review your support system on a yearly basis and decide which relationships are healthy and meeting your current needs. Sometimes we drift away from people because of distance or changing needs. These can be wonderful people, but their life paths lie in a different direction from yours. Perhaps one friend decides to have children, while you've decided to remain childless. Another friend likes daily social activities, but you prefer meditation and silence. Celebrate the time you've had together, but reduce the time you spend with these people so you have time to develop new relationships with people who share your current personal or work interests.

If you have tried many of these things in the past, and you still don't have a support network that feeds your soul, there may be a couple of reasons. The first could be that you look too desperate, too needy. Independent, self-assured people run quickly from needy, dependent ones. You might try cultivating second chakra qualities that others find attractive, such as humor, joy and enthusiasm. Next time you're in a group of people, watch those who are popular. They look welcoming and approachable and show interest in others. You'll probably notice a key talent that most possess: they ask questions about others' lives and listen attentively to the answers. These superior conversationalists validate others, so people seek them as friends and colleagues. They epitomize the best use of second chakra energy.

In *The 7 Habits of Highly Effective People*, Stephen Covey talks about the emotional bank account we have with people we know, be they family, friends or work colleagues. Covey says that if we keep our promises and do things that please others, we build up credits in their bank account. Then—when we need to ask a favor—we can withdraw on our balance in their account without endangering our relationship. Have you been depositing credits into the accounts of your family, friends and colleagues, and have they been depositing into yours? Relationships benefit from greater trust and enjoyment when the exchange is mutual.

Jill is a special education teacher who worked at a school for several years without a permanent contract. This school was unable to hire Jill permanently based on board policies outside their control. This was deeply disturbing for her because she was a single mom without any other source of income. But Jill didn't complain and did all work she was given and more. She felt that she was doing her soul's work, but it was still difficult financially. All the money Jill earned went to paying her mortgage, putting food on the table and making sure her children's needs were well taken care of. Little was left over for herself.

The day before Christmas vacation last year, her name was called over the P.A. and she was asked to report to the principal's office. She entered the office to find the principal dressed as Santa Claus, holding a big bag of presents for her. Bubble bath, earrings, gourmet treats and even nice underwear! Jill's colleagues wanted to show her how much she meant to them and they did so with joy, good humor and thoughtfulness. Jill and her fellow staff members epitomize what's best in second chakra qualities, namely, loyalty and concern for the well-being of others you know, be they family, friends or co-workers.

The 3•2•1 Rule

Choosing friends and work colleagues is one of the most important choices we make in life, because it either increases or decreases our chances of achieving the soul's purpose. Unfortunately, too often we associate with people out of habit or because we believe that individuals we would like to spend time with would not choose us. Selecting solid support is crucial to the success of our soul goals and needs to be an active, not a passive, process.

Barry Siskind, author of *Making Contact*, says that each of us has approximately two hundred people in our network of friends and colleagues. In order to have healthy, positive relationships, he recommends using a 3•2•1 classification system in selecting them. Individuals in the "3" category are achievers, people we *need* in our network who are willing to help us with our *specific* goals. For example, achievers could help us with a business plan, recommend us for a job or teach us a skill. The "2s" are nurturers, people we *want* in our network who support us in other parts of our life. Nurturers might be people interested in hearing about our successes and failures or who encourage us to go for our goals. Those in the "1" category are people we *like*, who are interesting, but neither nurture nor help us to achieve our goals. They may be people who are good company for dinner or entertainment events.

Siskind recommends that to build a successful network and support system, we need three achievers to every two nurturers and every one interesting person. I've asked hundreds of men and women who they chose for their support system and found that they sometimes have different priorities. Men tend to have more achievers and women more nurturers in their networks. Often, however, I've also found that *both* sexes experience difficulty in finding three achievers to help them with their soul goals. This is important because we achieve all goals more quickly and efficiently by adding achievers who are willing to help us.

Although some of our friends and colleagues fit clearly into one of these three categories of achiever, nurturer or interesting, others in our network may be combinations of these qualities. If we have people in our support network who meet all three criteria, we triple our good fortune, and it is a better use of both our time and energy.

Sometimes people change categories. I have a friend who is very loving and nurturing. She sends me cards on my birthday and calls when I'm back from some new venture to see how I've done. She has spent the first half of her life raising a family and although I love her and appreciate her support, I would not have said that she could help me *directly* to achieve my soul's goals. In other words, I thought of her as a nurturer and not as an achiever. She, on the other hand, courted me for her support network especially because I was an achiever and she appreciated the ideas that I gave her on how to start her business and the contacts that I was able to share with her.

One day I needed someone to be a phone contact for a *Take Your Soul to Work* seminar I was running and thought of my friend. She agreed to do it. But instead of just registering people, she proceeded to think of ways to get media coverage, places to advertise, etc. In other words, she became both a nurturer and an achiever—a friend and work colleague. At the same time, my friend started to see *me* as a nurturer as well as an achiever too because of the time that I spent with her children and the fact that I was there for her through some personal trials.

Obviously, I value this relationship highly because it works on so many levels. The more relationships we have that work on many levels, the more integrated we feel. We notice this especially in marriage. If we enjoy sex with our spouse but don't share many of the same interests outside the bedroom, the relationship lacks fulfillment. Likewise, at work we seek relationships that meet more of our needs, and we tend to prefer spending time with colleagues with whom we have many interests in common, and not just one—work. Using the categories of achiever, nurturer and interesting person, you might want to think of your current support system and determine which people—family, friends, work colleagues—can help you achieve your soul's goal. You can complete the following exercise with that goal in mind.

My Support System Using the 3 • 2 • 1 Rule

My soul's goal is: _____ .

1. List 3 people who can help you to achieve your goal.

    ❖ _____

    ❖ _____

    ❖ _____

2. List 2 people who nurture your life in other ways.

    ❖ _____

    ❖ _____

3. List 1 person you want in your life because she or he is interesting.

    ❖ _____

Do you see a pattern emerging? Do you have enough achievers to help you attain your soul's goals? Do you have enough nurturers to support you? And, are you spending enough time nurturing the people who are supporting you? It's wonderful to celebrate those friends and colleagues and if your support system is perfect just as it is, that is a true cause for celebration.

However, some people might decide to make a few alterations. If you spend a great deal of time with interesting people who are neither nurturing you nor helping you achieve your goals, you might never get your soul's needs met. Decide what changes you would like to make to your list; add the names of people you would like to cultivate and delete the names of those who are detracting you from your life's path. What actions do you want to take to increase the time you spend with the people you've chosen? In doing this, you will learn the appropriate use of energy in the second chakra—balance in relationship.

One Plus One Equals Three

When two people with cohesive energy are together, their energy is greater than either of them by themselves. Very few goals depend totally on ourselves for success. If we want to lose weight, apply for a job or write a book, most of us find it helpful to be surrounded by positive people who support our goal. If others support us, our chances of success are greater than if we are alone.

I refer to our chances of success as "plus three," although it could actually be "plus ten" or "plus one hundred," depending on how many people are helping us to achieve our goal.

Conversely, if our family members and work colleagues impede our goal and are not supportive, our chances of success are less than if we were alone. In this situation, let's call our chances "zero." Say we have one glass full of water and a second glass that is half full. After we mix them together and divide them equally, we will have two glasses that are each three-quarters full. The first glass has less water and the second glass has more. The same is true in a relationship with another person. If we devote our time and life energy to helping another person with his goal but he does not help us, we will have less chance of getting our goal than if we'd worked independently.

Therefore, it is essential to surround ourselves with people who are not only positive but who *actively* support our soul goals. As Stephen Covey said in *The 7 Habits of Highly Effective People*, "My parents were constantly affirming me in everything I did. Late at night I'd wake up and hear my mother talking over my bed, saying, 'You're going to do great on this test. You can do anything you want.'" And he did. He believed this affirmation and now heads a multi-million dollar business helping people to achieve their life goals.

Reciprocity is the key in the correct use of energy in our second chakra. When we have learned this spiritual law and are able to give and receive equally, we can then move to the unconditional love of our fourth chakra, interdependence. But it's hard to do this if we haven't yet learned the fundamental laws of relationship. I learned this law of reciprocity from my parents.

Both my mother and father worked full time in the family-owned hardware store, so from an early age my brother and I helped at home and in their store. My parents were always grateful for our help and I felt appreciated for my contribution. Each night at dinner my brother and I were engaged in conversation and encouraged to share our day's successes and failures. We were even consulted about major family decisions that would affect us all. Overall our relationship was generally one of interdependence.

Our family functioned as a "team," although these words were never used. There was an easy give-and-take and an accommodation to the needs of the others. All four of us knew and trusted the others to help us if we needed something. My parents taught me what the rule of one plus one equals three means. My parents were both masters of the art of what Tom Chappell in *The Soul of a Business* calls, "making goodness happen." They created an environment where both our personalities and souls would thrive.

My parents shared the same model of interdependence in their work life. They co-owned a hardware store, shared a bank account and made all decisions jointly, even though they respected the other's talents and interests in certain departments. For example, my father ordered the paint and tools and my mother the household goods. Yet both were familiar with each other's sections and waited on customers in all departments. And where did they learn interdependence? My mother was raised by parents who also had a business—a grocery store—and her aunt and uncle co-owned a hardware store, where she learned the trade. So I come from three generations of women who have worked and lived in partnership with men. For me the model of interdependence is patterned into my etheric body.

But even if you were raised in a family whose roles were based on one person being dependent and the other independent, you can change these patterns in your own life. My father, fourteen years older than my mother, was raised in such a household. His mother, raised by a governess in a well-to-do family in India, was taught to be dependent on others. His father was an independent, charming gambler who took the family from rags to riches to rags several times. But my father—a strong-willed, independent personality—was in his second marriage at mid-life, and found himself able to move to interdependence. He achieved this at a time when traditional roles were more locked in place than they are now.

Moving to interdependence is a natural state when the energy levels of two people are equally balanced. Then there is mutual respect cultivated, based on the talents of each person, so that they can step forward or move back as the situation warrants. The second chakra teaches us how to honor the differences of another person while celebrating what you can create together. Having learned the rules of the second chakra, which teaches us how to have positive relationships with our friends, family and work colleagues, we can now learn the laws of energy relating to the third chakra, mastering the material world.

Mastering the Material World

We must be the change we want to see in the world.

MOHANDAS GANDHI

The lower three chakras are concerned with the personality and how it relates to its environment. The third chakra is sometimes referred to as the mind of the lower body and is particularly concerned with applying our particular talents and skills in the outer world of action. To do this, we must be aware of our desires, which we learned about in the second chakra, and we must be grounded in physical reality, the gift of the first chakra. The third chakra is located in our solar plexus—the center for will and power. When in correct balance, we have high self-esteem, energy, joy and enthusiasm. When overused, we become egocentric, selfish and angry if we don't get our way. When underused or blocked, we are passive, listless and fearful. The third chakra is more yang, masculine and independent. When functioning positively not only do we usually have the self-esteem to help ourselves but we also have the power of personality to help others.

The Middle Path

Many spiritual traditions speak of the benefits of walking the middle path. Christian mystics call it the "via media" and Hebrews "the good way." In Mahayana Buddhism the middle path is the balance between wisdom and compassion. By walking this middle path in business and life, we create harmony between the goals of the personality and those of the soul. Tom Chappell, president of Tom's of Maine, bases his business on this principle:

> I've found the middle way for Tom's of Maine, where we use our head and heart in planning business strategies. We make room for spirit in the world of commerce. We have two aims, one that serves the individual and one that serves the common good.... Your personal values *can* be integrated with managing all the traditional goals of business—making money, expanded market share, increased profits, retained earnings and sales growth. Not only can your personal beliefs be brought to work, they can work for you.

The middle path is also the balance between fate and free will. Our soul has a purpose, but our personality has free will to choose how to manifest this purpose in our life and work. Some of our choices might be better than others. But by observing the consequences of our choices, we become conscious creators in the world. By walking the middle path, we learn to neither overuse nor underuse our wills—thereby balancing the third chakra. Overused, the third chakra inflates ego and leads us to choose goals that serve only the personality. We become driven by a desire for money, status and prestige. If we succeed, we are still not content but want more and if we fail, we blame others for having betrayed us.

Just as overusing our will deviates from the middle path, so does underusing it. When we set our sights too low, we are afraid that we can't achieve the soul's goal. Like those with inflated egos, we are allowing the personality—and not the soul—to run our lives. Management consultant Ken Blanchard, co-author of *The Power of Ethical Management*, clearly sees the problem of both under- and overusing free will in the workplace:

> Someone once told me that ego stands for "edging God out." It's interesting to see how self-doubt and false pride play out in managers. When they are addicted to either ego affliction, it erodes their effectiveness. Managers dominated with self-doubt are the "do-nothing bosses." They are described as never around, always avoiding conflict and not very helpful.... Under pressure they seem to defer to whoever has the most power. At the other end of the spectrum are the "controllers." These are managers dominated by false pride. Even when they don't know what they are doing, they have a high need for power and control. Even when it's clear to everyone that they are wrong, they keep on insisting they are right.

In the final analysis, not to use our talents and abilities is just as bad as using them for our own ends. Both extremes are a misuse of power. The middle path between personality and soul needs is concerned with finding the appropriate use of our gifts. Whether we are employees or managers, if we take this approach we help others to build their self-esteem—a quality of the third chakra—so that they, too, can more fully use their gifts in the world.

Showing Up

80 percent of success is just showing up.

Woody Allen

To master the material world we need to trust that we will be given exactly what we need each day. Not all experiences are pain-free, but every experience, great or small, painful or pleasurable, has been designed to stimulate our growth. Just as the strongest swords are the ones that are fired and struck repeatedly, we are often strengthened and molded by the difficulties we face, rather than by easy times. The importance of "showing up" is captured in the words, "You can't always change what you face, but you have to face it to change it."

Darshan Kailly started as a clerk in a large freight company, before rising through the ranks of several thousand employees to become its president. Well liked and competent, he continued using the traditional organizational structure through which he had succeeded until he realized that this structure was no longer allowing employees to quickly serve their customers' needs.

Breaking with tradition, Darshan invited the managers to a retreat—the first of its kind within the company—to discuss changing organizational procedures and roles. He was surprised and hurt when, instead of happily offering suggestions for improvement, his colleagues started dumping their grievances on him. A less mature soul would probably have shut them up and returned to the old system, but this leader trusted both himself and his managers to find a solution. Also Darshan realized that the fact that the managers spoke so frankly to him was a measure of how much they trusted both him and fellow colleagues. He recognized that speaking out was a sign of health in the organization and that most grievances stemmed from the managers' own fears of change and inability to succeed in the new system. Together, by showing up and doing their best—even though they had no previous experience in democratic or consensus management—they created a new organizational structure. Today the company, Canadian Freightways, is one of the largest and most forward-looking in its field in Canada.

Its strength lies in the way it treats both customers and employees. Before Darshan became president, new employees only received on-site training. Now they spend three days at head office meeting with him and other executives in order to thoroughly understand the company culture. And Freightways is just as forward-looking when it comes to customer service. The company asked its customers in which areas it could provide better service. Customers responded with six suggestions for improvement. These six areas of service are now guaranteed by Freightways and accompanied by partial or full money-back guarantees if these promises are not fulfilled.

Showing up and trying our best is easier for some of us than for others and depends on how much we want our goal and on how successful we have been in the past. How successful were you in school? In relationships? At work? In service to others? In answering these questions, be careful to measure yourself against your potential and not against your parents's, spouse's or culture's standards. You might have excelled in some, but not all, of these areas. Because the soul calls us to wholeness and balance in all areas of life, it is often necessary to stretch yourself in your weak area before moving ahead in a strong one.

I like to think of myself and others as "works in progress." This frees me from worrying about being perfect before acting. I don't know any perfect people—do you? With the right motivation we say and do the best we can in any situation while at the same time working on continual improvement. Nearly two thousand years ago, Plotinus, author of the *Enneads*, suggested that we look inside ourselves. Then we, like a sculptor, could "cut away all that is excessive, straighten all that is crooked, bring light to all that is overcast, labor to make all one glow of beauty."

And what are some of the things we could chisel out? Guilt, depression, holding on to past events and worrying about the future are all ways that we sabotage ourselves in the present. We might be totally committed to a goal, but are impatient and frustrated when it takes longer than anticipated. If we are too serious, lack humor and have lost the enjoyment of the journey, we can actually delay progress. Some individuals don't try at all and are bored, lethargic, uninterested and have no goals. Being uninterested is a way of protecting ourselves from disappointment, but it is also a denial of life and can lead to chronic depression. We must also avoid casting blame both on others or ourselves for past disappointments. This leads to a lessening of our life energy.

We learn our lessons, either quickly or slowly, easily or pain-fully. We can swim with or against the river of life, or float along without choosing a direction. It is our choice. However, showing up and using our will and power to the best of our ability is the quickest, most efficient path to mastering the material world and this is the function of our third chakra.

Sharing Your Gifts

Our gifts are so plentiful that it's hard to count them all; yet so often we think that we haven't enough talent, intelligence, skill or attractiveness. In a world where only recognized experts seem to be heeded, it's often hard to acknowledge our gifts. But this is exactly what we must do. We do not need to be certified as a healer in order to heal, or to make our living as a professional singer in order to sing. These sorts of mistaken beliefs diminish us and minimize what we offer to others and to the world.

In our society we have created too many fixed ideas about success, and those who do not fit into these categories feel they have no right to claim expertise. If we do not have a university degree, we have no right to teach. We have no right to our opin-ions unless we've published a book, and then, paradoxically, we are instantly recognized as an expert. So we study and struggle and wait to become perfect before feeling confident enough to step forward with our gifts.

We stop ourselves from contributing by saying, "No one wants to hear what I have to say because I'm not smart, well liked or articulate." Instead, we need to be like children who—loving both themselves and others—sing and dance and hug when they want. It's ironic that although we are hungry to learn, grow and experience, we hold ourselves back from feeling the joy we felt as children. Can this be progress for us as individuals? Does this make the world a better place in which to live? I don't think so.

For the good, not only of ourselves but also of others, we contribute far more by living and being fully who we are. This results in healthy self-confidence, a quality of the third chakra. Often, we do not need more education or mastery of someone else's techniques to live fully in the moment. There is a time and place for this, of course, but not at the expense of undervaluing our own talents. We will never become who we truly are by replicating someone else. When people do what they love, they sparkle. We excel at what we love, because learning about it is pleasurable and because we usually have talent in that area. The key in life is to follow what the soul loves and it will lead us to our talent.

A case in point is found in this story about a father and son. The father—a professional man—considered himself to be very intelligent, whereas his fourteen-year-old son was severely dyslexic and read at a grade-two level. This conversation transpired as they were putting a lock on my garage door.

"Dad, you're putting the lock on backwards."

"I am not!" The father replied instantly, refusing to believe that he could have done it incorrectly.

A few minutes later, I heard the father ask his son, humbly, "How did you say I should do it?"

"Like this," the son replied.

This boy fails repeatedly in school and has very low self-esteem. Yet, he loves cars and has a talent with mechanical things. In our present system of employment, his chances of getting a job he loves are slim. He will need a grade-twelve certificate to apprentice as a car mechanic—which he would dearly love doing—and achieving this might be unrealistic. However, if he could work in a gas station pumping gas and helping out the mechanics, he might find some degree of happiness, because his two loves are people and cars. In order to have a healthy center of will and power we must find a path of action for our talents. If we cannot do this, we tend to become either passive or aggressive, either giving up on life or using our power inappropriately in crime, violence or verbal abuse because of our anger and impotence.

Staying Open to Possibilities

We must allow the ebb and flow of circumstance,
of time, of luck, of serendipity, of inspired people,
of opportunity, to flow over us, guide us and
enlighten us.

CHRISTINE SILVERBERG

Physicists are now saying that any path or direction we choose is influenced, not only by the first steps we take in that direction, but also by the ongoing variation in events that this choice produces. We know this from personal experience. We seldom go from A to B predictably and to attempt to do so results in frustration. While keeping our goal in mind we need to surrender to the dictates of the universe. This means living in a "being" as well as a "doing" state in our day-to-day lives.

The being state is more feminine and accepts the world, people and events as they are. The doing state is more masculine and seeks to change and improve what exists. By mastering the qualities of the third and second chakras we can choose when it is advantageous to be in a being state and when in a doing state. Using the third chakra, we choose an action and, by employing our second chakra, we develop the flexibility to surrender our personal will to external circumstances that call for us to change.

We need to be like a river that adjusts to the terrain it encounters. When the earth is soft, the water flows straight, but when it meets rocks or other obstacles, it flows around them. When the river flows downhill, it speeds up and slows down when it comes to a plateau. By being flexible, the river creates diversity and beauty in its environment, but still eventually reaches its destination.

We might be fortunate and find, or create, a full-time job where we are able to do exactly what we want. But we also might need two or even three jobs—some of which pay and some of which do not—to meet all of our soul's needs. This has been the path of my own career. Since the mid-70s, I've conducted workshops, both for traditional corporations and for spiritual centers, and have learned—through much trial and error—what is appropriate for each environment. I do not teach esoteric spiritual truths at IBM but—as part of my workshop on managing stress—I teach the employees meditation, goal-setting and guided visualization. In doing this, I meet my client's needs and, to some extent, my own.

However, if I worked only with traditional corporations, I would be unable to take my soul fully to work because I feel called to teach deeper spiritual truths. Therefore, I have created two other areas of work to meet these less traditional needs. One is teaching at spiritual centers and the second is taking groups of people to sacred sites of the world. I have found that to achieve my soul's purpose I needed not one, but all three areas of work. If I had tried to make myself fit into just one job, I would have frustrated not only myself but everyone around me. By learning to flow with the river of life, I've found my own path.

Persist, but Know When to Cut Your Losses

Be not afraid of going slowly. Be only afraid of standing still.

Chinese proverb

Showing up and sharing your gifts are not enough by themselves. You also need to be consistent and persistent in the pursuit of your goals and to refine your talents and skills. The third chakra overcomes inertia and gives you the drive to do this. First, you need to find out if the kind of work you want to do exists and if anyone else is doing it. If someone is already doing the kind of work you'd like to do, you could try to arrange a meeting to get a more realistic view of that job and their approach. The goal is not to duplicate another's work but to learn how to use the tools and techniques that others have discovered in order to increase your chances of success.

If no one has done the work you want to do, determine if the idea or product is needed. It's not enough for you to think that people need something; they must also perceive that they do. You can't interest people in meditation or tai chi if they don't think they need it. If you have followed all these techniques and nothing is working, ask yourself why. Is your goal timely and needed? What feedback are people giving? Is the product aimed at the appropriate people? Reassess! Sometimes you need to redefine your direction many times before something clicks.

At the same time, we mustn't give up too soon. We need to keep a clear vision and work daily to achieve the soul's goal. Successful athletes, musicians, writers and business people practice their crafts for hours every day. To attain our goals we need to start down the path, listen for feedback from the environment and then adjust our course accordingly. There may be many paths to a goal and, if one does not work, we need to be flexible in changing or modifying our approach. If, after doing this, the goal still remains out of reach, we need to consider the possibility of other options and goals. We need to surrender our personal will to the divine. As Jesus said to the Creator, "not my will but Thy will be done."

For seven years Sam had a toy company. He did just about everything you could think of to make it successful. He investigated the toys his competitors were making and did market research to determine which toys were successful and which weren't. He read about toys, created various prototypes and even visited customers personally to get their feedback. To manage his money flow he got his family involved in packing and shipping. Sam lived and breathed toys for seven years—but what he didn't do was make his business a success. Finally, after a fire damaged the building where his toys were made, he stopped to rethink what he was doing.

Sam had learned a great deal about the qualities of persistence and exerting his own will, but now he was called on to learn another skill—that of knowing when to cut his losses. Calling up his competitors, he told them what had happened and of his desire to sell his business. He was able to sell his equipment and recommend his workers to other employers, but no one wanted his smoke-damaged toys. Sam decided to host a cut-rate sale one Saturday, complete with children's music, balloons, clowns, and salespeople (actually, his family) dressed in costumes. The children loved it, as did their parents, and what Sam didn't sell, he gave to charity.

Sam did not waste energy after he had made his decision to cut his losses. He quickly dispensed with the business so that he could get on with other goals. This is an important lesson for all of us to learn if we are attempting to function well in the third chakra. Whatever you decide to do, put all your energy into it and if it doesn't work out, quickly cut your losses and redirect your energy to another area. Sam is now a successful business consultant who travels internationally teaching people how to create outstanding trade shows. Many of the skills he acquired in his first business he was able to apply to his second one.

Attracting and Using Money

Money is a form of energy that has value because of our thoughts about it. It's very difficult to manifest what we want in the world if we have not learned how to attract and use money. Financial difficulties, depending on the cause, could stem from a lack of understanding in the first, second or third chakras. If organizations and people have continual financial difficulties, it could be a first chakra problem in that they don't know how to control their basic needs of survival. If organizations or individuals spend or give away more than they receive, it could be a second chakra issue, because they do not know how to balance their needs with the needs of others. If organizations or individuals manage small amounts of money well but have difficulty handling large sums, it could be a third chakra issue, concerning their ambivalence about fully manifesting their power in the world.

We need to accurately assess how much money we need in order to accomplish our soul's purpose. The answer will be different for each of us. Seldom is the soul's goal to live in poverty, but many "spiritual" people erroneously believe that poverty makes them more spiritual. Poverty is something that is imposed on us because we have not learned the rules of survival from the first chakra. Simplicity in life—although it may look like poverty to an outsider—is in fact very different and is a chosen path. When we achieve that state of simplicity we can ask for and receive however much or little money we need. Gandhi and Mother Theresa, for example—while living in voluntary simplicity themselves—knew the rules of manifestation well enough to attract millions of dollars to their causes. Knowing how to manifest and use money, while remaining unattached to it, comes from mastery in the first, second and third chakras.

Each of us has different levels of skill with the various tools we are given for mastering the material world. Some are good at showing up, while others, like Sam, are skilled at persisting. All of us must learn to manage money, as we see in Carol's case. Carol had mastered the ability to handle small and medium amounts of money, but she had difficulty both asking for and accepting large amounts of money. Some years ago she was offered twenty-five acres of property, complete with a home and barn, by an older friend of hers. His hope was that Carol would turn it into a retreat center. Overwhelmed with the responsibility of accepting his gift, she refused and started looking around for others to whom he could give the property. She found two well-respected Tibetan teachers, who were very happy to accept the property, and, in witnessing their willingness, Carol realized that she had an issue with material prosperity.

Her ambivalence towards money stemmed from her childhood. Carol's parents did not have much money, but paid their own way through life, never accepting money from others. Her frugal economic independence had been a source of pride for Carol—as it was for her parents—but lately she realized that she had been refusing to accept abundance from the universe. Not long ago, a friend of Carol's asked, "How much money would you like to make each year?"

The question caught her by surprise and raised all her issues about money. "Net or gross?" Carol asked, hedging for time.

"Net," her friend replied.

"I'd like to clear $40,000 a year," Carol said. As soon as she spoke, Carol realized that she'd already done this for several years and that she'd created a financial limit beyond which she would not go. To remove that self-imposed barrier to prosperity and abundance, she decided to try out what to her was a gigantic figure.

"No, I've changed my mind," Carol said, "I'd like to make $300,000 a year, gross."

As soon as she said this Carol started choking, coughing and spluttering. The difficulty she had in asking for this much money, because of feelings of greed, fear of failure and fear of responsibility, resulted in a physical reaction. This experience was a great teacher for her. So great was her resistance to asking for a large sum of money that she knew she must do just that. Avoiding this challenge was to stay closed to divine abundance and to the proper use of energy in the material world.

To improve our relationship with money we, like Carol, need to examine any areas where the channels and chakras might be blocked. Here are a few questions to help you clarify your relationship with money.

❖ Do you like money?
❖ Do you have enough money?
❖ Does it come easily to you?

❖ Are you afraid of losing it?
❖ Is there a balance between how much you receive and how much you spend or give away?
❖ Are you equally comfortable with small, medium and large amounts of money?
❖ What patterns do you see in your relationship to money?

If you have ambivalent feelings towards money, it's unlikely you'll be good at attracting it. To overcome this, you might try thinking of all the good things you could do with money, things you couldn't do without it. Money is neither negative nor positive; it's what we do with money that determines the right use. If you are comfortable with small, but not large, amounts of money, you might be struggling with issues of greed or a lack of worthiness. Using the techniques I discussed in Chapter 7, "Reprogramming Yourself for Success," you may find you are able to ease this restrictive pattern of behavior. Think of money as energy that flows better when it is circulating. To cure a fear of scarcity, give money to others until you have given enough to restore the balance between what you give and receive. You will know that you have mastered the first, second and third chakras' relationship with money when you have all you need to fulfill your soul's mission.

Influencing Others: Seven Powers to Increase Effectiveness

Power—the ability to influence others to do something we would like—is under the auspices of the third chakra. Like money, power is neither positive nor negative; it is what we do with our power that determines if we are using it for good or bad. Many of us—because we are afraid of overusing our power—actually underuse it, and this too is a misuse. The wise use of power is to influence others to develop more love and wisdom and to create more beauty in the world. There are seven major kinds of power:

legitimate, association, charismatic, love, persuasion, wisdom and ethical. These powers are associated with the seven chakras and are listed in ascending order.

When asking ourselves if we are powerful, we too often focus on our job title—but this is only one kind of power. If we are called president or CEO, we are often perceived by others as having legitimate power. I refer to this type of power as "legitimate," because it is legitimized by political, societal and organizational structures in the material world. People who have powerful jobs and titles usually do so because they excel in the ability to fit in and be accepted by others.

We are more likely to succeed in our goals if we are perceived to fit into the prevailing patterns for success. Do we look the part? The Cherokee say that we must stalk the tyrant, by which they mean we must look desirable to the people we want as allies. Our dress code for business is much more relaxed than it was even five years ago, but we still must be seen to fit in. My rule of thumb is that the more controversial my words, the more conservatively I dress. Sometimes our choice becomes, "Am I willing to compromise my dress and how I express myself to do the work I love, or are my appearance and forms of expression more important to me?" If our goal is to make people like us and be willing to be influenced by us, we achieve this more easily if we look and speak like them.

Although power is a quality associated with the third chakra, the physical manifestation of it—such as clothes and titles—is connected to the first chakra. To fit in and achieve credibility we might need a business card, brochure or product, and, if we have two or three kinds of work, we might need different cards and products for each area. Everything should be of top quality. If we want to be well paid for our services, we must look like we are used to being well paid. In addition, we must match the price for our product with what people expect to pay. Discover what the going price is for someone with your experience and ask for that fee. Asking too low a figure often results in people undervaluing your service.

The power connected to the second chakra is that of association. This means knowing powerful people and being able to count on them to help us meet our goals. Even if we do not hold legitimate power in an organization, if we have the support of a person with legitimate power, we can use this as leverage to influence others. Association power—often held by women and by volunteers—has often been overlooked and devalued in our society. Many secretaries and administrative assistants have association power and support their managers and presidents, who usually have legitimate power and receive the recognition. Many wives have often had association power. How many of us can name Gandhi's wife? Would he and many other men have accomplished as much without the continual support of their wives?

Charismatic power means being able to influence others by personality and is a third chakra characteristic. People with charismatic power have a uniqueness about them and follow the beat of their own drummer. Both Hitler and Jesus possessed the gift of charisma, illustrating that any power can be used for good or bad. Other charismatic people include Pierre Elliott Trudeau, Madonna, Elizabeth Taylor, Pope John Paul II, Mikhail Baryshnikov and Princess Diana. You don't have to be especially talented, attractive or intelligent to be charismatic, but you do have to have the ability to attract and then hold people's attention and interest. Although arguably some people are born with more charisma than others, we can strengthen it by developing our gifts and using them with self-confidence.

The power of love is located in the heart chakra. People who have this power are doing their best to create a better world. Others recognize this and are drawn to help. Some of these people are well known, but most are not. Beth Elise Sutherland, a university professor, has founded the Bali Book Project. For three years now, she has gathered money from friends to buy books and supplies for eight schools in Bali. Last year she and her traveling companion, Randell Hayward, also bought clothes for 250 children who had very little. What unsung heroes do you know who manifest this power of love?

Individuals with persuasive power, which is associated with the fifth chakra, have the "gift of the gab," and are able to persuade others to their way of thinking. Using persuasion, they might *intentionally* dangle a carrot to attract someone's personality—knowing this is the only way they'll get his or her attention. Some people who have this power use their intelligence to find the correct data to convince others. Germaine Greer, Gloria Steinem and William Buckley are current-day examples, while Socrates, Cicero and Julius Caesar are past ones. In some people the power of persuasion might also be combined with intuition, in which case they are able to "read" others and influence them. To develop the power of persuasion, put yourself in another person's shoes and ask yourself, "What's in it for them to be interested in what I have to say?" As soon as you have the answer to your question, give the person the reasons they seek.

Wisdom is a power of both the sixth and seventh chakras. This is more often a power of age than of youth, although there is a lower form of wisdom that is desired in organizations—that of information. Wisdom comes by digesting information and selecting the particular parts of that information that could best serve the organization or world long term. Information power—having facts that are necessary to others—is a transient power and not to be counted on exclusively. Information is expendable. It might be worth millions one minute and nothing a few minutes later. For information power to be effective it needs to be shared. Hoarding it like gold, because we are afraid we will be replaced if someone else has the information to do our job, makes us unpromotable and more expendable. To be successful in the changing job market, we can no longer depend on information exclusively, but must develop other powers. Wisdom power is developed as we decide which knowledge and information is important for the well-being of the world and which is not.

The power of being ethical is associated with the seventh chakra. This means being trustworthy, honest and living by the golden rule of doing unto others as we would have others do unto us. Ethical power is sadly missing in our corporations and government—yet this way of influencing others is intrinsic to taking the soul to work. If we follow the dictates of the soul, we cannot help but be ethical, for we are guided by the highest motivation. Also, ethical power can create great good in the world.

One such example is that of Stonyfield Farm Yogurt in New Hampshire, which was started by Samuel Kayman and Gary Hirschberg in 1983 as a means to raise money for an organic farming project. Stonyfield's corporate mission reflects Gary's personal goal to make a positive contribution in the world. In conversation with me, he confided, "My wife Meg and I lost money for the first eight years, but we couldn't pack it in because so many friends had invested and believed in us."

Gary's comments are an example of ethics in action. He and Meg were more concerned about not harming others than meeting their own needs. And their motivation paid off. Last year Stonyfield grossed over $40 million.

"What makes Stonyfield different from other companies?" I asked.

"We give 10 percent of our profits to environmental causes," replied Gary, "and pay farmers not to use synthetic growth hormones in the milk that we purchase to make yogurt. Also, we are committed to decreasing our manufacturing emissions by 15 percent every year. We buy treed land with our profits so that our production will have zero impact on the planet and not contribute to global warming. Even our product packaging advocates environmental causes. One package design, which contained information on how to support cleaning up the environment, resulted in 200,000 e-mails being sent to the White House."

Whereas their competition is growing at only 2 percent, Stonyfield's growth rate over eight years has been 36 percent, making it the fastest growing company in its market in the United States. Their secret is ethical power. When customers were asked why they bought Stonyfield yogurt, seven of the ten reasons given had to do with Stonyfield's dedication to helping the environment.

"Another thing we're happy about," said Gary, "is that our competition has now launched similar environmental campaigns.

So we are having an impact on the way this entire industry is run."

Stonyfield is truly a David and Goliath story of how a few people with an ethical vision can take on corporate giants and succeed, not only in winning market shares, but in changing forever the way in which business is conducted.

Ethical power, like Gary and Meg's, can have a great impact when all seven chakras are functioning. We are only able to fully use our power when all our chakras are open and balanced. Up until recently, the major center of functioning in the developed world has been the third chakra of independence, supported by the first and second chakras. These lower three chakras are concerned with the personality and how the individual relates to their own energy in the first chakra, to others in the second and to what they want in the third.

The fifth, sixth and seventh chakras—in the throat, third eye and crown, respectively—are more concerned with how the soul can use the personality and the five bodies to be more effective in a larger sphere of influence in the world. The link between the lower and higher chakras is in the heart—where we become a soul-infused personality able to balance the needs of both the personality and the soul.

Walking the Path of Heart

Only when the will of the personality and the will of the soul come together evoked by love does the soul dominate the material light of the personality.

ALICE BAILEY

We make a quantum leap when we move the center of our consciousness to the heart chakra, the fourth and central chakra of the seven. Here the material realm of the personality merges with the divine realm of the soul. Working in this chakra, we are finally able to take our soul-infused personality to work. Concern for other humans and the world merges with our concern for ourselves. We understand that what we do for another we do for ourselves and this knowing opens us to interdependence—not just in theory, but in reality. In the current emerging cycle of human evolution, we will work more consciously with the heart chakra. This occurs when love, wisdom and will flow through our hearts out into the world as in the contemporary mythic story of *The Wizard of Oz*.

The Three-Fold Flame of Love, Wisdom and Will

The movie and book *The Wizard of Oz* has enthralled millions of people, both the young and the young at heart—because it contains a profound truth in the guise of an entertaining story. This mythic story feeds not only the personality but the soul.

Dorothy runs away from her physical home to find fulfillment and is knocked unconscious when she tries to return home before learning her spiritual lesson. In her unconscious state she has a profound dream where she is blown "over the rainbow." In the dream she learns of an all-powerful wizard who could help her return home, so she sets out to find him. Along the way she encounters three characters: a tin man looking for a heart, a scarecrow looking for a brain and a lion hoping to find courage. During the journey, Dorothy suffers through many trials but her friends never desert her. Eventually she reaches the Emerald City, only to discover that the wizard—a second-rate magician—cannot get her home. But he does give her some important advice. He points out that everything she has been looking for has been with her all along. He has a similar message for her companions as well—that the love, wisdom and courage they have been seeking are qualities they already possess. All Dorothy needs to do is to *believe* that she can return home and she will.

Dorothy's journey is ours. We are all seeking our true home—our soul—and through trial and error discover that our soul resides inside, not outside, ourselves. Greek, Roman and Egyptian philosophers located the soul either in or around the heart. To them, the heart held the seed of our true being and called us to our destiny. Many Eastern religions would concur that it is through our hearts that we manifest our higher selves in the world. Buddhists believe that in each of our hearts is a three-fold flame of love, wisdom and the will to actualize. This is strikingly similar to the Christian concept of the Holy Trinity, which is the merging of the divine will of the Father-God with the feminine wisdom of the Holy Spirit, brought into the world by Jesus, the Son, whose teaching was love.

The three-fold flame is linked to the three channels of energy that run up the spine, feeding the chakras. These channels are the masculine, feminine and the child—the child being birthed from the merging of the other two channels. Some of us have a two-inch flame and others, like Jesus and Buddha—because they are totally soul-infused personalities—are *all* flame. To become conscious creators and work fully with our souls in the world, we must develop the three qualities of the flame in equal proportions. By doing so, we balance the energies of our heart chakra.

Love-Compassion

My occupation: love. It's all I do.

St. John of the Cross

We practice love in its non-personal form as compassion when we observe someone in physical, psychological or spiritual pain and wish to ease it. Likewise, we are moved by love-compassion when we create healthy workplaces where people will thrive and develop their potential. With love-compassion we seek harmony and good relations with friends, family and co-workers.

Love-compassion—in its evolved form—is detached. This means having empathy for others without becoming overwhelmed by their feelings. In the second chakra, individuals learn to love family and friends and, perhaps, even co-workers, in a personal, subjective way. This paves the way for a higher expression of love in the heart chakra. People in healing professions either master the detachment of the fourth chakra or eventually burn out, because individuals in pain drain energy from others. When we love with detachment, we don't see people in pain as victims, but as personalities handed an opportunity to grow.

We can learn to care for ourselves with the same detachment. When we are turned down for a promotion, let go in a downsizing or are prevented from working on a project we love, we are presented with an opportunity for growth. Through these trials the universe teaches patience, forgiveness and compassion. Sometimes the personality grows more quickly through suffering than if it got what it wanted.

A doctor I know was given a "family physician of the year" award. During his acceptance speech he talked about his own battle with depression over the last few years. Through his own wounding he had opened up more to love. He said that although the medical guidelines state that physicians should not touch their patients other than professionally, he was no longer able to comply. He regularly gives hugs to old ladies and patients battling cancer or other serious diseases. This doctor is taking the high road in healing and his motivation is love. Hugs are healing. We have to stop making rules to fit the one in one hundred people who could make trouble and start making rules for the ninety-nine who need hugs!

Wisdom

> *To attain knowledge, add things every day.*
> *To attain wisdom, remove things every day.*
>
> Lao-Tzu

The second quality of the three-fold flame is wisdom. And using our wisdom to benefit others will help us align ourselves with spiritual laws. In this computer age, when we can obtain all the information we want in a matter of minutes, wisdom is knowing which pieces of information are useful. Wisdom—unlike knowledge—is concerned with quality, not quantity. More than just searching for answers, wisdom seeks to ask the right questions, from which the answers come of themselves. Wisdom is knowing the appropriate amount of information to share with others at a specific time. If we speak to show how clever we are, we are motivated by ego and pride. This is knowledge, not wisdom.

Thich Nhat Hanh says, "In Buddhism, knowledge is regarded as an obstacle to understanding, like a block of ice that obstructs the river from flowing." It is only by letting go of our attachment to knowledge that we reach understanding—wisdom.

In seminars I am often faced with a dilemma. I think of many things that could help participants, but know that they will only hear one or two things before being overwhelmed with information. During those moments, I ask myself the question, "What could I say or do that would make the *most* difference to this person at this time?" This question helps me sort through my knowledge to find the one most important thing to help. More is not always more. More is sometimes less. The soul is wise and knows when to speak, and when not to. The personality, on the other hand, likes to show off how much it knows.

Medieval theologians called this kind of soul wisdom "connatural knowledge." They thought of it as being not so much intellectual as intuitive or body knowing. The 13th-century Christian mystic Meister Eckhart shed light on the quality of wisdom when he said, "Only the hand that erases can write the true thing." We receive information and knowledge from our environment and by refining it can uncover the simplest, purest truth of that knowledge. This discernment is wisdom.

Will to Actualize

Do it now; if you see what needs doing, do it.

DHYANI YWAHOO

Power is to will what knowledge is to wisdom. The desire to use personal power is a quality of the third chakra, as when we say that someone has will power. In the heart chakra, we align our personal will with divine will. Actualizing the divine will is the third quality of the three-fold flame in our hearts. It is an active principle that wants to say, do and create positive things in the world. We are creating a wasteland for ourselves because of misuse of the personal power of the third chakra. And many well-motivated men and women are hesitant to use their power because they are aware of this danger. As Abraham Lincoln said, "A lot of people can withstand adversity. If you really want to test someone's character, give him power." However, to underuse our power, because we fear being inadequate or wrong, is as poor a choice as overusing it. The soul gives us desires and goals in life so that we will take action to achieve them.

> It is as if God has deliberately put unfulfilled desires into our hearts so that our hearts may be stretched beyond their present capacity. Soul making requires this kind of stretching. It is not enough to know about soul making.... We become more and more who we are...when we struggle with... love, death, power and time.
>
> ALAN JONES, DEAN OF GRACE CATHEDRAL, SAN FRANCISCO

We must release the energy that we've built through love and wisdom by taking action in the world. If we don't, we can never become a conscious creator and perform the soul's work. It is crucial that all well-intentioned people do everything of which they are capable. To not do so is to abandon the Earth to those who use their power to serve their personalities and not their souls. American career consultant Marilyn Moats Kennedy said, "It's better to be boldly decisive and risk being wrong than to agonize at length and be right too late." By balancing the will of the personality with the will of the soul, we can create in the world through the heart.

Each of the three qualities increases the three-fold flame in our heart chakra and by developing these qualities in harmony with each other, the personality can accomplish what the soul wants. People who incarnate with will as their strongest gift, for example, often rise early in life to positions of power. But they may find it difficult to relinquish their personal power to learn love and wisdom. However, this is exactly what they must do to achieve balance. Other individuals are born loving, but love indiscriminately, without standards of excellence either for themselves or for others. These loving men and women must learn wisdom and discernment so that they can develop their potentials and encourage others to do the same. Still others, born with wisdom, might find it painful when their wisdom and "knowing" are unrecognized. But wisdom untempered by love is cold and inflexible. By learning love through suffering, these people bring long-lasting solutions that serve the hearts, as well as minds, of others. Don't forget that while each of us is unique, we are all moving to the same place.

Opening Your Heart to Love

What matters is not to think much, but to love much.

St. Teresa of Avila

Will, in its lower form as power and wisdom, in its lower form as knowledge, have both been accepted in the business world more than love-compassion. To develop love-compassion we need first to value it. If we view love-compassion as sentimentality, or think it could result in being a pushover or never getting what we want, it does not seem desirable. Earlier in the book we discussed subatomic physics, which demonstrated that the atoms of all things continually move and interpenetrate each other. All human beings are linked and what we do for another, we also do for ourselves. By loving and helping others to achieve their goals, we actually serve ourselves. I am discussing the reasons for developing love-compassion in this self-serving way in order to convince even the most hardened skeptics that the benefits of being compassionate outweigh any liabilities.

How do we learn love-compassion? The path to love is through feeling, and there are many role-models who light the way. One great one was Mother Theresa. She, either directly or indirectly, helped millions of dying people, not only on the streets of Calcutta, but in hospices she helped to set up around the world. When asked how she could work with the destitute and dying year after year, she replied, "I see my Lord in each of their faces." Mother Theresa saw the soul of each person and this is the key to developing love. Buddhism puts this practice a similar way by saying, "Treat every being as your mother." Mother Theresa was also a wonderful example of will and of achieving a goal through sheer persistence. She said, "If I never picked up the first person, I'd never have picked up 42,000. So I think one, one at a time."

Some people are called by their soul to work directly with those in need and this service strengthens the heart chakra. These men and women raise foster children, look after handicapped adults or work with the dying. Professions such as social work, counseling and teaching develop our love-compassion, but we don't need to work full time in these professions to learn to love. We can practice love on a daily basis with everyone we meet.

Loving helps not only others, but ourselves. Allan Luks, executive director of Big Brothers/Sisters in New York City, conducted a national survey involving 3,300 volunteers. He discovered that taking care of others significantly improved the health of the volunteers. People who volunteered regularly were ten times more likely to be in good health than those who either helped others only once a year, or didn't help at all. Benefits included emotional uplifts—called the "helper's high"—reduction in chronic pain, fewer colds and improved eating and sleeping habits. But we don't need to volunteer at social service agencies or hospitals to serve others, we can do it in our everyday work and lives.

Acts of Kindness

True generosity grows in us as our heart opens.

Jack Kornfield

Over the last few years I have asked thousands of people this question: "What did we have in the world ten years ago that you miss most now?" Their answers are often variations on the same theme: "That I matter as an individual; that I'm not just a cog in the wheel; that people care for me as a person; that people know my name." Sound familiar? In our fast-paced technological world, we are becoming anonymous and losing our humanity. People feel they don't matter any more. Today it often seems like voice mail has replaced the human being, bank machines have replaced tellers and sex on the Internet and on the telephone have replaced loving relationships. It is because our need to be loved is not being satisfied that I think one of the greatest trends in the next decade will be personal contact with customers. If you need a marketing advantage for "doing unto others as you would have them do unto you," there it is.

All of us have stories of acts of kindness and I'd like to share a few of mine. Ten years ago when I became interested in ethical investment, I wrote to well-known Canadian environmentalist David Suzuki and suggested that he might want to write a column on this topic. He wrote back—not a form letter but a handwritten card—responding to my suggestion and telling me to keep up the good work. Not only do I still have this card, but for the last three years I have worked with David, his wife Tara and the environmental foundation they created. His card has translated into ten years of loyalty from me and I know that he has written thousands of personal cards to others. People need to feel recognized and appreciated and David has a gift for doing that.

The Earl's restaurant chain in Calgary also has this gift. Each staff person at Earl's is given three days of intensive training before they ever see a customer, and it shows. If there's a line-up when you arrive—and there often is because it's so popular—you are greeted by friendly staff who offer you hors d'oeuvres while you're waiting. Then you are seated and the waiter, who has tasted all the specials and different kinds of wine, offers helpful advice. The service is courteous and efficient and the staff appear happy and genuinely glad to see you. Once I complained about a dessert and not only was I given another dessert at no charge, but a customer service representative came to ask how they could serve me better. I felt as if they really wanted my opinion and would implement it.

Acts of kindness are acts of love and they open our heart chakras. Do you give your seat on the bus to someone who needs it more than you do? Do you hold open the door for those who follow? Do you give change to a street musician who is bringing beauty into the world? Do you stop to talk to those less fortunate than yourself? Do you thank people for what they do for you and show appreciation in many ways? All of these things, as well as assisting the elderly, being a good neighbor, playing with children and helping your community, are also acts of compassion.

Jack Kornfield, a meditation teacher, talks about the three stages of generosity. The first stage is called *tentative giving*. We are fearful to give because we are afraid of being deprived later on. Yet, after our initial reluctance we experience the first joys of giving. In the second stage, *brotherly or sisterly giving*, we openly share what we have, both in energy and material ways with others and experience joy and friendship in doing so. The most developed kind of generosity is *royal giving*. We delight in the welfare and happiness of all beings and give the best we have to them. We never consider scarcity and our hearts are abundant like kings and queens.

A school principal who is a friend of mine told me a story that exemplifies royal giving. Over a period of weeks, the staff-room at her school accumulated more and more dirty dishes. Teachers with high cleanliness standards were bothered a great deal by the mess. Others—probably the culprits—appeared not to notice the problem. One of the teachers, without drawing attention to herself, started washing the dishes each night before leaving. The tension in the staffroom was immediately dissipated by this act. When the principal pointed out that she didn't have to do the dishes, the teacher replied that she liked to create an atmosphere where everyone would feel comfortable. This teacher, through her small, consistent act of kindness, affected the lives of many others. Not only was she strengthening her own heart chakra through service to others, she was also opening up other hearts by her generous action. She was not concerned with doing something that was beneath her and realized that soul work is what we do every minute of every day.

Serving Others in All Jobs

> *When you work you fulfill a part of Earth's furthest*
> *dream, assigned to you when that dream was born,*
> *And in keeping yourself with labor you are in truth*
> *loving life,*
> *And to love life through labor is to be intimate with*
> *life's inmost secret.*
>
> KAHLIL GIBRAN, THE PROPHET

Some time ago, I was staying in a hotel in Barbados. From my balcony I noticed an old crippled man try unsuccessfully to rise from his chair in the courtyard. A maid, carrying dirty laundry, saw his plight, dropped the laundry and ran to his assistance. Motivated by compassion, she acted quickly to prevent this elderly man from falling.

In the same hotel, I went into a shop to buy groceries and encountered the shopkeeper, who was snippy and curt both with me and her other customers. For the next few days, on my trips to her shop I engaged her in conversation about her long hours, asked her advice on products and commented on what a good job she was doing of meeting people's food needs. When I went in to buy garlic she told me that it was too much bother to sell fresh food. I replied that I loved garlic, but understood how difficult it was for her to stock everything. The next morning when I entered the shop, she smiled happily and gave me a bulb of garlic she'd brought from home. This is what our interactions with people can be like when we spend time appreciating them, their life and their work.

When I mentioned to people that I was writing a book called *Take Your Soul to Work*, several of them replied that it was not possible to do so in all jobs. I was asked, "How do bartenders, maids, hair-stylists, secretaries and construction workers take their souls to work?"

It is a commonly held belief, although erroneous, that some jobs are soulful but others aren't. Our soul is interested in us developing love, wisdom and the will to self-actualize so that we can become conscious creators. And we can do this in *any* job. Let's look at the jobs that were just mentioned to see how we could take our soul to work. Bartenders are lay counselors because customers often confide their life stories and problems to them. This is often true of taxi drivers as well. Maids and housekeepers create beauty and comfort so that their clients are in harmony and can do better work. Massage therapists, beauticians and hair-stylists relax us and give us physical tune-ups so we can recuperate from stressful work. Secretaries and assistants help others to manifest their dreams and goals in the world. All of these people mentioned have two choices about how they do their work. They can do it just for money or they can do their work with love and the spirit of service—which creates a happier, healthier atmosphere for their customers.

Builders, painters and factory-workers serve the world in different ways. If they believe in the product they are creating, they birth something better into the world. Only if they have an aversion to what they are making (for example, war products, harmful chemicals or ugly buildings) is their work soul-destroying. Even in the worst work environments we can work with the three-fold flame of love, wisdom and will in the heart chakra to improve the lives of our fellow workers and by doing so we work with our soul.

Erin Feuerstein, owner of Malden Mills, a company that makes PolarTec® fleece, has had a first-hand experience of serving others with love—even when it entailed a personal financial sacrifice. When his plant burned down in December 1995, he vowed to rebuild and, while doing so, to keep all his employees on the payroll. It took a year to do this, and during that time he kept up his payments to over one thousand people. The life of one person was able to affect the lives of a great many.

Although we might not have such dramatic stories to tell, each of us working with open heart chakras can have a great impact on the world. In fact, no other chakra has as great a power for good as the heart. Why? Because the heart is the center of synthesis between the lower world of our personality and the higher world of our soul. Even physically it resides in the middle place in our body and is the central chakra. The heart and its focus on love-compassion and service to others is ultimately the reason for our evolution. We are not on the planet to develop our creativity and communication skills—the function of the fifth chakra—nor to develop our intuition—the function of the sixth—or even to live in harmony with natural cycles—the function of the seventh. The purpose of human evolution is to learn to become creators of good in the world and that cannot be achieved without a strong heart chakra.

Creating Organizations with Soul

The world in which we live has been created unconsciously by unconscious intentions.

GARY ZUKAV

As we have seen, each of the chakras has a specific talent and the talent of the fifth chakra, located in the throat, is manifesting in the world. To do this, it has characteristics that are higher functions of the second and third chakras. Like the yin, feminine center of the second chakra, the throat is designed to give birth, although its children are books, technology, inventions, communication and ideas. And like the third chakra, the fifth has yang energy and a more masculine, external focus in the world. But the fifth chakra differs from both the second and third chakras in that it manifests by employing the higher energy of divine will. The second and third chakras, on the other hand, are more concerned with manifesting what the personality wants, whether that be a child of your own or developing your self-esteem through becoming financially successful.

We have heard it said that our thoughts determine our reality and this is the function of the fifth chakra. The fifth chakra is activated by our thoughts, so it is essential to ensure that they are of the highest good. We accomplish this by aligning our thoughts with divine will, using the spiritual gift of clairaudience and listening to our higher self, our soul, to get messages of what to do. But the fifth chakra involves more than just listening. It also involves speaking, creating plans and forming strategies. When our fifth chakra is functioning well, we are able to take a vision seen in our sixth chakra—the third eye—and find creative strategies to turn this vision into reality, while at the same time communicating our ideas persuasively to others so that they will wish to assist us with our goal.

We are not equally strong in all chakras and it might be helpful to examine these differences. While acknowledging the limitations of stereotypes, men and women generally excel in different chakras, and their talents correlate with whether the chakra is yang or yin, masculine or feminine. It could be argued that men are usually stronger physically—the realm of the first chakra—and women more interested in relationships—the realm of the second chakra. Men are often more successful in manifesting their talents in the world—the domain of the third chakra, whereas women are more concerned with love and service in the world—the domain of the fourth. Following this line of thinking, one would point out that men seem to be more noted for their inventions, technology and interest in politics and ideas, the talent of the fifth chakra. Women, on the other hand, are noted to be more intuitive—the talent of the sixth. The crown chakra involves the merging of both yin and yang channels and so is equally accessible to both genders.

Regardless of whether we are men or women, we must develop all chakras to become a soul-infused personality—but the use of some chakras might come more easily to us than others. This particular chapter is devoted to the creation of organizational forms and structures that are aligned to higher purpose and divine will. Creating healthy organizations is not just the re-sponsibility of CEOs and senior managers, but of all of us.

Small Is Beautiful

Current workplace trends in North America indicate that more people—of their own volition—are choosing to work either in smaller companies or on their own. Many individuals have de-cided that the price they pay to work in a large, successful or-ganization is not worth their physical, emotional, mental and spiritual health. There is also a growing need in both men and women for creativity and self-expression—both qualities of the fifth chakra—and these people feel they will be better able to meet these needs in small organizations.

A 1996 poll conducted by Angus Reid found that 33 percent of Canadians either run their own businesses or plan to start one within five years. The poll also discovered that 62 percent of Canadians believe that entrepreneurs are happier than employ-ees. Similar results can be found in the United States, where there is a growing trend away from working for large organizations and towards working for smaller ones. *Fortune* magazine re-ported that in 1996 only 13 percent of new MBA graduates from Columbia University joined large manufacturers, down 25 per-cent from just six years earlier. The same trend is reflected at Stanford University, where the number of business graduates joining companies with more than one thousand employees had decreased by 20 percent over the same period.

I believe this trend towards self-employment and working in smaller companies will continue to grow for several reasons. First, companies are shrinking, decentralizing and dividing into smaller units to serve their customers more efficiently. This means fewer jobs in large organizations. But there are still jobs; they have just been re-arranged. David Birch, an economist with a research organization called Cognetics, studied the U.S. job market from 1987 to 1991. He reports that while big firms laid off 2.4 million workers in that period, firms with fewer than twenty employees added 4.4 million new jobs.

The second reason for people choosing to work in smaller organizations is that they better feed people's hearts and souls. I believe smaller organizations work best not just because of efficiency, but because of intimacy. Management guru Tom Peters has documented many cases of organizations breaking down into smaller sizes to thrive and believes that 150 members is a natural size and that anything larger results in absenteeism and sickness. Bill Gates of Microsoft—whom one would think an unlikely proponent of small organizations—agrees that small is best and sets his preferred maximum to 200 people within a unit.

This trend could indicate a pendulum swing back to an earlier time in North America, where success was built on family and small businesses. Charles Handy, in his book *The Age of Paradox*, talks of the strength of the small- to medium-sized family companies that are the backbone of German and Italian business. There are approximately 300,000 firms in Germany with 10 to 3,000 employees and the same phenomenon is found in Italy with companies that specialize in knitwear, textiles, furniture and hydraulics. Both countries want global reach—but not global size—and specialize in what they do well. They think long term about doing their work profitably and enjoyably and invest enormous sums in innovation. These businesses are run by heads of families who think in term of decades, not quarters, and who look after their employees' children as their own.

I'm not saying that I think Italian or German organizations are perfect. Their approach is centered in the second chakra, where your employees and your nation are like your family. Companies in Italy, Germany and Japan need to work on moving preferred feelings about their own people to the heart chakra, where they will see *all* humans as family. Still, these three nations that emphasize the importance of "the group" have only one part of the learning. North Americans, with their third chakra emphasis on the independence of "the individual," have the other part. Although they start from different places, all countries will eventually move to the heart chakra in the fourth cycle of interdependence

This is already happening through the European Common Market, free trade between Canada and the United States and similar alliances that are forming among South American and Asian countries. This movement towards working interdependently with other nations might be motivated by national self-interest at present, but creating this new structure without national boundaries will in the long term lead to better cooperation between people of different nationalities. The fifth chakra works with the paradox of being able to understand both our unique individuality and our similarities with others. New organizational structures that allow us to work in small independent work units while maintaining contact with the global market will recognize this paradox.

We're All in This Together

> *Treat a man as he is and he will become as he is.*
> *Treat a man as he can and should be and he will*
> *become as he can and should be.*
>
> GOETHE

Developing the power of the heart in organizations comes not only from the "size," but also the "kind" of work that people do. Jeremy Rifkin, author of *The End of Work*, says that the largest growth sector in North America includes social service agencies, not-for-profits, the arts, volunteer and underground economies. Why? Because individuals are searching for soulful work where they can make a difference in the world.

But the changes that I'm suggesting and which are occurring in the workplace transcend a concern for each individual and demonstrate that all living beings are woven together in the same web. As Reverend Martin Luther King Jr. said in *The Trumpet of Conscience*, "It really boils down to this: all life is interrelated. We are all caught in an inescapable network or mutuality, tied into a single garment of destiny. Whatever affects one directly, affects all indirectly."

Both Germany and Japan see the inter-relationship between the individual, the company and the country, and they structure their systems accordingly. In Germany, business is seen as serving *all* the people—not just shareholders or employees. Workplace training is regarded as essential to the strength of the country, even if companies don't employ the workers they train. Pension money is held within the company with two built-in assumptions: the business will always be around and workers will want to work there all their lives. Establishing company policies to support employees is a positive use of the fifth chakra in business.

Continuity in Japan—as in Germany—is for the good of all. Employees are loyal to their organization as well as to their country and invest in long-term plans instead of short-term gain. By law in Japan, any merger or takeover requires agreement from a majority of directors of the company, almost all of whom are employees. Also, senior managers in Japan are not rewarded—as in Britain or America—with share options, but are linked through a bonus system to the performance of their workforce. Because of the long-term commitment of these national governments to companies and companies to people, contested takeovers are almost unheard of in Germany and Japan.

The laws and company policies in Germany and Japan serve to break down the barriers that separate "them" and "us." We would be more effective at creating healthy workplaces in North America if company policies reflected some of these principles. Positive use of the fifth chakra is to create company policies and procedures that help people take their souls to work. Ultimately, though, we as individuals are responsible for the ways we foster this within our sphere of influence. How do we treat our co-workers, clients, those we report to and those we supervise? It doesn't matter how many spiritual books we read or courses we attend; the proof is in action and not talk. Some of the best managers I know don't use buzz words like "empowerment," but do practice it.

Ross Risvold is one such manager. He has perfected a way of working with the three-fold flame to empower his staff. Motivated by love, Ross trusts his wisdom to discern people's talents. Then, using his will to actualize, he takes action to help employees develop their potential. His staff and colleagues love working with Ross because he recognizes their gifts and rewards them with work at which they excel.

As old hierarchical organizations die, new organizational forms are being born. But executives, managers and staff are all confused as to the best way to proceed in this sensitive time of transition. Through this time of chaos and uncertainty, we need to allow the barriers between management and staff, and leaders and followers, to fall and together embrace the unknown with positive motivation and trust. By doing this we create organizational forms with the fifth chakra that are designed to develop each person's potential.

Embracing Diversity

The fifth chakra works well with diversity. Diversity, whether in our individual bodies or the bodies of our organizations, is crucial to good health. Diversity adds flexibility and additional perspectives, which create depth and breadth for a company's structure, products and services. We know, for example, that people are more productive at solving simple problems when they are in *like* groups (e.g., age, race, values, gender) and more effective solving complex problems in *unlike* groups. It takes longer for unlike groups to make decisions, but their answers are almost always better, because they are more inclusive and allow for more variables. The serious problems we face in our organizations and world today are more likely to be complex than simple, so to make better decisions we must involve people of many different cultures and backgrounds.

Embracing diversity is essential not only to create better products, but also to improve our company's bottom line. Working with others from different races, genders, ages, values and learning styles offers us opportunities for soulful growth. Carol Pearson and Sharon Seivert, authors of *Magic at Work*, support this view:

> The more homogeneous the mix of people in our organizations, the more comfortable we get—so comfortable, in fact, that more and more parts of our psyche go to sleep. As a result, we become less and less able to respond to new challenges with energy and vigor. We may experience a sense of being jolted awake when we have to work with people who are very different from us. No longer can we assume everything. We have to think all the time—and in new ways.

Our world is diverse and that is its beauty. One kind of tree does not make a forest and the more varieties of flora and fauna in an ecosystem, the stronger it is. It's a wonderful time in our evolution when people from all races, religions and values are intermingling throughout the world. This is not a time for coasting. Our psyches are awake and trying to figure out how to meet individual and collective needs. A love of diversity is a function of the fifth chakra, and we use it to create. If we listen to each other, are flexible and motivated to create something we can all enjoy, we will succeed in creating a beautiful world.

Discernment: Separating the Wheat from the Chaff

*Can you discern and penetrate in every direction
without pretense and presumption?*

Tao Te Ching

We don't switch from old- to new-style organizations, or from old to new ways of thinking overnight. Years can be spent with a foot in each camp while this transition takes place. During this time we need to separate the wheat from the chaff and celebrate what was good about the past, while releasing what holds us back from a positive future. We might, in fact, discover many qualities from old-style organizations that are both valuable and necessary and incorporate them into our transformed business.

Old-style organizations valued their people and took care of them by assuring them long-term—and often lifetime—employment if they did a good job. Leaders more often rose through the ranks and got to know employees as individuals. So these leaders helped to create a kind of family feeling. Unfortunately, through downsizing and economic cutbacks, human lives have too often been sacrificed on the altar of the bottom line. Although organizations are no longer able to assure long-term employment, they can guarantee that employees are treated fairly, with respect and are given opportunities to develop their hearts and minds at work. Revolutionary economist E. F. Schumacher spoke of the need for discernment:

> You are put into this life with the task of learning to distinguish between that which is really real and really important and permanent and of true value on the one hand, and things trivial, amusing, ephemeral, and of no real value on the other hand.

Discernment is essential and to learn it we need open, inquiring minds. Great thinkers of all ages have had the ability to do this by stepping outside of their own personal story and era in order to see the greater picture. Earlier in this book you were asked to question all your assumptions about yourself. This helped you become discerning about your own life. To practice discernment in business, you need to question all your assumptions about what your customers *really* want, and discern whether you are meeting their needs. Are you meeting their long- as well as short-term needs? Are you meeting their soul as well as personality needs? I believe we can meet the needs of customers and employees in both the way we treat them personally and with our products professionally.

To do this, we must also be discerning about people. Gay Hendricks and Kate Ludeman said, in *The Corporate Mystic: A Guidebook for Visionaries with Their Feet on the Ground*, "Corporate mystics develop a double vision, at once to see the mask and the essential person inside." We must be able to see both the personality and soul of each person with whom we interact, and discern what food to give each one to develop her potential. All of us, regardless of our job title, can build up a sense of accomplishment in those people with low self-esteem. Conversely, we need to create a hunger to strengthen the souls of individuals with too strong an ego, even if this means denying their personalities. Putting our discernment into action like this strengthens our fifth chakra.

This is easier to do with those we supervise than with those who supervise us, but we can still do it in more subtle ways with our boss. For example, if you have to stay late because your supervisor continually gives you work near the end of the day, you might wish to have a confidential talk with him. State that you are most happy to do the work but that you need more notice in the future. Negotiation and speaking up for yourself are both qualities of the fifth chakra. Maybe you will receive 100 percent cooperation and maybe only 25 percent. If you don't take the risk, you'll get zero and have to live with the continual frustration of your current situation. These are not easy choices, but working effectively with the fifth chakra is like being a good cook who knows how much of each ingredient to use to make a tasty and wholesome dish.

Rituals of Healing

The key to recognizing effective rituals is the aware-ness that ritual is not performance art—it is partici-patory prayer.

MATTHEW FOX

Rituals employ the power of the throat chakra to de-manifest old forms and patterns that no longer work and create new ones. Rituals can help us grieve the passing of an era in our organiza-tion or they can help us celebrate our successes. They assist us in recognizing and honoring each other. There are rituals that work best for groups of women and ones that work best for men. Outward Bound specializes in physical challenges that work well to build team spirit and to overcome physical fears. These chal-lenges take potentially dangerous situations—similar to the ritual rites of passage that are mostly missing in our modern world— and apply them to organizations in order to build group cohesion.

I use a wide range of rituals in corporate settings. A few years ago I was invited to lead the annual retreat of the executive train-ing department of a university. These participants were a highly skilled group of professional trainers who were having serious communication problems. In the past they had tried many ways of "talking about" their problems but were not able to break through old patterns and behavior. At the retreat I asked them to use their bodies to create an image of how their organization looked. They were invited to stand beside those with whom they felt close; away from those they did not; and to assume the body posture that represented how they felt at work. They did this in silence.

For at least half an hour people wandered through the maze of bodies, moving towards one person and then another until they finally found the position in the organization that felt like them. They froze in place and we looked at what they had created. The executive director was totally alone in the middle, touching no one; the assisstant director had several people holding on to her for dear life and one manager was almost out the door.

This ritual conveyed the alienation and desperation that people felt but could not express. The executive director was deeply moved, as were they all, and was able to discuss his ambivalence about staying in the organization and how his physical separateness mirrored his emotional separateness. Together, through some tears, all members spoke about healing the relationships and creating a new pattern. They experimented bodily with some new forms to discover which felt best to them. Soon afterward the executive director had the courage to leave his position to do his soul's work and the group was able to form the new pattern they desired.

Another ritual helpful in eliminating negativity and non-productive behaviors is to ask each individual to write on a piece of paper an undesirable quality or behavior of theirs that they would like to eliminate. They then tell the group about the behavior they are eliminating and burn the paper in a bowl. Writing down what they want to eliminate and acknowledging it verbally to others ensures their commitment to action. And the bowl is a vessel containing a sacred fire of purification to transform their negativity.

As well as eliminating negative behaviors, it's important to strengthen positive feelings in organizations, too. Not long ago, I was conducting an annual retreat for a healthy work group whose staff and board members liked each other and were committed to similar goals. We'd celebrated their successes, but I realized we were missing something when three people, independently during the day, asked me if something was wrong. I thought this a strange question and when I asked them to explain what they meant, none of them was able to articulate the reasons for their feeling. I meditated on what to do and realized that they were asking me to go deeper with them.

When we convened the next morning, I spoke of the synchronicity of the three comments and brought out a sacred talking stone, given to me by the Waitaha/Maori people of New Zealand. I invited each person to hold the stone and speak from their heart about what they liked in their organization and what they felt was missing. I was nervous doing this as the participants included two new board members. Yet, I felt a sense of rightness about the process and continued. Before long, the staff, board members and the executive had all shared that they wanted more time to play together. They valued their work tremendously but felt that they never took any time to just enjoy each other. We acted on their suggestions immediately by having a picnic lunch by the sea and a barbecue that evening.

Our everyday life abounds in rituals—having a shower every morning, reading the paper with our morning coffee, driving the same way to work every day, making a "to do" list before leaving work, changing into comfortable clothes when we get home from work and going to bed at the same time every night—but are they life-sustaining or denying? Some of these rituals bring us comfort, some may have a negative impact.

Ask yourself what rituals you have at work presently. Which are energy enhancing and which ones are depleting? Positive work rituals might include making a daily "to do" list and continually returning to top-priority items during the day. It could also be bringing flowers to work every Monday to brighten up your office. Some people might enjoy going to the pub Friday after work with their department or sharing doughnuts with co-workers at Friday's coffee break. Negative rituals could include having meetings even if there's nothing of importance to discuss and doing low-priority items because they're easier than tackling the more difficult top-priority work.

Most people complain that they attend too many meetings. If so, what choices could you make to improve the *quality* and *quantity* of the experience? Ross Risvold—the manager I mentioned earlier who used the qualities of love, wisdom and will to help his staff develop their potential—employed an efficient ritual for meetings. He decided to streamline meetings by having them standing up at the coffee machine in the morning. Ross called these "tailgate" meetings, named after the guys who discuss important things as they're unloading goods from their trucks. Because people couldn't sit down and get comfortable, the amount of time spent in the meetings was kept to a minimum. Also, Ross took advantage of the already existing ritual of people stopping for a chat while they got their coffee. In this way, he focused the discussion on information that was important to the entire group. People enjoyed these meetings so much that they kept holding them, even after his departure.

Creating Environments That Inspire Joy

The greatest and simplest power of a teacher is the environment of their own freedom and joy.

JACK KORNFIELD

More than twenty years ago I was a high school teacher and counselor at a school with sixteen hundred students. To build a sense of community, I suggested to the administration that teachers and students take a day to play together. They thought it was a good idea and asked me to help organize it. A committee was formed composed of teachers and students who each made suggestions about what they'd like to do. The activities that passed the criteria of being interesting, safe and involving physical, emotional or mental learning were offered to both teachers and students, who all selected one in which to participate. Among these choices were visiting the zoo or an art gallery, attending the theater, skiing, rollerskating and cooking with a professional chef.

The day was a tremendous success. Devoting time to play together built camaraderie and good relations—and it was fun!

In a 1970s Harris poll, Americans reported working an average of forty-one hours a week, with twenty-six hours available for leisure. Twenty years later, work time has increased to forty-eight hours and leisure time has shrunk to sixteen, a 40 percent reduction in leisure time. I find this distressing and have two obvious solutions. First, decrease the number of hours we work and, second, make sure that work is play or involves a great deal of play.

Oscar Wilde said, "Work is more fun than play." Do you *enjoy* your work? It is crucial to the well-being both of the soul and personality that you do. Without joy there is no optimism and without optimism there is no hope for solutions to existing problems. If we approach our work with the playful spirit of a child trying out new things, we are likely to enjoy it more. Play is not only fun, it increases our creativity, which in turn facilitates our discovery of innovative solutions for complex problems. Without play, people with a strong throat chakra might have wonderful ideas, but they may come across as a bit stern and cool. Let's examine the effect that play and creative environments have on intelligence.

Neuron cells in the brain don't reproduce, but there are cells connected to intelligence that do. These "glial" cells—from "glia," the Greek word for glue—support and surround every nerve fiber in the body. Glial cells increase synaptic connections, which facilitate thinking in both speed and different patterns. This allows people to think of a problem from varying points of view, a quality much desired by the fifth chakra with its liking for creativity. Neuron cells make up only 10 percent of the brain; 90 percent of brain cells are glial cells. When Albert Einstein's brain was investigated after his death, it was found that he had 72 percent more glial cells than the average person. Although there was only one Einstein, we can all create environments at work and home that increase the amount of glial cells in our brains.

Dr. Marion Diamond, a neuroanatomist at Berkeley, pioneered research in this area in the 1970s. Rats were tested to see how many glial cells they had and then were placed in an environmentally rich atmosphere—a rat heaven full of mazes and interesting toys. After ninety-one days they were retested and found to have 20 percent more glial cells. Next, the rats were placed in an environmentally deprived atmosphere and ninety-one days later they were found to have 19 percent *fewer* glial cells than they had had originally. In other words, they actually were *worse off* than when they started the experiment.

Human intelligence, like that of rats, is affected by environment. Our work and home environments can either increase or decrease our intelligence. Could this be why upper- and middle-class children with do better in school than working-class children *the same* IQ? Upper- and middle-class children often have a more enriched environment—more books, music classes, computer access, holidays to other places—in which to thrive.

Rats, whether through heredity or the morphogenetic fields that Rupert Sheldrake describes, pass their newly acquired intelligence on to their offspring. Intelligence, for humans as well as rats, can be cumulative from generation to generation. To create a world where we all rise to our potential, we must ensure that our young are given stimulating, enjoyable environments in which to learn. And we need to take responsibility for doing the same for ourselves and others in the workplace.

There are many ways to do this. To support creative play in our organizations, we might have a contest for a funny company slogan and put the winner on mugs and sweatshirts. We could also play baseball together, hold business meetings while walking in the forest or have annual organizational retreats at a spa. Let's not wait for others to make our work environment fun; let's do it ourselves. The soul loves to play and have fun.

Also, having a sense of humor decreases stress and helps us to develop life balance. The "ha ha" sound of laughter opens our heart and brings love through our throat into the world. A while ago, I was giving a seminar to chartered accountants who were working long hours with little fun. I asked them what they found helped them to reduce their stress. One of them—Bob—started chuckling to himself. "Have you got a technique you could share with us Bob?" I asked. Beaming, he responded, "For years I've been a perfectionist and a workaholic. Things have been getting worse and my doctor told me that my workaholism was affecting my health. I decided to enjoy life more. I put a sign on my bathroom mirror so I can see it first thing every morning. It says, 'Bob, this is God speaking; I won't be needing your help today.'"

Having a sense of humor, smiling, having fun—all is food for the soul. It doesn't take more time to have fun; it actually saves time. A monk who had been meditating seriously all his life finally had a breakthrough during his meditation and met the Buddha. "It's been such hard work getting here, but it was worth it," the monk said. "Ah," replied the Buddha, "You would have gotten here faster if you'd laughed more."

Practicing Abundance Mentality

The fear of scarcity—that there is not enough money, power or love and that we have to guard against those who want to take everything from us—is an erroneous thought that creates great pain. Believing this, we see our world, workplace and others as dangerous and think only of what we can get for ourselves. These thoughts create stress, a lack of happiness for us and a lack of generosity and love for fellow workers. Yes, there are predators in the workplace who are dangerous because of their drive to satisfy only their own needs. We give them power by fearing them and allowing them to influence us but we can protect ourselves from them by visualizing a shield between us and them and by reducing or eliminating the time we spend with them. However, the greatest danger is not these predators, but believing in scarcity ourselves.

The soul lives in abundance and knows that we will be provided for in just the right way at just the right time. It knows that the enemy is not out there but within. To practice abundance mentality we must learn to act with trust and face our own fears of scarcity.

If you tend to hoard information, share your knowledge with others who would benefit from it. If you think there isn't enough time to help others and still do your own work, confront that thought by changing your behavior and acting as though there *is* enough time. Live in the moment. Celebrate the successes of fellow employees, assist them with problems and devote time to them. Happy people do better work. Whether you are a manager or not, you can improve your work environment by leaps and bounds by being accessible to listen and speak with people on an ongoing basis. In other words, practice abundance mentality and believe that there is enough time, information, people and money to create a prosperous and soul-filled company.

It is impossible to function fully in the fifth chakra if we cannot think big and believe that the universe will manifest our dreams. Practicing abundance mentality has many benefits, including raising the quality of our products or services because we have more ongoing, open discussions and more practice solving the causes (not symptoms) of problems. But the greatest benefit will be the enjoyment that people will have at work. This enjoyment will spill into relationships with customers and at home with family and friends.

Leaders Who Foster Trust

The best rulers are barely known to men.
The next best are cherished and extolled.
The lesser are feared, and the least are scorned.
Distrust cannot summon trust.

Lao-Tzu

What are the essential qualities of business, political and social leaders who will create workplaces and countries where all can thrive? Jack Hawley, in *Reawakening the Spirit in Work*, suggests several characteristics that he believes are needed. These include virtue, equanimity, inner peace, service, spiritual awareness, unity, gratitude, being a sense-maker, an embodier of truth and also a worker for the higher good.

These qualities hearken back to the priest-kings of Egypt, Sumeria and early Greece, where leaders in the outer, physical world were also leaders in the inner, spiritual world. This is not such a bad idea, as we can never teach or lead people where we haven't gone ourselves. Soul-infused individuals make the best decisions for everyone. These individuals have gone through the various tests and stages that Perceval confronted in his quest for the Holy Grail. They have the compassion and wisdom to ask the central question, "Whom does this serve?"

We have many role models already available of this kind of leader. The Dalai Lama, both the political and spiritual leader of the Tibetan people, exemplifies these qualities. Not only does he lead his own people, he attempts to help all beings in the world. Even in countries where religion and politics are separate, we have leaders such as Nelson Mandela who embody these qualities. Tom Peters devotes an entire chapter in *Liberation Management* to the quality of trust, which he calls "the missing X factor." Trust would be a non-issue if more leaders of our companies and countries embodied the spiritual qualities of which Hawley speaks.

I have noticed over many years that A managers hire A employees and B managers hire C employees. What I mean by this is that the best managers have high self-esteem and encourage others to develop their potential, whereas mediocre managers feel continually threatened by others who might take something from them. Managers and executives who are the most successful know that if their departments do well, it reflects on them. The success of their employees make them more, not less, promotable in their organization. Jack Welch—CEO of General Electric—said, "A company cannot distribute self-confidence. What it can do, what we must do is to give each of our people the opportunity to dream, risk and win, and hence earn self-confidence."

I believe that building people's self-confidence is the foundation for their learning to take risks, overcome fears, make better decisions and feel better about themselves and others. And how do we build self-confidence in others? We must trust them. John Goodman, managing partner of Sage Company, summed up this attitude by saying, "If employees are to become all that they can be, first you must trust them. When you assume that their best efforts will be made, you have bestowed respect. In turn, employees develop self-trust."

A company which exemplifies this principle of trust is Semco, an equipment manufacturing company in Brazil, run by Ricardo Semler. Virtually all the employees set their own hours and there is no organizational hierarchy to speak of. Some individuals with valuable skills even make more money than their bosses. Employees at Semco make most of the important corporate decisions, including finding new factory sites. More than 150 of the management people set their own salaries and supervisors are hired and evaluated by future subordinates. Semco provides classes in financial data so each employee can understand balance sheets and cash-flow statements in order to increase his own productivity. And it has. Semco is one of Brazil's fastest growing companies and was voted the best company for which to work in Brazil.

> *Don't hire extraordinary people; get ordinary people to do extraordinary work.*
>
> AUTHOR
> UNKNOWN

What Ricardo Semler demonstrated at Semco was that when leaders delegate authority to those who are doing the work, a remarkable thing happens—individuals rise to the responsibility and make excellent decisions. Because of the speed with which our technology and information is changing, no one can be an expert in every job. Therefore, the hierarchical organizational structure, where a few bright executives at the top tell all the less bright workers what to do, no longer works. Schumacher refers to this as a *moron shortage* in our world. By this he meant that because we all have access to education—where we are taught to think for ourselves—we desire to solve problems that concern us. Men and women who do the work often have better solutions to their problems than their managers who only hear about them. Employees must be given the authority to solve the problems that directly affect their jobs.

Research on productivity has proven repeatedly that people work harder when they are involved in solving their problems, rather than when they are told what to do by others. Authority, commensurate with responsibility, needs to be delegated so that people receive signing authority for the number of people, things and the amount of money they need in order to accomplish their tasks. This is empowering. By giving employees responsibilities that are greater than their authority, we sabotage their effectiveness. This is disempowering.

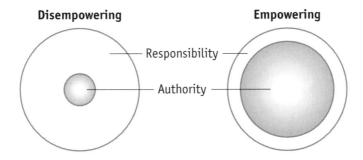

Rather than making employees fit into a set organizational pattern, soul-filled organizations—which function well in the fifth chakra—make the most of their employees' unique strengths and talents. Employees who are encouraged to work in their areas of excellence achieve more for their company and feel good about those who encouraged them. This is the way to create prosperous organizations.

However, the responsibility for empowerment does not rest solely on the shoulders of the company or manager. It is also the responsibility of employees. After identifying areas where we can make a positive difference, we need to step forward and make suggestions, not wait for our bosses to ask us. If we are not acknowledged or recognized, after repeatedly offering our talents to our employer, we might need to seek another job where our talents will be valued. Sometimes we outgrow our job and, rather than shrinking ourselves in order to keep it, we need to leave our job and have faith that the universe will find another place for us to continue our growth.

The Willing Pit Pony Syndrome

There are two things people want more than sex and money—recognition and praise.

Mary Kay Ash

In Welsh coal mines, before automation, pit ponies were used to haul out the coal. In working with the ponies, miners noticed that some were far more willing to work than others. In fact, some ponies worked willingly hour after hour, day after day, until they dropped dead; whereas other ponies resisted working and stayed in the barn eating the hay.

We must avoid the *willing pit pony syndrome* in our corporations by not asking willing workers to work through lunches, stay late or come in on weekends. Overworked employees burn out, have nervous or physical breakdowns and end up being replaced. It is the responsibility of employers to share the work equally among employees and not give in to the temptation to give more to the willing worker. Likewise, it is the responsibility of each employee to know her own limits and to be assertive in saying what she can, and cannot, realistically do.

New Criteria for Success

> *The primary purpose of an organization is not to make a profit. It is to help human beings grow, express their creativity, contribute their life-force and make the world a better place. Above all, the role of an organization is to be an efficient means of distributing knowledge, and improving human conditions and happiness.*
>
> LANCE SECRETAN

Traditionally, success in organizations has meant a substantial annual profit. Corporations interested only in accumulating money have seldom concerned themselves with either the short- or long-term effects of their products on the world. They have been solely interested in short-term financial gain, which often results in a long-term loss of human and environmental health. This adolescent approach of unlimited growth is unsustainable in the long term.

Irresponsible Growth

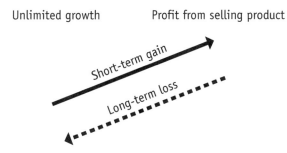

Unlimited growth   Profit from selling product

Short-term gain

Long-term loss

Cost to make product

Companies and individuals each have two kinds of bank accounts. The one we all recognize is determined by how much money we have. A second—and more important one—is a "karmic" bank account where we measure how much we give to and take from the world, everything from how much food, water, minerals and forest products we in the Western world consume to how much food we eat compared to individuals in other countries. Using this way of calculating our present situation, citizens in the Western world are extremely overdrawn and the time to start paying back has arrived.

Is it by accident that the United States, the greatest consumer of the world's resources, is also the greatest debtor nation? Or that its export of toxic wastes to Third World nations has now resulted in its own people eating food contaminated by chemicals now banned? Or that its increase in arms and military power against others has been equaled only by the increase in violence in its own streets and homes?

All countries, companies and individuals have what Carl Jung referred to as a "shadow" personality. These are the undesirable aspects of ourselves that we do not want to recognize, preferring instead to attribute these qualities to others. For example, we hotly condemn Brazil for destroying its rain forest, while we in Canada and the United States have destroyed far more. Peace and health can only occur if we acknowledge our shadow and clean up our own backyard. By doing this we change consciousness around the world.

Nelson Mandela's life and work is an uplifting testimony to the power of transforming the collective shadow of South Africa. Mandela, after being imprisoned for twenty-seven years for his resistance to apartheid, worked with those who had imprisoned him to create a new era of peaceful cooperation with all races. Mohandas Gandhi, Eleanor Roosevelt, Florence Nightingale, Albert Schweitzer and Tommy Douglas were—like Mandela—all great humanitarians and soul-infused personalities whose lives and work were dedicated to making a better world.

It is of paramount importance that organizations, like these individuals, make products and offer services to create a better world and not add to the addictions of sex, shopping, drugs, TV and food that imprison so many people. We need to develop criteria for responsible growth in organizations, such as, "Does the organization benefit the world in the long as well as the short term?" Companies should not go broke making sustainable products and, if this does happen, they have not mastered the laws of manifestation as they relate to the third and fifth chakras. Through knowing how to use these centers, we become masters of knowing how to make our products and services fit in the everyday world and we can do this without compromising our values. Through the fifth chakra we can know the best way to market and package our products to get the best results.

The Body Shop is an example of a new-style organization— a business founded on spiritual values—that set out to create goodness in three ways. First, its products include healthy ingredients designed to benefit others. Second, staff are allowed half a day a month of paid time to take part in a community project of their choice. Third, the Body Shop gives money directly to charities and helps underdeveloped countries in its Trade Not Aid program. Recently, the Body Shop has been criticized for not living up to its stated mission and it's commendable that the general public is calling it to account. The public is disappointed and want the Body Shop to do what they promised because the Body Shop's mission appeals to the heart. There are many more blatant offenders of the karmic bank account than the Body Shop, but they are not being judged by the same high standards. In future I hope they will be.

Responsible growth, based on a healthy use of fifth chakra energy, is a three-step process, as illustrated in the diagram below. The first step is to examine the cost both to the organization and to the environment of making the product. Second, the organization determines the profit it accrues from selling its product. This step takes into account the cost to the company's workers—physically, emotionally, mentally, spiritually and financially. Third, the organization determines the cost to the company and the world to recycle the unwanted castoffs of this product back into the environment. This three-step process may not be as profitable for the company in the short term, but in the long term it is more sustainable and soul-filled for the organization, their employees and the world.

Responsible Growth

Profit from selling product

Cost to organization, cost to environment of making product

Long-term gain

Cost to recycle products back into the environment

Today companies are experimenting with healthier and more comprehensive criteria to measure their *real* success. IBM, for example, measures its success using the criteria of four financial numbers (revenue growth, profit, return on assets, cash flow) and three new measures (customer satisfaction, quality, employee morale). On the global scene there are also signs of progress. The United Nations asks all member organizations to include their environmental policies, capitalization on environmental expenditures, environmental liabilities and disclosure of anticipated environmental expenditures in their annual reports.

Let's examine some of the new criteria for evaluating the "success" of our companies. As well as creating products and services that help the world, is our company directly benefitting the community? Do we employ local people? Does the construction of our products cause noise or pollution where they're produced? Do the services we offer ask people to compromise ethics? Do we send our toxic waste to the Third World or find ways to reduce and recycle it ourselves? These criteria are organic and circular, unlike the more linear process of determining financial success employed by most companies in the past, and are in keeping with the divine use of will in the fifth chakra.

Behaving Ethically

Brian Hall, in his book *The Genesis Effect*, says that as our values evolve, society evolves. He argues that our inner values act upon and transform our world and that an inner ethical vacuum creates a void in our outer life. Hall's words are in keeping with a Native American code to which I adhere: "Do what is good unto seven generations." This is the kind of ethical vision around which our organizations need to re-form.

By rewarding ethical people and penalizing unethical people, we build trust and commitment within our companies. I believe a time will come when companies who are not exhibiting ethical and/or environmentally sound practices with regard to their staff, customers and products, will cease to exist. Even if not for any moral reason, good business sense alone would dictate this. John Dalla Costa in his book *The Ethical Imperative* reported that "in 1997 alone, losses due to unethical behavior equaled more than the salaries of 12.5 million workers, or the profits of the top forty corporations in North America." In fact, there are now laws to punish companies such as Exxon—they paid a $5 billion fine for the *Valdez* oil spill. How many fines like that can even a massive company absorb?

Individuals, as well as governments, are being given the power to fight environmental offenses. Environmental protection acts—often referred to as "citizen suit laws"—give any person the right to sue for the protection of air, water, land and natural resources. The first such law was passed in Michigan in 1970 and many other American states now have them too. In 1988, the Canadian government enacted the Canadian Environmental Protection Act, which provides the right for two persons to request an investigation of suspected environmental offenses.

Still, rather than dwelling on punishing offenders, I prefer to observe how the universe is rewarding those who are ethically and spiritually responsible. Over the years, more individuals have become interested in investing money in areas that will benefit the world. The Social Investment Forum estimates that $500 billion is now being invested by American citizens in areas of ethical, social and environmental concern. VanCity, Canada's oldest high road financial investment institution, invests $5 billion each year in these areas and there are other funds such as the Environmental Equity Fund in Ontario that do the same.

Companies have realized that it's good business to give money to charities and projects that their consumers favor. *Cause marketing*, as this trend is called, has become one of the fastest growing ways in which corporations get consumers to choose their brands. *Time* reported in 1997 that companies poured $535 million into cause marketing—up $75 million from 1988. Examples of successful cause marketing include Avon's support of breast cancer research and Kraft General Foods' donation of 25 cents from sales of specially marked products towards scholarships for African-American college students. Some companies, such as Barnes and Noble bookstores, which promote literacy, have causes that are directly linked to their customers and products.

Whether we believe that these companies are sincere or not, we do know two things. Giving money to these causes helps their communities and the world and it increases the companies' profits. The *Time* article also reported that 66 percent of 1,981 consumers polled claimed they were likely to switch brands if the purchase supported a preferred cause; and 12 percent said that helping a cause was one of the *most important* factors in their purchasing decisions.

In daily life, whether at work or home, we are faced with continual temptations to satisfy either the immediate needs of the personality or the sometimes longer-range, more difficult, needs of the soul. Our work is a continual proving ground for our resolution and practice. Very often we are the only judge of the struggle that is going on within us as we decide to take the low or high road at work. There may be no observable penalties for taking the low road and no immediate rewards for taking the high road. Quite the opposite, we may attract unwanted attention for stepping outside the accepted rules and codes of our organization and colleagues. The fifth chakra is associated with clairaudience, which is hearing our conscience tell us what to do. It is also associated with the kind of creativity and clear thought that helps us find the information we need to support our case for taking the high road. The gift of the sixth chakra—intuition—contributes even more to this process.

Activating Intuition: The Soul's Tool

Life is painting a picture, not doing a sum.

OLIVER WENDELL HOLMES JR.

How the Mind Works

Intuition, imagination, vision and clairvoyance are the gifts of the sixth chakra. The speed of light, which the sixth center accesses, is faster than the speed of sound related to the fifth chakra. The masculine and feminine channels of energy come together in the sixth chakra and give intuition an androgynous quality. Whereas the throat center is more yang and masculine in nature, the sixth center—sometimes called the third eye—is thought at first glance to be more yin and feminine. Receptivity and surrender are necessary for intuition to work and these qualities have a softness characterized by the feminine. Still, for intuition to be employed as a reusable tool, clear focus and intention—qualities more characteristic of the masculine—are also important.

How does intuition work? Neuroscientist Karl Pibram said that the mind works like a hologram and that memory is stored "omnipresently" throughout the brain. He reached this conclusion by studying how the brain works in rats. When he removed a sample of brain tissue of rats, he found that memories of what they could do previously became fuzzier, but did not disappear. Along the same lines, physicist David Bohm has described a model which suggests that the universe itself might be a kind of hologram. He calls this *holoflux*, because the universe is continually in a state of flux and change. The brain is a part of the larger hologram of the universe and the two continually interpenetrate and reflect each other. At this time Pibram's and Bohm's ideas remain theory but they have shaken their respective fields and the entire area of consciousness.

Employing this holographic model, we can direct our mind to call up any image that we want and it will search through internal and external records to correlate information to give us the desired image. This image is called intuition or vision. Not being limited by time or space, our mind can move backward and forward in time, into the microcosm of the individual and the macrocosm of entire human history, to retrieve the data we seek. Intuition is not limited by factual data but can as easily use dreams, myth and metaphor to find the "right" answer. It works with information from the personal unconscious and the collective unconscious of humanity to do this.

> *Even when the experts all agree, they may well be mistaken.*
>
> BERTRAND RUSSELL

This process works best when we have no preconceived ideas that might eliminate relevant pieces of information. An example of this concerns recent discoveries about Egyptian mummification. Some time ago a French researcher, examining a mummy, discovered that tobacco had been used in the mummification. How could this be, when history asserts that tobacco did not exist in ancient Egypt but had been brought to Europe from the Americas around the time of Columbus? This researcher's colleagues accused her of contaminating research and denied her findings. Many years later a researcher in another country found the same thing with other mummies. Once again, most Egyptologists denied the new facts but some were prepared to check the findings and discovered them to be accurate. As there was no tobacco grown in ancient Egypt, this could mean that trade with the Americas existed some four thousand years ago.

By changing one "fact" in a system of knowledge, the entire system often changes. This is why researchers often discount and even deny new information. In fact, many Egyptologists to this day dispute this new information. It is quite frightening to live in a world where there is no certain knowledge, but this is the realm where intuition often dwells. By continually increasing our knowledge—both in factual, historic domains as well as in the unconscious arenas of dreams and myth—we make a larger library. Then, by using intuition to retrieve this information, our clairvoyance increases.

The Intuitive Personality

When asked the secret of his game, the great hockey player Wayne Gretzky answered, "I see where the puck will be and then skate to meet it." Gretzky is a high intuitive who is able to see the future and plan his strategy while other hockey players are still embroiled in where the puck is presently. The fact that Gretzky is outweighed by twenty to forty pounds by the competition does not render him ineffective in a very physical profession. His intuition, the function of the third eye chakra, gives him an advantage.

Carl Jung—himself a high intuitive and strong believer in listening to the voice of the soul—defined intuition as "a function that explores the unknown and senses possibilities and implications which may not be readily apparent." It is very hard to "prove" that either intuition or the soul exist, yet we observe the impact of them on our life every day. Intuition is a tool of the soul. It is a lens that can glimpse the soul's purpose and a way that the higher Self can communicate with the lower self to give it practical answers to problems we face. By developing intuition, we align ourselves to the soul and enlarge our capacity to bring it more fully into our day-to-day existence. Not only does this benefit us as whole people, but our organizations also benefit from our talent at solving their complex problems and making them more productive and marketable.

We are born with intuition and creativity and, like soul, these qualities are unique to each of us. Dr. Marylin Kourilsky, former dean at UCLA's Graduate School of Education, reports that 97 percent of kindergarten children are original thinkers, and only 3 percent form their thoughts in a structured conforming manner. By the time students graduate from high school, however, the balance has changed to 46 percent creative thinkers and 54 percent structured thinkers. By age thirty we have all but lost our individuality in thinking with only 3 percent still being original thinkers and 97 percent conforming to social correctness and orthodoxy.

Howard Gardner's research on creative intelligence concurs with Kourilsky's. He said that two qualities found in creative people are "ego strength and willingness to defy tradition." This means that people who have developed ego and will, located in the third and fifth centers respectively, might have a better chance of developing their sixth chakra. Gardner also stated that there is a "lack of a relationship between scores on creativity and on more conventional tests of intellectual strengths, at least above a certain level of IQ."

These findings indicate that our traditional educational process penalizes creative thinking. This has also been true of most organizations and is still true of some. True original thinking is rare, but it is the older sibling of intuition. I believe that as we deprogram ourselves from society's myths and values to determine our own inner truth, we free the latent creativity and intuition that we had as children. This is also the path to becoming a soul-infused personality, whereby we regain childlike wonder, trust and openness towards our world. Perhaps this is what Jesus meant when he said, "The little child shall lead them." He was not thinking of five-year-olds as CEOs, but of the transformed, soul-infused personality which is the wise child in each of us.

Initially, in the first stages of our transformation, we might employ intuition to satisfy such ego needs as making more money and manipulating others to do what we want. But once activated, intuition will not be easily shut off. We see more clearly what our actions do to others and we hear our conscience more acutely. We might choose to ignore these messages from the soul, but if we do so, we don't rest easily. The soul dangles intuition like a worm to tempt the personality, and when it's caught by the promise of a delicious meal, we are reeled in. The soul promises the personality success in its endeavors and it delivers on its promise.

Weston Agor, who conducted a study of intuition on five thousand managers, discovered that the higher their intuition, the greater their chances of success. Agor found that senior managers in the private sector had a mean average of 6.5 out of 10 points on the intuition scale, whereas middle and lower managers ranked at 5.8. The results were similar in the public sector, where managers at the national level ranked at 6.7, compared to 5.9 at the municipal level. Agor's study also indicated that individuals whose work was helping others to use their talents—such as in organizational development and personnel—are more intuitive than those who enforced standardized rules on others—such as those in finance, the military and engineering.

Elliott Jaques, a British consultant and writer, also discovered that people rise to the level of their vision. He refers to this as their ability to manage a larger time-span of abstract work. According to Jaques' findings, corporate CEOs working internationally envision and plan for ten to twenty years in the future. Presidents, senior VPs and general managers work with a time-span of between two and ten years. Individuals who control the specific operation and implement these plans work with a time-span of between three months to two years. Those who are told what to do by others work with a time-span of one day to three months.

But vision alone—according to Jaques—does not determine success in organizations. He learned that individuals with less vision often resent those with greater vision, especially if the person with greater vision is a subordinate. Why is that? Others recognize the power of intuition even if they don't know what to call it. I have found that people with high overall orende—regardless of their level of intuition—are generous to others. They foster the "cohesive" relationships of which I spoke earlier. If people are operating from a scarcity mentality—that you have to protect what you've got—they might block others from manifesting their potential. These blockers often have "repulsive" relationships with high energy people.

It takes great courage for visionaries to speak about what others do not see or know. As Schopenhauer wrote, "All truth goes through three steps: First, it's ridiculed. Second, it is violently opposed. Finally, it is accepted as self-evident." Yet, great spiritual, political and social visionaries have the ability to ground their intuition in the reality of the material world which is the ability to work with all chakras. We see this with Nelson Mandela, Gandhi, Mother Theresa and the medieval German abbotess Hildegard of Bingen, whose sage counsel was sought by Popes and political leaders. Reverend Martin Luther King Jr.'s "I have a dream" speech is one of the best examples of how one person's vision of a better future can inspire millions of people.

Techniques to Activate Intuition

I must Create a System or be enslav'd by another Man's.
I will not Reason and Compare; my business is to Create.

WILLIAM BLAKE

It's my imagination! I made it up! It's make-believe! Sound familiar? These are the phrases that we, or others, use to discount intuition. Although these phrases have a negative connotation, they are all true. The word "imagination" means that the mind creates an image and this is what intuition does. "Make-believe" means to make something from our beliefs and because our thoughts create form, this comment is true as well. When we get into the realm of the two higher chakras, the sixth and seventh, it becomes increasingly difficult to *prove* their legitimacy by using the data and facts that we find in the lower realms. I'm reminded of Hamlet's words to Horatio—a man who only believed the proof of his four senses, "There are more things in heaven and Earth, Horatio, than are dreamt of in your philosophy."

Scientists are finding proof of the mind's ability to perceive reality without the use of the four senses of sight, hearing, touch or taste. Experiments reported by Charles Honorton and many others have proven that meditation, hypnosis and dream states can increase ESP (extrasensory perception) or what in science is called PSI (supposed parapsychological faculties). Honorton and his colleague Daryl Bem of Cornell University used what they call "the ganzfield procedure," which is a "remote viewing" technique to simulate the effects of meditation. By placing the subject in an isolated room, everyday sensory "noise" is filtered out. It's this noise that prevents us from receiving weak PSI signals associated with meditation, hypnosis and dream states. In the experiment, the subject closed his eyes and in another room a computer screen showed images. The subject was then asked to describe the images and achieved an average hit rate of about 35 percent instead of the 25 percent hit rate expected by chance. The test subjects were average people and were not particularly selected for their intuitive faculties. The odds of these results occurring over so many experiments by chance are a billion to one and a person with this margin of success would get rich very quickly at a casino. Honorton also tested creative or artistically gifted people from the Juilliard School in New York City. Overall these students received a hit rate of 50 percent; musicians were particularly successful at 75 percent. From the results of these experiments, we learn that meditation, working with our dreams and developing our creativity through the arts are all techniques that increase our intuition and strengthen our sixth chakra.

The University of Nevada has a gaming institute where research was conducted to determine if people could increase their odds of winning at gambling by using thought alone—in other words, could the mind create reality? A machine was built to replicate the random odds of winning at slot machines. Subjects sat in front of this machine and asked it to give them as many chips as possible. The majority of subjects were unable to improve on the odds of chance but three people in fifty did significantly better. One very successful woman subject actually talked to the machine like a person and had developed a relationship with it.

In the ganzfield procedure, the subjects used their intuition more passively and at the University of Nevada more actively, to create the desired effect. I believe that a combination of these two techniques—one more yang and the other more yin—increases the effectiveness of intuition. The more individuals develop both masculine and feminine aspects, the greater their potential for intuition. Many of the methods we described for accessing our soul—solitude, walking in nature, meditation and prayer—work well for activating and expanding the more feminine aspects of intuition. Some people also have insights while driving their car and might want to carry a tape recorder to record their ideas. Still others have dreams that answer questions and solve their problems and they make it a practice to write them down on waking. A man I know has had many flashes of intuition while showering, so he's now placed a waterproof pen and pad in the shower to record his thoughts.

People need to find a process to listen to the soul that works for them. Here's a technique that I've found very effective in combining both the receptive yin and the active yang aspects of intuition. It was discussed in more detail in Chapter 7 under "Reprogramming Yourself for Success." Every morning in meditation, go to your favorite place, visualize what you will do that day and ask your higher self for assistance in doing it. During the day, recall your visualization and reinforce that image. Then at night—just before bed—meditate and review the day's events to discover what you have and what you have not done well. Forgive yourself and others for what has not gone well and visualize the situation corrected. By doing this, you will erase the negative memory of the past and reprogram a new, more positive, image in the present. Not only does this technique expand your intuition, it also strengthens your connection to your soul, so that you can see and hear what it would like you to do.

Intuition is a very effective problem-solving tool, but preferences on how to use it vary. Here are some more yang, intentional approaches to intuition. We might, for instance, determine our past patterns for success and repeat these. Some people find it helpful to immerse themselves totally in an issue to look for patterns where none seem to exist. Others like to identify pros and cons in a situation and then, using their intuition, assess their feelings about each option. Another technique that works is to discuss the problem with friends and colleagues with different perspectives. One might also try playing freely with ideas without a specific goal in mind, or grab one part of a problem and run with it to see where it leads.

To be successful in any of these options, it is usually preferable to consider a difficult problem when you are most alert and can have a "creative pause"—a time of doing nothing to let the universe shuffle things into order—before reaching a decision. Don't count on instant success. Intuitives accept ambiguity and lack of control, and practice flexibility and staying open to unknown possibilities. If you trust your own internal cues, have the courage to face the unknown and see the world as it is and not as you wish it to be, you cultivate what the Japanese call *sunao*, "the untrapped mind." Intuition comes from the space *between* what is said, not from what is said. It arises when you are following, not resisting, your life purpose. We cannot make intuition happen; it is a gift from the higher self. If you maintain a good sense of humor, don't press too hard for an answer and retain childlike wonder, intuition will flourish.

Fostering Intuition in Your Organization

Intuition, as Joel Barker says in his video *The Power of Vision*, is "the ability to make good decisions with little information." Developing intuition and the sixth chakra is essential for two reasons. First, we don't have time in this present age to wade through facts and figures to make sure we are making the right decision. Second, the problems we face in our world can only be solved through creative and original thinking. With this idea in mind, let's look at ways to nurture creativity and intuition in the workplace.

Are you encouraged to suggest improvements to your supervisor and colleagues without fear of reprisal and with reward for your contributions? If so, your organization engenders trust and empowerment that, in turn, foster innovative and soulful contributions to the business.

Intuition and creativity flourish where they are valued, so we must attempt to create an atmosphere at work that values intuition and soulful practice. Some of this may be outside your control if you are not self-employed and work in a very traditional company, but you may be able to implement some ideas. For example, have a "closed-door policy" for an hour every day to give employees the space and time to think about difficult problems—their AI priorities. This needn't be the same time for everyone, and could be arranged beforehand so that the phones are answered and customers are served. Another idea is to write a problem you are trying to solve on a white board placed in a central location to encourage suggestions from fellow employees. Be a positive listener and learn to suspend critical judgment during idea generation. There will be a time for it later. It's important not to confuse a poor presentation of an idea with the idea itself. An employee could have wonderful intuition but be lacking in presentation skills.

> *Without this playing with fantasy no creative work has ever yet come to birth. The debt we owe to the play of the imagination is incalculable.*
>
> CARL JUNG

A conducive physical environment is also important. If possible, decorate the office attractively with nice colors, plants and pictures and—while still being professional—dress comfortably. Dress is not just cosmetic, it sets a tone for either rigid or creative thinking. Some years back, I was waiting for a plane when the current prime minister of Canada disembarked with eight of his assistants, all of whom were dressed identically in blue pinstriped suits, white shirts and blue ties. My immediate thought was, "How are these people going to solve Canada's problems when they're carbon copies of each other?"

Having enough sleep and not being overworked is also important in fostering intuition and in developing the use of the sixth chakra. Exhausted people cannot think new thoughts, so assess the appropriate amount of work that you can do and create a space daily to allow new ideas to come in. Leonardo da Vinci, arguably the most creative person who ever lived, recommended this same action. "Every now and then go away, even briefly, have a little relaxation, for when you come back to work your judgment will be surer, since to remain constantly at work will cause you to lose power." In writing and editing this book I worked unusually long days, but I made sure I devoted one to two hours to walking in the woods. During that time the material I was working on sorted itself out into more usable categories and forms. In walking, I grounded my intuition in concrete, practical reality so that when I returned to the computer, I was able to write more coherently.

Our physical and emotional environment either fosters or hampers the use of intuition. If we are fearful, angry, tired, confused, sick or discount our own feelings to accommodate the feelings of others, we won't be able to fully use intuition. If we are rushed to make a decision, fail to get the necessary background facts or act impulsively, we do not create enough space for our intuition to rise. Also, if our ego is attached to an outcome—such as wanting to get a specific job, marrying a certain person or landing a desired business deal—we might not have the necessary detachment to use our intuition accurately. For intuition to work during information-gathering, we must be able to go into neutral when searching for ideas and detach ourselves from the outcome.

To develop quality of vision, companies might consider organizing annual staff retreats that focus on self-examination and restoring physical, emotional, mental and spiritual balance. We give our cars spring tune-ups to increase their efficiency, reliability and longevity—so why not offer our employees tune-ups as well? This is not the same thing as organizing strategic planning sessions or aligning employees to the organizational vision, although these are two qualities in which the sixth chakra excels. What I'm suggesting is a chance for individuals to realign their individual vision to the company vision. Employees who feel that the organization is interested in their personal lives, and not just for what they can do for the company, are much more willing to go that extra mile for their employer. My colleagues and I have noticed an increase in the number of organizations who are committed to helping their employees to develop themselves. Visionary companies are creating time and space to let go of the old so that new visions can emerge for themselves and their employees.

The Third Option

> *It was the best of times, it was the worst of times, it was the age of wisdom, it was the age of foolishness, it was the epoch of incredulity, it was the season of Light, it was the season of Darkness, it was the spring of hope, it was the winter of despair, we had everything before us, we had nothing before us.*
>
> A TALE OF TWO CITIES, CHARLES DICKENS

Our Western culture has taught us to think in terms of two options: either/or, black and white, right and wrong. Using this way of thinking we have either friends or enemies; one is either a good or bad employee; we are either winners or losers. Such simplistic thinking has led us to the brink of disaster in our world. Life is not this simple. If we are to solve the problems facing us—while living a balanced work and personal life—we need to practice *both/and* ways of thinking. This is what I call "the third option."

Both/and thinking is integrated whole-brain thinking and it is a function of the sixth chakra. It means finding the balance between facts and intuition, between quantity and quality, between serving the personality and serving the soul. Making the leap to both/and thinking is a quantum leap; love of knowledge is replaced by love of wisdom. Once you have discovered both/and thinking, it is not more difficult to practice—it's easier.

To practice both/and thinking we need to examine areas where we commonly use either/or. Here is an example of either/or thinking: "If I give my employees what they want—fewer hours, more pay—my company won't make a profit." Both/and thinking rephrases this thought into a question. "How can I help my employees feel financially secure and healthy, while still being a profitable company?" Either/or thinking tends to divide the employees and employer into two camps—much as unions and management have done. When this happens, both camps want to get the most for themselves because they think there won't be enough for both. This thought is representative of scarcity mentality. Both/and thinking does not divide people into camps of winners and losers, but looks at the interests that all the people have in common. Examining these interests unfreezes people from the polarization that accompanies positional thinking.

In the example of the company and employees who appear to want different things, using both/and thinking might result in the company hiring more people so that the present employees don't have to work so many hours and burn out. Granted, employees might make less money in the short term, but they gain time to do what they want. The company's advantage is not paying for people who are absent or on sick leave because of burnout, so the company's money goes directly to people doing work.

If the company then makes a better profit—and it should with this strategy—it could return this money to the employees in the form of bonuses, training or shared profits. In this way, both parties benefit.

In employing both/and thinking, a company seeks to satisfy the needs of both its employees and customers. The company works cooperatively with its competitors so that they both succeed in their areas of expertise. With both/and thinking employees attempt to be productive at work while leading a balanced life outside work. They seek to create a healthy workplace and financial prosperity both in the short and long term. By using both/and thinking, employees meet the needs of both their soul and personality, as well as the needs of their organization. This kind of thinking is necessary for a healthy future.

Balancing Chronos and Kairos Time

There is more to life than increasing your speed.

MOHANDAS GANDHI

The sixth chakra alters our perception of time and space and allows us to access information in many dimensions. There are two kinds of time—*chronos* and *kairos*. Chronos is clock time—doing time—and by utilizing it we can create in the material world. If we don't have a good grip on chronos time, we miss planes, are late for appointments and generally make a nuisance of ourselves. Kairos time—being time—is that of the eternal moment when we enter into a rhythm with the divine life force. It cannot be contained by our physical sense of reality and often expands or diminishes when it enters chronos time. Intuition lives in kairos time and this is why it's sometimes difficult for people to know exactly when the intuitive vision they see will take place in physical reality. Psychics and mediums, for example, are often highly accurate at predicting events but get the time wrong.

Today, many people complain that there is too much to do and not enough time to do it. They feel that the amount of time that they are working is out of balance with the priorities—spouse, children, hobbies, alone time—in the rest of their lives. A 1995 study by The Families and Work Institute reported a "time famine," and said the greatest family worry of women in the United States is not having enough time with their families. Reinforcing this message, author Michael Ventura wrote an article entitled "The Family Interrupted" in *The Family Therapy Networker*, where he reported that the average working couple, because of all their other commitments, spends only twenty minutes a day together.

> *Everything depends on the quality of our acts and experiences. A multitude of badly performed actions and of experiences only half-lived exhausts and depletes our being. By doing things badly we make ourselves less real.*
>
> THOMAS MERTON

Why is there a shortage of time, and why does time appear to be speeding up? Individuals living in "developed" countries value quantity over quality in most areas of life. For example, more money is better than less, more friends better than less and more education preferable to less. However, sacrificing quality for quantity of experience puts us squarely in chronos time and results in the feeling that there is not enough time, or that time has accelerated. Focusing on quantity creates a feeling of meaninglessness in life because our experiences lack depth. But it's more than that. Overwork is actually killing us. In Japan, they have a word—*karoshi*—which describes work addiction that kills, and it is estimated that ten thousand Japanese die from this every year. I wonder how many North Americans suffer from the same disease in its obviously fatal or more subtle forms?

Taking your soul to work entails re-establishing the balance between quality and quantity, between kairos and chronos time, and between being and doing. This often means reducing the quantity of work that we do. We must be ruthless in determining what is important and say "no" to distractions, low-priority items and quantity of experiences that keep us from states of peace that are found in a more leisurely life. This could be taking only one trip to the grocery store instead of four, meaning we'll have to plan better for what we'll be needing for the entire week. It could be restricting our use of television because its hypnotic, mind-numbing vibration can rob us of energy and consciousness. At work, it could mean doing top-priority items that have the greatest chances of positively impacting our world, such as market plans, product development, following up with clients, rather than doing the easy things that make little difference to achieving important goals, such as paying our bills daily, continually tidying the office or redoing the filing system. Yes, of course, these things are necessary, but they must be offset by the amount of time we spend in doing high-priority items.

By adopting these measures, we develop the sixth chakra and learn to work in "magical time," where both chronos and kairos meet and extend both the quantity and quality of time. This might seem unlikely, but all of us have had experiences where time seemed to stop and we were able to accomplish an apparently impossible amount of work. McLaughlin and Davidson, authors of *Spiritual Politics*, say:

> As we move towards soul consciousness, our vibration speeds up, energy is released and time is experienced differently. We become more detached from events and begin to see "the big picture." As we think more clearly and make better decisions, more is accomplished in less time. We work *with* time rather than *against* time, being flexible in adapting to changing circumstances and waiting for the right time to make a decision. When in a higher state of consciousness our timing is perfect. We begin to recognize how the flow of all events is coordinated from a higher level by the one Soul of all.

Working with the Space/Time Continuum

We might easily wonder how intuition actually works. The sixth chakra is open to all times—past, present and future. By employing intuition through meditation, we can travel in time to see past events, or future ones that have not yet happened in physical reality. Physicist Jack Saratti suggests that the universe is composed of "quantum foam," which consists of mini "wormholes," approximately 10^{-33} cm in diameter. These wormholes are beyond space and time and connect every point in space to every other point in space. Saratti's findings, like those of Bohm and Pibram, indicate that we can access any information we wish; we are only limited by our skill in using focused intuition.

Intuitive individuals perceive the energy fields that are creating the forms that will eventually manifest in physical reality. Hindus call these fields the Akashic records and locate them in the ethers, where everything that has happened in all times and space is recorded. Intuitives, by focusing their attention, can call up the appropriate record and interpret the information it contains.

The soul, dwelling more fully in the seventh chakra, lives in space outside of chronos time. It sees the past, present and future *simultaneously*. Descending into the sixth chakra and working with the personality, the soul can choose to move forward or backward in time and space. It is only the personality—anchored in chronos time as it is—that sees time as linear, with the past behind and the future ahead. In order to effectively work with both the soul and personality, we need to combine the space (soul) dimension with the time (personality) dimension of the material world. The more open we are in both our seventh and sixth chakras, the more we can move in both space and time.

The Romans had a revered place for sacred space, which they called a "focus"—the Latin name for hearth. They created sacred spaces in their homes where people would gather to discuss philosophy and life meaning. We need to create both an interior and exterior sacred space for ourselves. We need to take time daily to center ourselves and return to this balanced point within. Living in sacred space and time was a part of us in our youth and it can be reclaimed. Poet Sven Birkets describes this magical time:

> Back then it was not one thing or another, just a way things had of happening natural and unquestioned. I was full to the brim, with nothing lacking; space and time were not yet separate concepts at all. "Weren't you ever bored?" Dear God, I was in ecstasy of boredom! I was so bored that time would back up on itself and start flowing in a new direction.

What Birkets is describing are "peak experiences." Maslow says that "in all the common peak-experiences which [he has] studied, there is a very characteristic disorientation in time and space." Soul-infused people have more peak experiences of heightened creativity, love, insight and awe and during these experiences time either speeds up or slows down.

I have found the symbol of the Celtic cross very helpful in ascertaining how best to live in this magical space and time. The Celtic cross has two axes; the horizontal axis represents time, the vertical axis represents space and a circle of energy is created in the center where time and space meet. By focusing our attention within this magical circle, we will be amazingly productive with little effort and accomplish much more in a shorter amount of time. If we anchor ourselves in the material world, we are focusing only on the horizontal time axis. This limitation of existence provides several results. First, we will repeat what we are doing with few new thoughts; there is little growth in our lives and work. Second, as we get older, time runs faster on this axis, so we have less time to accomplish what we want.

The vertical axis of the Celtic cross represents space. Unlimited possibilities and potential exist in the higher realms of space. As we develop our spiritual abilities, we have increasing access to these realms and are able to bring those possibilities into our physical world.

The Magical Circle

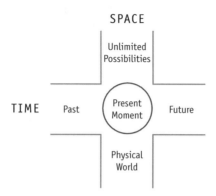

SPACE

Unlimited
Possibilities

TIME   Past   Present
Moment   Future

Physical
World

There is a technique you might practice to work within the magical circle. First, through the visualization exercise I outlined in Chapter 6, send out a clear message to the universe about what you want to do/be/have. Then, let go of your attachment to the end result of whether you will reach your goal or not. This will ensure that you move into the magical circle. Next, meditate to determine what you need to do to assist the universe. Finally, wait for the universe to create the opportunity and, when it does, act without hesitation. What I'm suggesting may appear contradictory, but it moves you into the magical circle where both your will and divine will meet. In this place, state what you want while accepting whatever the universe gives to you. This is how you can become a conscious creator.

Living within the present moment where space and time meet means living in the flow. This method of time management is effortless. We enjoy the quality of the moment knowing that there will be enough time to do everything of importance, and we create a space for the universe to surprise us with magic. When we live only in the physical world, we are so full of doing that we have no space left for magic. By living and working in the magical circle, we do and be simultaneously. We do not push against closed doors but wait for the doors to open of their own accord and if they don't, we move on to another door that interests us.

By living in the present moment, you'll find time for meaningful work, visiting friends, reading, walking in nature and sleeping. There's also enough time to do absolutely nothing, which creates the magical space for new ideas to enter and start moving down the pipeline into manifestation. Living within the magical circle allows us to practice what the Buddhists call "the journey without the goal." Although we have goals for the future, our attention is focused on what we can do/be in the present moment. By acting in the present, we encourage our goals to manifest in the future.

There is a poem called *The Station*—attributed to Robert J. Hastings—which summarizes the importance of living in the present. It was sent to me years ago by a participant in one of my seminars. Despite the fact that I've been unable, after much effort, to confirm the title or author, I'd like to share it with you:

Tucked away in our subconscious is an idyllic vision.
We see ourselves on a long trip that spans the continent...
But uppermost in our minds is the final destination...
Sooner or later we must realize there is no station,
No one place to arrive at once and for all.
The true joy of life is the trip.

Trusting Synchronicity and "the Force"

The universe gives us many hints about the direction it wants us to walk, but we have the choice to follow these nudges or not. If something happens to us once it may be an accident, but if a pattern emerges more than once, we are involved in it in some way. The puzzle is to discover what the lesson is and what we are being asked to learn.

We see this happening to Luke Skywalker in the movie *Star Wars*. Luke has been training to recognize what his teacher Obi-

Wan Kenobi calls "the force." The force is the universal life energy that is in and around all of us and which we can use to manifest our desires. In order to survive, Luke is required to let go of his training as a fighter pilot and allow the force to guide him. *Star Wars* has remained one of the biggest box office attractions in movie history because its story is mythic and meaningful for all of our lives. To master the material world, we must learn to surrender to the force—which, from the personality's point of view, looks like a quick path to self-destruction.

Over the years I have come more and more to trust synchronicity and have created a kind of "soul rule." If something is mentioned to me more than once I pay attention and take any action that's needed. A few years ago three different people, over the space of several months, mentioned a man they thought I should meet. He was a senior executive in a large traditional resource-based company. Following my soul rule, I called him up and told him that three people had suggested we might have something to discuss. He commented that he also had heard my name mentioned. This strengthened my feeling of synchronicity. With no other information, he invited me to meet him at his company's head office.

Dressing the part of a corporate consultant, I arrived for the meeting and was greeted politely by a man fitting the image of a corporate executive. He invited me to sit and asked me why I had thought we should meet. I immediately launched into describing my work in creating healthy organizations, thinking this must be what the universe wanted. Although slightly interested, I could tell he was largely unmoved. It was as if only our personalities, rather than our souls, were communicating. In one of those moments we've all had, when we leap into the abyss, I opened my mouth and said, "I'm a closet mystic." These words emerged from me without thought. It was as if the essence of who I was spoke to him with absolutely no attachment to outcome.

Immediately, he leaned forward, looking at me quite differently, and said, "Now, I'm interested." By both of us being willing to throw our personality roles aside and trust ourselves and each other, our relationship had moved immediately to a much deeper soul level. Sitting there in his corporate office, we closed our eyes and proceeded to meditate together to discover what we were supposed to do. After some time, we returned to a conscious awake state and compared our experiences. We both had received similar guidance—that we were to do nothing at that point but get to know each other and that, at a later time, we would discover what to do.

Every few months we talked by phone and occasionally met for coffee. One day he asked me to come to his office as he had something to tell me. His company had just decided to embark on policies that sounded like just the kind of thing I had originally discussed with him. The time for us to work together had arrived. By waiting without attachment to results, both of us had allowed the universe to align our vision in the physical world. I have been working with that company for three years now.

Can you think of synchronicities in your life that pointed you in the right direction? Do you remember times when "the force" was with you in your work and you found yourself doing something which your personality thought was either crazy or misguided? When we work with, and not against, the universal plan, doors open that never would otherwise—or perhaps with only a great deal of effort.

Working with the universal plan is a function of the crown chakra, not a center of doing, but being. This seventh chakra uses the other chakras as tools to manifest in the world. Even the intuition and clairvoyance of the sixth chakra are tools. Moving to the crown chakra we expand beyond our individual personality and even our soul and glimpse a conscious universal mind connected to all living beings.

Living in Harmony with Natural Cycles

The way through the world is more difficult to find than the way beyond it.

WALLACE STEVENS

Merging with the Soul

The nature of consciousness is both to manifest and liberate—to create form and to help form return to pure consciousness. The crown chakra, the pinnacle of the seven chakras, is a center of knowing. Its function is being, not doing. From here our consciousness can descend into form or ascend into formless transcendence. We can learn to control and use the lower six chakras to make something occur in the world of form. In the lower chakras we learn to work within constraints and boundaries. The seventh chakra is different. We do not just act; we are acted upon as we merge and flow with the divine energies of the universe. No longer is there a separation. The yin energies of the Earth and the yang energies of the Soul blend to create a child: the soul-infused personality.

Have you ever noticed the innocence and childlike quality that many spiritual people, such as the Dalai Lama and Mother Theresa, have? These conscious beings experience so much joy in every moment that their joy is contagious. They have, or perhaps are, clear awareness that lives in communion with the divine. Consciousness is a *force* inside us, around us and through us. It is not something we try to attain, but something that exists and, by opening to it, we recognize that it has been there all along.

The crown chakra is the central point on the wheel of life, where the world of the individual and the world of all humans and the universe meet. To access this place, we must move our attention to the very center of the magical circle I talked about earlier—the hub of the wheel that turns to create the cycles in which we live. There *are* higher chakras than the seventh and our transformation and evolution does not end with the opening of the crown chakra. But we started our journey by discussing the experience of unity with the Earth found in the root chakra. Now with the seventh chakra, we again feel unity—and this time with all creation.

Hundreds of years ago, Plotinus said that the soul moves in circles and if we examine our lives, we can see that this is still true today. We tend not to progress by moving straight ahead from point A to point B. Instead we fall off track, relearn lessons, get back on track, move with the flow, fall off the path and get back on again. By the time we enter middle age, we begin to see patterns emerging in our life and realize that many of these patterns are spirals. A spiral is created by putting a line and a circle together. We exist in time; we are born, age and die. This is the time line. But *learning* occurs more like a circle. Learning does not take place once but over a series of episodes during which we circle back to repeat cycles of learning. Like peeling the layers of an onion, as we circle and recircle we come to understand and learn about ourselves at deeper and deeper levels.

A. Bartlett Giamatti, lawyer, president of Yale and baseball commissioner, writes beautifully of how baseball—with its patterns and cycles—helped to frame his life. Writing about his fortieth year, he says:

> There comes a time when every summer will have something of autumn about it. Whatever the reason, it seemed to me that I was investing more and more in baseball, making the game do more of the work that keeps time fat and slow and lazy. I was counting on the game's deep patterns, three strikes, three outs, three times three innings, and its deepest impulse, to go out and back, to leave and to return home, to set the order of the day and to organize the daylight.

Although Giamatti is describing what happened to him in midlife, in essence he's describing the soul's way of using time to create patterns and rituals for our life. By living and consciously working with these rhythms we live in the being state of the seventh chakra.

The Four Seasons

> *To everything there is a season, and a time to every purpose under the heaven.*
>
> ECCLESIASTES, 3:1

To live with soul, it is important to live and work in accordance with the cycles in nature. By doing so, we move with—rather than against—the natural flow of life energy. There are many cycles in nature that affect us, including the annual solar cycle of the four seasons, the monthly lunar cycle, and the daily cycle of light and dark. These are the obvious cycles but there are less obvious ones too, such as the movement of the stars, that also affect us. By observing nature's cycles and our own inner rhythms, we can work far more productively and healthily in accordance with our seventh chakra.

Cycle of the Seasons

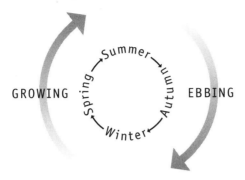

Spring is the season of new growth, the time when the Earth gives us abundant energy to break new ground. This is a pioneering energy that can be used at work to sweep away resistance, just like a seed breaks through the hard-packed winter soil to create a new plant. Spring is a good time to birth new ideas, start projects or try things we've never done before.

Summer is the season of fertility. It takes a lot of energy in the spring to start something new and summer uses this momentum to continue what we started. Summer is a time of productivity and abundance, when the crops grow and the flowers bloom. Nature is able to accomplish a great deal in a little time during the summer season. For us, summer is also a time of success and accomplishment when doors open easily in our work. It is the season with which our organizations feel the most comfortable, as it fits the prevailing traditional North American mind-set. Organizations prefer the abundance of money and products and customer appreciation that comes during its summer season. It also prefers employees who are in the summer of their cycle and are able to accomplish a great deal with ease. We are speaking here not about the actual summer season, as many employees take vacation at that time and businesses slow down, but of a summer cycle of a person or a business that could go on for many years.

Autumn is the season of reaping in wheat and leaving behind the chaff. It is a time to re-assess and celebrate what we have accomplished and to eliminate what is no longer working. It is a time to finish projects and decide what work or which clients to keep, reduce or eliminate because they are not in keeping with our goals. We are still productive in autumn, but work tends to slow down in preparation for winter.

Winter is the season of rest and a time to cocoon and let go of everything that is not in keeping with what your soul wants you to do now. Often, winter calls us to leap empty-handed into the void, with only faith and trust that something new will come. This can be a time of leaving jobs or of working the minimum number of hours necessary in our existing job. It is not laziness, but a time of self-reflection and just being.

Individuals and organizations often find winter the most dif-ficult season because our society, as a whole, does not value emptiness, silence or reflection. We don't want to let go of what we've got until we have something else to replace it. However, without winter there is no fallow time to allow the deeper urges of our unconscious to surface, which is necessary for the activa-tion of the creative process. We need winter if we are to give rise to a fully formed seed in the spring. If we are so full of doing that we have no time for being, new ideas cannot enter our lives. This can leave us feeling hollow and depressed. Winter allows the time for deep rest and it is in our long-term best interest to flow with it, rather than fight against it.

Monthly Cycles

The Jewish religion uses a lunar, not a solar, calendar to teach the full cycle of birth to death, which we experience in the course of each year. Just as the ebb and flow of the tides are affected by the moon, so our blood and the fluids of our bodies are affected. Being aware of monthly cycles and working with the lunar energy helps us to flow with this energy. The new moon carries spring en-ergy; the full moon represents summer; the waning moon is like autumn; and the dark of the moon is like winter.

Using these cycles to plan our monthly work can improve our productivity. For example, I find that the bulk of my creative work happens from new to full moon and then I do more routine work during the waning moon. A writer friend of mine works in accordance with lunar energy, but his process is a bit different. He creates his original work from the first quarter to the third quarter of the moon and edits during the other two phases. There are many ways to work with the natural cycles and, sometimes without even being aware of it, many of us develop a preferred way of doing this. What is important is to recognize how much these cycles can affect us and to use them to enhance both our creativity and the ease with which we do our work.

Daily Cycles

Within each thirty-day period of the lunar cycle we experience a microcosm of the 365 days of the year, and within each twenty-four hours in the daily cycle we experience an even smaller version of the same principle. In the daily cycle, morning is like spring, afternoon is summer, evening is autumn and night is winter. Using this cycle, we do our new, or difficult, work in the morning and early afternoon when our energy is rising. We do our routine work in the later afternoon when our energy is plateauing. As evening arrives, we need time to reflect on the day's events, to integrate learnings and let go of outdated or limiting feelings or ideas. Our nights—the winter of the day—are for sleeping, to give our subconscious time to process the day's events and our body time to re-energize for the next day.

Some people say that they do their most creative work at night. There may be several reasons for this. Perhaps the rest of their day is so cluttered with other people's priorities and business that they have no empty space to think a new thought for themselves. Or maybe they live in a highly populated area where the ethers are so crowded with activity during the day that they can only intuitively access the information they need in the hours between ten p.m. and eight a.m. when most people are asleep. Yogis believe that spiritual energy is highest when the sun rises and sets because it is at that time that the Earth and cosmic energies are in balance. Many yogis meditate at those times to maximize the effect of their meditation and we might want to follow their example. As we work with the natural cycles of both nature and our inner life, we enter a deeper harmony with the universal life force of the seventh chakra.

Examining Your Life Patterns

The greatest revelation of my generation is the discovery that by changing the inner attitudes of your mind, you can change the outer aspects of your life.

WILLIAM JAMES

Our individual lives have their own unique cyclical patterns with recurring themes that, if understood, shed light on our process of learning and on how our sixth and seventh chakras function. Our minds create energy fields, or thoughtforms, composed of wave patterns that repeat in certain predictable patterns (scientists call them fractals). If something happens to us once, we might think it's an accident, but when there is a recurrent pattern it is important to realize that we are responsible. These patterns are life themes, many of which we have in common with others. Some examples are: "I always do things for others and no one does anything for me" or "I'm excited when I start projects but I get bored easily and have a tendency not to finish what I start" or "I'm misunderstood. No one sees how brilliant, noble, perfect, etc., I am."

When we examine our life patterns, we often find both positive and self-sabotaging thoughts existing side by side. The positive message is what gives us the energy, focus and right motivation to accomplish our goals, but often we sabotage our effectiveness by restricting our success or not persisting. It is crucial that we examine our patterns to see what is working, what is not and then consciously create another pattern to move in harmony with the natural cycles of the universe so we can fully manifest our gifts. Opening to the soul's guidance through the crown chakra will help us to do that, if we are prepared to follow its advice even when it is not easy.

Bill is an idealist who has experienced great difficulty in creating a positive life pattern with regards to money. He publishes magazines to help the world and is well liked by all. There's only one problem—he continually struggles financially. He spent many years in a monastery in his younger years and seriously considered becoming a monk. During his time in the monastery, he was taught the "evils" of money. After leaving the monastery, Bill became the personal assistant of a powerful spiritual teacher while maintaining his own spiritual practice. For many years, he dedicated his life to this man's teachings and was barely paid for his service. He never thought to ask for more because that would not have been spiritual. Years later, Bill married and was raising a family when he felt a call to start publishing magazines devoted to creating good in the world. He has done this for over a decade now and has struggled with a lack of money the entire time. Bill realizes that he is blocking himself from financial prosperity, but appears to be unable to release his previous thought patterns. As long as he maintains his old thoughts about money, he is reinforcing the mental thoughtform and energy field.

Bill's situation is not unique. But to become fully conscious, we must transcend old programmings and break both conscious and unconscious patterns. It is most important that we become conscious of the way we think and talk to ourselves in order to change the root thought, thereby changing the entire energy field. This goes beyond thought. We must actually *believe* that we can change the pattern. We must have total faith and trust in the process because doubt sabotages reprogramming. Trust and faith are both qualities we learn from the crown chakra.

Wanya is a woman who took an unusual path to eliminating past programs. She is a Reiki master, which is a form of healing working with spiritual energy. Wanya, like Bill, is a very spiritual being and motivated to serve in the world. In fact, her entire life has been service and others see her as kind and considerate. One of Wanya's Swedish students was staying with her when I went over for a visit. This student was attempting to meet all of Wanya's needs and perhaps was a little over-zealous in the process. Dinner time came and the student could be heard in the kitchen starting the food preparation. "Don't make the dinner!" yelled Wanya, "Tanis is cooking for me, tonight." I could tell from the long silence that the student had taken Wanya's words as rejection.

"Wanya," I said quietly so as not to be overheard, "It's unlike you to be so firm with someone." She leaned closer and smiled at me confidentially, "I've done all my bad karma. Now I'm working on the good." She was totally conscious of what she was doing. Acting to break her previous kind and loving thought-form helped Wanya to avoid programming herself to be good or pleasant always. She was also helping her student to break *her* thoughtform of dependence and seeking approval. Wanya knew that the journey to consciousness is not always pleasant. Teaching tyrants are sometimes loving but at other times might be perceived as cold and firm as they help others break negative patterns. This is transcendent love, the kind that knows the soul of the other person and acts in the best way to help that soul grow.

Working with the Flow

Working with the flow means working in tune with our own biorhythms, the rhythms of others who affect us and the universe as a whole. By doing this, we allow energy from our seventh chakra to move down into the others in order to work with being and doing time simultaneously. Using this system of time management, we call clients when the time "feels right" and we start projects, continue them and complete them using the same sensitivity.

As we all know, there is a great deal of energy needed to start something new. It's harder to write the first fifty pages of a book than the last fifty, because a momentum is created and the book starts writing itself. I agree with Aristotle, who said, "We are what we repeatedly do. Excellence is not an act; but a habit." If we repeatedly practice something we improve and become consistently excellent. We increase the magical circle of space and time and spend more time working with the flow and are able to accomplish far more with less effort.

Finding the optimum conditions for creation in the workplace is not always easy, but this is what we must try to do. Is your work environment conducive to creativity and happiness? Some of us prefer four-day work weeks; others need to have an office window; still others are more productive if they walk outside during lunch hour. It's time for organizations to start paying people for what they produce, and not for how many hours they sit at their desks. If someone can accomplish the same result in half the time, they should be rewarded for their productivity. Moreover, they should be able to choose their rewards. Some might want money; others might prefer time off; still others might prefer to work at home. Working from nine to five, five days a week, is a leftover concept from the industrial age and it is not the best work cycle for some people.

Being attuned to what the universe wants and working with the flow has led me into some fascinating circumstances. Many years ago I was invited to conduct a sacred ceremony at the ancient serpent mounds in Peterborough, Ontario, with a Native man named John, whom I had never met and knew nothing about. I had a sense that I should just accept and did so. The day arrived and many people gathered for the ceremony. An older Native man, dressed casually but who carried himself with confidence and power, approached me and introduced himself as John. I offered my name and, without further pleasantries, we immediately launched into our joint purpose—creating a ritual that merged the male and female energies of the serpent mound, so that all could participate. Even though John and I had never met, there was a comfort and trust in the way we worked together that allowed both of us to move forward or back as was necessary, to balance the yin and yang currents.

After the ceremony, John generously invited the group back to his home on Rice Lake for a salmon barbecue. It was very relaxing and we were sitting enjoying the day when it occurred to me that John's manner was not only that of a spiritual guide but also of a business leader. "John," I asked with curiosity, "What do you do when you're not leading rituals at the serpent mound?"

He smiled at me, with a mischievous glance that acknowledged that I'd looked through one of his personas to see another.

"I'm the chairman of the Atomic Energy Commission of Canada," he replied. "And what about you?" indicating by his look that he knew that I too had another line of work.

"Oh," I replied without hesitation, "I'm a consultant and the Atomic Energy Commission is one of my clients."

We both broke into laughter at how the universe had brought us together in such a strange way. John and I had very similar points of view regarding our willingness to work in whatever setting was necessary in order to help others become more conscious.

Creative Destruction and Renewal in Organizations

If either individuals or organizations resist natural cycles, nature will force change on them. As Lao-Tzu wrote two thousand years ago in *Tao Te Ching*:

> Does one want to take the world and tamper with it?
> I see he will not succeed.
> The world is a sacred vessel which none should spoil.

One who tampers with it spoils it,
One who grasps it loses it.
There is a time for surging ahead and for staying behind.
A time for breathing softly and for breathing strongly,
A time for vigour and for withdrawal,
A time for soaring upwards and for lying low.

Nature has its own cycles and resisting them will create future problems. Forest fires illustrate this principle perfectly. Left to nature, periodic forest fires burn out decaying trees to make way for new trees and plant growth. The devastating fire that raged through Yellowstone Park a decade ago happened mainly because humans had been holding back this natural cycle while trying to maintain old growth. Human interference resulted in a high level of forest decay so that when the fire did start, it wouldn't stop.

Destruction and renewal is a natural cycle. Beavers dam streams to make ponds for themselves, but also create a place where other creatures can thrive. Water erodes rock to create rivers from streams. Destruction—whether in nature or in organizations—is not bad in itself but needs to be in keeping with long-term environmental health.

3M in the United States practices "creative destruction." Its policy—that 25 percent of sales must be from products less than five years old—ensures that new products are always entering the market and that only the best of the old survives. At the same time 3M practices creative destruction, it also supports "creative renewal," by allowing employees to devote 15 percent of their time to projects that interest them. This is how the famous Post-it notes came into being. By giving employees time to follow their own creativity, 3M builds a continual cycle of new birth into its organizational structure. These cycles not only make the employees happy and more productive, they ensure prosperity for the entire company.

Working with organic cycles and seasons is good for the soul of the business and for the souls of individuals. By doing so, we work not just with the seventh chakra, but all chakras.

Progress is no longer linear, but in harmony with ourselves, others and the Earth. As Kornfield says:

> We are not trying to get somewhere better next year or in twenty years... We are learning to open to the timeless universe unfolding in our lives, being in greater harmony with what is, with a greater inclusiveness of our hearts to all the seasons of our life.

Transformation: The World as Our Workplace

> *A person works in a stable. That person has a breakthrough. What does he do? He returns to the stable.*
>
> MEISTER ECKHART

Taking our soul to work means doing what we can, where we are and with whom we can. We need to eradicate the continual inequities that make some people more important than others in our workplace and society. All of us are unique and each of our soul's missions—regardless of whether we are a CEO or a plumber, a physician or an office worker—are of equal value. Our responsibility, as I see it, is to create home and work environments where souls and personalities can grow in harmony and thrive.

Personal and even organizational transformations are not the end of the journey. In fact, they are the beginning of another journey, another cycle, whose purpose is dedicating ourselves to serving others regardless of our work. By doing this, we place our talents and gifts in service—not to the personality—to the soul. But there is more than just our individual souls. We share a common consciousness with others and with what Greeks called *psyche tou kosmow*—the soul of the world.

In the Buddhist tradition, individuals on the verge of enlightenment take a vow to continually reincarnate until all beings are enlightened, referred to as the "boddhisattva vow." Enlightenment occurs when our individual personality needs are no longer as important as our concern for the whole. Because we can only be fully effective in transforming our workplaces and our world if we put our own house in order, this must be the first step we take. Yet we cannot wait to be perfect before acting in the world and—if we allow it—our work and life will transform us on a daily basis. Flawed, imperfect, but with the right motivation, we must take the steps our soul shows us, however unclear or confusing.

The Butterfly: Symbol of Transformation

> *What the caterpillar calls the end of the world, a master calls a butterfly.*

RICHARD BACH

Butterflies epitomize the inevitability of our path to consciousness. Just as there are thousands of species of butterflies, each one of us is totally unique, but our process of transformation leads to the same final result. There are four cycles that the butterfly undergoes in its transformation: egg, to caterpillar, to cocoon, before finding its final grace and beauty as a butterfly. These stages are ones that we also undergo in our journey from unconsciousness—dominated by the personality—to consciousness—partnered with the soul.

Individuals in the egg—the first stage of transformation—are unconscious. Obedient and never questioning the rules, they are at the mercy of their environment. Because they are passive, others control them, and their careers are usually unplanned. These unconscious individuals buy the lottery ticket of life and hope that—through luck but no effort to become conscious—they will win the big payoff. Men and woman in the egg stage do not consciously harm others or their environment, but neither do they consciously improve it.

The second stage of transformation is that of the caterpillar. Our world and organizations have been run by caterpillars, who, with an insatiable appetite for more, have destroyed our environment. People in the caterpillar stage of transformation step over others in their path in order to reach their ego-centered goals. They want to have the most money and the best that money can buy and have little conscience as to how the needs of others are met. I am not suggesting malevolence, just a "me-first" attitude. Natural resources exist only to meet the needs of the caterpillar. Individuals in this stage do not act as if they care how many trees they cut down, minerals they extract or whether they pollute the air. Whereas the egg is passive and dependent, the caterpillar is aggressive and independent. Although it still cannot create new life, the caterpillar is further along the path of transformation than the egg because it makes choices. It chooses which plants to eat and can move to an environment more suited to its preferences.

The cocoon is the third stage in transformation and it is a time of rest and seclusion. People cocooning withdraw from the world and prefer to stay home and enjoy simple pleasures. Men and women might cocoon by leaving their highly paid, high-stress jobs with large organizations to work at home for themselves or to take a lower-paid job with less responsibility. Cocooning also happens when individuals take a sabbatical to meditate and reflect on their life purpose or move to the country for a more peaceful environment. You might cocoon and still remain in your present job, but now decide to work only eight-, not twelve-hour days, refuse to take work home and, instead, spend your evenings and weekends with family and friends. Cocooning is an inner time. On the surface it doesn't appear as if much is happening, but the transformation from caterpillar to butterfly is occurring.

At this time in our human evolution, many men and women are going through this cocoon stage. They know that being an egg or a caterpillar is no longer an option. They have the desire to become a butterfly and so withdraw from their previous ways of being to reflect and meditate. These individuals are creating a space to allow the universe to complete their process of transformation. We become what we must be and by surrendering to the process of divine will, the transformation will naturally take place.

Butterflies are the last stage in the process of transformation. Butterflies feed on nectar and water and are creatures of beauty who destroy nothing in their path. Butterflies are also the breeders—the fertile ones who create the eggs to ensure the continuance of their race. But they do more than this. They fly from flower to flower pollinating them, thereby assuring the continuance of other species in the world. Butterflies are beings of air and soul and are not bound, like caterpillars, to the earth. They are delicate and can be easily damaged by an unfriendly environment. But they are also tenacious and—as with monarchs—can fly thousands of miles to find the right environment to create new life.

Men and women in their butterfly stage are free of both their culture's rules and their personality's drives. Formerly, they were found more often on the fringes of society living alternative lifestyles. Often they were the craftspeople, artists, writers, environmentalists, social activists, healers, spiritual teachers or others who brought beauty, love and wisdom into the world. For some time there have been butterflies in the traditional workforce, and I believe that their numbers are increasing. Butterflies are those soul-infused women and men who assist others on their paths to consciousness. Fertile and creative, they catalyze new growth in other people and in the organizations they work for. As we enter the fourth cycle of human evolution, it is these individuals who will be the forerunners and the way-showers of the principles of interdependence.

Bibliography

I list here only the material that has been of use in the making of this book. This bibliography is by no means a complete record of all the works and sources I have consulted. It indicates the range and substance of reading upon which I have formed my ideas. Every effort has been made to ensure that sources are correctly credited. Any corrections brought to my attention through the publisher will be entered in future editions of the book.

Introduction

Moore, Thomas. *Care of the Soul.* New York: HarperCollins, 1992.
Schumacher, E.F. *Good Work.* New York: Harper & Row, 1979.

Chapter One

Campbell, Joseph. *Reflections on the Art of Living.* New York: HarperCollins, 1991.
Fox, Matthew. *The Reinvention of Work: A New Vision of Livelihood for Our Time.* San Francisco: Harper San Francisco, 1994.
Mascaro, Juan, trans. *Bhagavad Gita.* New York: Penguin Books, 1978.

Chapter Two

Eisler, Riane. *The Chalice & the Blade: Our History, Our Future.* San Francisco: Harper San Francisco, 1987.
Hultkrantz, Ake. "Conceptions of the Soul Among North American Indians." In *Soul: An Archaeology of the Spirit:*

Readings from Socrates to Ray Charles. Edited by Phil
Cousineau. New York: HarperCollins, 1995.
John of the Cross, St. *The Collected Works of St. John of the
Cross.* Translated by Kieran Kavanaugh and Otilio
Rodriguez. Washington, D.C.: ICS Publications, 1979.
Sanford, John A. *Soul Journey.* New York: Crossroad
Publishing, 1991.
Teilhard de Chardin, Pierre. *The Phenomenon of Man.* New
York: Harper, 1965.

Chapter Three

Campbell, Joseph. *Reflections on the Art of Living.* New York:
HarperCollins, 1991.
de Troyes, Cretian. *The Quest for the Holy Grail.* Translated
by P.M. Matarasso. New York: Penguin Books, 1969.
Eliot, T.S. "Four Quartets." From *Collected Poems 1909–1962.*
London: Faber and Faber, 1974.
Kornfield, Jack. *A Path with Heart.* New York: Bantam Books,
1993.
Maslow, Abraham H. *Motivation and Personality.* New York:
Harper & Row, 1970.
Whyte, David. *The Heart Aroused: Poetry and the Preservation
of the Soul in Corporate America.* New York: Currency and
Doubleday, 1994.

Chapter Four

Berry, James. Editor's response. In *BusinessSpirit,* June/July 1998.
Fox, Matthew. *The Reinvention of Work: A New Vision of
Livelihood for Our Time.* New York: HarperCollins
Publishers, 1994.
Globe and Mail, May 24, 1997.
Gold, Kerry. "Plant hailed for garbage-to-fuel technology." *The
Vancouver Courier,* October 23, 1996.

Halstead, Ted. The Genuine Progress Indicator is available from: Redefining Progress, One Kearney Street, Fourth Floor, San Francisco, CA 94108.
Henderson, Hazel. "False Economy," In *Creation Spirituality*, September/October, 1992.
Schumacher, E.F. *Good Work*. New York: Harper & Row, 1977.
Wheatley, Margaret. *Leadership and the New Science*. San Francisco: Berrett-Koehler Publishers Inc., 1992.
Wilson, Lionel. "Green Bank Prompts Eco-Enterprise." In *Shared Vision*, December 1997.

Chapter Five

Maslow, Abraham H. *Motivation and Personality*. New York: Harper & Row, 1970.

Chapter Six

Hillman, James. *The Soul's Code: In Search of Character and Calling*. New York: Random House, 1996.
Kornfield, Jack. *A Path with Heart*. New York: Bantam Books, 1993.
Silverberg, Christine. From a speech delivered to Women in Business Conference, University of Calgary, May 1997.

Chapter Seven

Chopra, Deepak. *Ageless Body, Timeless Mind*. New York: Harmony Books, 1993.
Descartes, Rene. *Essential Works of Descartes*. Translated by Lowell Blair, New York: Bantam Books.
Friedman, Howard and S. Boothby-Kewley. "The Disease Prone Personality: A Meta-Analytic View." In *American Psychologist* 42, 1987.

Goleman, Daniel. *Emotional Intelligence: Why It Can Matter More Than IQ*. New York: Bantam Books, 1995.

Schweitzer, David. "New Insights in Thoughtform Photography." In *Common Ground*, August 1997.

Shoda, Yuichi, Walter Mischel, and Philip K. Peake. "Predicting Adolescent Cognitive and Self-regulatory Competencies from Preschool Delay of Gratification." In *Developmental Psychology* 26, 6, 1990.

Ywahoo, Dhyani. *Voices of Our Ancestors: Cherokee Teachings from the Wisdom Fire*. Boston: Shambhala, 1987.

Chapter Eight

Ywahoo, Dhyani. *Voices of Our Ancestors: Cherokee Teachings from the Wisdom Fire*. Boston: Shambhala, 1987.

Chapter Nine

Gardner, Howard. *Frames of Mind: The Theory of Multiple Intelligences*. New York: Basic Books, 1983.

Goertzel, Mildred and Victor. *Cradles of Eminence*. Boston: Little, Brown, 1962.

Chapter Ten

Hammarskjold, Dag. *Markings*. New York: Knopf, 1964.

Helliwell, Tanis. *Decoding Destiny: Keys to Mankind's Spiritual Evolution*. Toronto: T.A. Helliwell Publications, 1988.

Chapter Eleven

Judith, Anodea. *Wheels of Life*. St. Paul, Minnesota: Llewellyn Publications, 1997.

Leadbeater, C.W. *The Chakras*. London: The Theosophical Publishing House, 1979.

McLaughlin, Corinne and Gordon Davidson. *Spirituality in Business*. Puerto Vallarta: November 1997, conference.

Chapter Twelve

The orende system is taught by Harley Swiftdeer Reagan. DTMMS Doorways, P.O. Box 12397, Scottsdale AZ 85267. The physical, sexual, emotional and mental charts are in keeping with the Twisted Hair tradition. I have compiled the section on spiritual orende from many different traditions.

Chapter Thirteen

Covey, Stephen. *The 7 Habits of Highly Effective People*. New York: Simon and Schuster, 1989.
Siskind, Barry. *Making Contact*. Toronto: Macmillan Canada, 1995.

Chapter Fourteen

Blanchard, Ken. "Self-Esteem and the Managing of Others." In *Heart at Work: Stories and Strategies for Building Self-esteem & Reawakening the Soul at Work*. Edited by Jack Canfield and Jacqueline Miller. New York: McGraw-Hill, 1996.
Chappell, Tom. *The Soul of a Business: Managing for Profit and the Common Good*. New York: Bantam Books, 1993.
Plotinus. *Enneads*. Translated by Stephen McKenna. Larson Publications, 1992.

Chapter Fifteen

Luks, Alan. "The Healing Power of Doing Good." In *Natural Health*, 1996.
Petrie, Ann and Jeannette Petrie. *Mother Theresa*. San Francisco: Petrie Productions, Dorason Corporation, 1986, video.

Chapter Sixteen

Angus Reid poll for accounting firm Ernst and Young in Toronto. Reported in *Business in Vancouver,* 1996.

Dalla Costa, John. *The Ethical Imperative: Why Moral Leadership Is Good Business.* Toronto: HarperCollins Publishers, 1998.

Goodman, John. "Managing from Within." In *Heart at Work: Stories and Strategies for Building Self-esteem & Reawakening the Soul at Work.* Edited by Jack Canfield and Jacqueline Miller. New York: McGraw-Hill, 1996.

Hall, Brian. *The Genesis Effect.* New York: Paulist Press, 1986.

Handy, Charles. *The Age of Paradox.* Boston: Harvard Business School Press, 1994.

Hawley, Jack. *Reawakening the Spirit in Work: The Power of Dharmic Management.* New York: Fireside, 1993.

Kadlec, Daniel. "The New World of Giving." In *Time* magazine, May 5, 1997.

King Jr., Martin Luther. *The Trumpet of Conscience.* New York: Harper & Row, 1967.

Pearson, Carol S. and Sharon Seivert. *Magic at Work.* New York: Currency and Doubleday, 1995.

Pulos, Dr. Lee. Specialist in brain functioning. In conversation, May 10, 1997.

Schumacher, E.F. *Good Work.* New York: Harper & Row, 1977.

Chapter Seventeen

Agor, Weston, ed. *Intuition in Organizations: Leading and Managing Productively.* Newbury Park, CA: Sage Publications Inc., 1989.

Andrews, Valerie. "The Soul Hunger of Children." In *Soul: Archaeology: Readings from Socrates to Ray Charles.* Edited by Phil Cousineau. New York: HarperCollins, 1995.

Bem, Daryl J. "Ganzfield Phenomena." In *Encyclopedia of the Paranormal*, edited by G. Stein. Buffalo, NY: Prometheus Books, 1996.

Gardner, Howard. *Frames of Mind: The Theory of Multiple Intelligences.* New York: Basic Books Inc., 1983.

From the poem "The Station" attributed to Robert J. Hastings.

Jaques, Elliott. *Requisite Organization: A Total System for Effective Managerial Organization & Managerial Leadership for the 21st Century.* Kingston, NY: Cason Hall & Co., 1989.

McLaughlin, Corinne and Gordon Davidson. *Spiritual Politics: Changing the World from the Inside Out.* New York: Ballantine Books, 1994.

Pibram, Karl. "Interview." In *Omni* magazine, October 1982.

Radin, Dean. *The Conscious Universe: The Scientific Truth of Psychic Phenomena.* New York: HarperCollins, 1997.

Secretan, Lance H.K. *Reclaiming Higher Ground: Creating Organizations That Inspire the Soul.* Toronto: Macmillan Canada, 1996.

Talbot, Michael. *Beyond the Quantum.* New York: Bantam Books, 1986.

Ventura, Michael. "The Family Interrupted." In *The Family Therapy Networker,* January/February 1995.

Chapter Eighteen

Giamatti, A. Bartlett. "The Green Fields of the Mind." In *Soul: Archaeology: Readings from Socrates to Ray Charles.* Edited by Phil Cousineau. New York: HarperCollins, 1995.

Hurst, David K. *Crisis and Renewal: Meeting the Challenge of Organizational Change.* Boston: Harvard Business School Press, 1995.

Kornfield, Jack. *A Path with Heart.* New York: Bantam Books, 1993.

Lao-Tzu. *Tao Te Ching.* New York: Concord Grove Press, 1983.

General:

Vardey, Lucinda, ed. *God in All Worlds: An Anthology of Contemporary Spiritual Writing.* Toronto: Vintage Canada, 1996.